Terrorism, Security, and Computation

Series Editor

V. S. Subrahmanian, Department of Computer Science and Institute for Security, Technology and Society, Dartmouth College, Hanover, USA

The purpose of the Computation and International Security book series is to establish the state of the art and set the course for future research in computational approaches to international security. The scope of this series is broad and aims to look at computational research that addresses topics in counter-terrorism, counter-drug, transnational crime, homeland security, cyber-crime, public policy, international conflict, and stability of nations. Computational research areas that interact with these topics include (but are not restricted to) research in databases, machine learning, data mining, planning, artificial intelligence, operations research, mathematics, network analysis, social networks, computer vision, computer security, biometrics, forecasting, and statistical modeling. The series serves as a central source of reference for information and communications technology that addresses topics related to international security. The series aims to publish thorough and cohesive studies on specific topics in international security that have a computational and/or mathematical theme, as well as works that are larger in scope than survey articles and that will contain more detailed background information. The series also provides a single point of coverage of advanced and timely topics and a forum for topics that may not have reached a level of maturity to warrant a comprehensive textbook.

Anatolii Marushchak · Anayit Khoperiya ·
Mykola Balaban · Stanislav Petrov

Counter Disinformation System Development in Ukraine

Springer

Anatolii Marushchak
International Information Academy
Kyiv, Ukraine

Mykola Balaban
Center for Strategic Communications
«SPRAVDI»
Kyiv, Ukraine

Anayit Khoperiya
Center for Countering Disinformation
of the National Security and Defense
Council of Ukraine
Kyiv, Ukraine

Stanislav Petrov
The Institute of Special Communication
and Information Protection of the National
Technical University of Ukraine "Ihor
Sikorsky Kyiv Polytechnic Institute"
Kyiv, Ukraine

ISSN 2197-8778 ISSN 2197-8786 (electronic)
Terrorism, Security, and Computation
ISBN 978-3-032-24730-8 ISBN 978-3-032-24731-5 (eBook)
https://doi.org/10.1007/978-3-032-24731-5

This Springer imprint is published by the registered company Springer Nature Switzerland AG
The registered company address is: Gewerbestrasse 11, 6330 Cham, Switzerland

Foreword

Ukraine has been at the forefront of receiving and disproving Russian propaganda for decades. Since the Euromaidan, Ukraine has regularly been accused of being "neo-Nazi", genocidal against Russian speakers, and a "puppet of NATO". While Ukraine was quick to understand the threats that such disinformation could pose to its people, the West at this time tended to view Russian digital propaganda through the lens of election interference. This compartmentalisation skewed Western perceptions of Russian influence into discreet events with limited goals, such as interference in the US Presidential Election in 2016 or the 2017 French Presidential Election.

The Ukrainian experience, however, reveals the stark reality of "the most intense information onslaught in modern European history". Ultimately, Russia's goal has been to undermine Ukrainian sovereignty to the degree that the history, identity, and autonomy of a people can be erased. Ukraine's ability to analyse and counter Russian disinformation, through strategic communication as well as through strategically communicated actions, is not simply about protecting an event; it is existential.

The experience of Ukraine in dealing with information influence operations should therefore be of profound interest to anybody who has an interest in the future of democracy. This volume is the first to comprehensively explain how the Ukrainian institutions, methods, and co-operations developed. In particular, there is much to be learned about how strategic communication was professionalised after 2014, which in turn supported a unification of Ukraine's national messaging and narratives. At the same time, government institutions had to learn how to work together, with civil society, and with allies to maintain trust with general publics as well as with decision-makers at home, in the temporarily occupied territories, and abroad. The challenge could have been insurmountable; but as with so many examples since 2022, Ukraine's ingenuity and resolve continues to surprise and impress.

This volume will no doubt be seen as the authoritative resource on Ukraine's response to the informational components of Russia's war of aggression. It is written by genuine experts who were there when the response was being built. It was written while the war was ongoing, while Russia still targets innocent civilians with missiles and drones night after night—war crimes that serve no legitimate military purpose. The stories told and lessons learned should be measured against Ukraine's refusal to be influenced by physical and informational attacks.

For many readers, one of the most important insights will be how the Ukrainian will to defend is bound up in this informational work. Another key insight will be the organic interactions between government, civil society, and the private sector to build both capability and capacity. Without this cooperation, Ukraine's strategic communication would be a fraction of what it currently is. Any reader interested in how to protect democracy from those who would destroy us will be interested in this important work. Slava Ukraini!

February 2026

Dr. James Pamment
Psychological Defence
Research Institute
Lund University
Lund, Sweden

Competing Interests The authors have no competing interests to declare that are relevant to the content of this manuscript.

Contents

About the Authors

Prof. Dr. Anatolii Marushchak is a human rights researcher who specializes in information and cyber law, with a specific emphasis on disinformation. He co-founded and serves as a strategic advisor (pro-bono) to the International Information Academy, a non-governmental organization in Ukraine that conducts research and provides training on cyber and information law, as well as counter-disinformation tactics.

Marushchak has been a lecturer at the National Academy of the Security Service of Ukraine since 2008, where he trains employees from the Security Service and other Ukrainian law enforcement agencies. His academic and professional work combines legal study, national security, and applied policy, with a focus on preserving human rights in the digital and information spheres.

Professor Marushchak is the author of over 200 academic publications, books, and theses on information law, cybersecurity, and information security. His expert briefs and analytical materials on information law and cybersecurity have been used domestically by key Ukrainian institutions such as the National Security and Defense Council, the National Institute for Strategic Studies, the National Academy of Legal Sciences of Ukraine, and the Security Service of Ukraine.

Dr. Anayit Khoperiya is a Ukrainian policy expert specializing in countering disinformation and information-related threats to national security. She serves as the deputy head of the Center for Countering Disinformation under Ukraine's National Security and Defense Council in Kyiv, where she contributes to the development and implementation of state-level responses to information threats and foreign influence operations.

She holds a Ph.D. in Law, having completed her postgraduate studies at the Burchak Research Institute, and earned her Master's degree with honors from Taras Shevchenko National University of Kyiv. Her academic background underpins her analytical and evidence-based approach to information security and public policy.

Dr. Khoperiya actively promotes cooperation with international partners and coordinated, whole-of-society approaches to strengthening resilience against disinformation. Her work focuses on bridging analytical research, strategic communications, and applied policy solutions in the field of information security.

Dr. Khoperiya has been recognized for her professional contributions on multiple occasions. She received commendations from the National Security and Defense Council of Ukraine in 2022 and 2024 and in 2025 was awarded a distinction by the Main Intelligence Directorate of the Ministry of Defence of Ukraine for her support to Ukraine's military intelligence. Her work combines academic expertise, international cooperation, and practical experience in the national security domain.

Dr. Mykola Balaban is a Ukrainian historian, policy analyst, and strategic communications expert specializing in disinformation prevention, historical memory, and information integrity. He serves as the deputy head of the Center for Strategic Communications and Information Security, where he contributes to the development of state-level responses to information risks and foreign information manipulation.

Since 2021, Dr. Balaban is a research fellow at the Center for the Study of Memory and Public History, Ukrainian Catholic University. In 2019, he was a junior visiting fellow in the Ukraine in European Dialogue Program at the Institute for Human Sciences (IWM), where he conducted doctoral research within an international interdisciplinary environment.

He earned his Ph.D. in History from the Ukrainian Catholic University with a dissertation on localized violence in Lviv during the early phase of the German–Soviet War in 1941. His academic training also includes a Global Dialogues Fellowship at the New School for Social Research.

Dr. Balaban's writing has appeared in EUvsDisinfo, Ukrainian Pravda, and Eurozine. He has also served as a national consultant on disinformation for UNDP Ukraine. His work bridges historical scholarship, public policy, and applied analysis of contemporary information warfare.

Dr. Stanislav Petrov is a Ukrainian cybersecurity expert and legal scholar with extensive experience in information security, digital transformation, and data protection. He has degrees in law and economics and worked in Ukraine's state security and intelligence agencies from 2003 to 2023, specializing on cybersecurity and the legislative frameworks that regulate computer systems.

Petrov was actively involved in developing Ukraine's Cybersecurity Strategy and constructing the country's national cybersecurity system, providing policy insight as well as practical implementation guidance. He possesses a Doctor of Law degree and has authored over 50 research publications in legal and cybersecurity disciplines.

In 2023–2025, he was the asset recovery and management agency's deputy head for Digital Development, Transformation, and Digitalization (CDTO). Petrov oversees efforts to safeguard and upgrade the Agency's information systems and institutional infrastructure. Petrov also promotes ARMA globally, presenting his work on information system protection and database security at key forums and conferences, as well as encouraging collaboration with European partners on cybersecurity standards and practices.

1 Introduction

Truth is becoming increasingly scarce in our environment, much like clean water. Even though everyone is aware that lying is a psychological trait that has existed for centuries, disinformation is a systemic issue facing humanity today that distorts the expression of will, blurs the truth, alters priorities, and puts a person under the influence of adversaries.

The public operations of special services were previously unaware of the existence of disinformation. However, as information technologies and information transmission methods have advanced, disinformation has become a common way to influence populations, nations, and geographical areas.

For all democratic states worldwide, Ukraine's experience combating disinformation, especially from the Russian Federation, is exceptional. These institutional capacities, which were developed since 2014 following the Russian Federation's annexation of Crimea and reinforced following the Russian Federation's full-scale invasion of Ukraine in 2022, can serve as models for states that uphold human rights, safeguard the right to information, and allow free expression of will without outside interference.

Since Russia's initial aggression in 2014, Ukraine has been a key testing ground for a sophisticated form of information warfare, which utilizes a range of tactics from historical revisionism to mass-scale disinformation campaigns. The struggle for a country's truth and sovereignty in this new era of hybrid combat is fought not just on the battlefield but also in the media, on social media, and in people's hearts and minds. Due to its hard-won experience in this battle, Ukraine has become a global pioneer in the fight against disinformation, having built resilience out of necessity.

Using theoretical and methodological underpinnings from the academic environment, the authors of this book actively implement ways to counter Russian disinformation, both through the mechanisms of state bodies and civil society.

A. Marushchak et al., *Counter Disinformation System Development in Ukraine*,
Terrorism, Security, and Computation, https://doi.org/10.1007/978-3-032-24731-5_1

This enables the use of contemporary instances to demonstrate the most recent developments in the system for combating disinformation in Ukraine. This book compiles examples of Ukrainian experiences at the state and civil society levels with regard to the creation and growth of an ecosystem to combat Russian disinformation, the introduction of media literacy, collaboration with foreign partners, and the execution of the most recent projects based on emerging technologies and the realities of war.

Summing up, the history of Ukraine's struggle against Russian propaganda, fakes, and false narratives that became a part of the Russian war against Ukraine serves as an example of the experience of combating disinformation. This fight is tinged with the blood of our people, who were frequently misled by Russian disinformation operations.

This detailed study delves into Ukraine's multilayered battle against Russian disinformation, tracing its historical roots and legislative measures aimed at combating it. It investigates Russian disinformation tactics and provides analysis of legislation from around the world, giving readers a comprehensive picture of how states respond to information threats. The book highlights Ukraine's ongoing efforts to build national resilience through detailed case studies and insights from the Center for Countering Disinformation (CCD) and the Center for Strategic Communication and Information Security (CSC), as well as lessons learned from operational practices. It also includes the Kyiv StratCom Forum (2021–2025), demonstrating how annual discussions have improved public communication and inter-agency collaboration in times of crisis.

Beyond government structures, authors explore the larger ecosystem that promotes information integrity, such as media literacy training, fact-checking networks, and international collaboration. It covers activities led by the CCD and CSC, ranging from public awareness campaigns to collaborations with worldwide technological companies and academic institutions, demonstrating Ukraine's unique approaches to countering disinformation. The book addresses the rising issues posed by AI-powered disinformation, including solutions for detecting, preventing, and responding to technologically amplified dangers.

This book is essential for scholars, policymakers, and anyone interested in modern information warfare. It presents both a historical perspective and a forward-looking plan for developing information-secure societies.

History and Legislation

2

Disinformation has attended human societies since rule became organized. From rulers and politicians to interest groups, from one era to another, the history of political discourse has been dominated by selective truths, embellishments or sheer fabrication in order to boost authority, rally supporters, or crumble down opponents. The technologies and tools of dissemination may have shifted, from ancient proclamations and religious texts through the era of the printing press to mass media and now digital networks, but the underlying logic remains constant: shaping perception in order to alter behavior.

This issue has been addressed throughout history by various kinds of regulation. From ancient edicts regulating public oratory to medieval controls over unlicensed printing, and through the twentieth-century's various propaganda laws and broadcasting regulations, law has often been the chosen instrument for maintaining social peace and preventing citizens from being led astray. Today, governments and international organizations are still trying out different legal frameworks—from thwarting foreign interference to holding digital platforms responsible for harmful content. These efforts raise challenging questions about the balance between protecting democratic debate and the dangers of censorship and overregulation.

In order to understand these developments, one must put them in a longer sweep of history. And in each era, responses have been developed: censorship systems and propaganda controls, legislation aimed at curbing information flows.

The shaping of a new environment, not the mere presence of disinformation, poses the defining challenge of our time. Information never moved with the speed, reach, or virality that it does today. In the digital public square, disinformation is magnified by algorithms, replicated by bots and supported by distributed partisan audiences who often consume news in separate information bubbles. It poses an issue of trust, as cultures grapple with who to believe and who is playing them.

A. Marushchak et al., *Counter Disinformation System Development in Ukraine*,
Terrorism, Security, and Computation, https://doi.org/10.1007/978-3-032-24731-5_2

Thus, let's dig into these historical patterns that help us understand how the contemporary era of disinformation is both continuous with, and significantly different from, the past. By examining how state regulations, societal responses and international cooperation have evolved, we are better placed to judge how future laws and public conversation might affect the world's approach to disinformation in the years ahead.

2.1 Disinformation Across History

The Cold War made disinformation a permanent, systemic feature of geopolitics. The Soviet Union institutionalized a diversified range of political warfare activities, referred to as "active measures", inside the KGB.

Disinformation did not begin in 2014, it is a nearly two-thousand-year-old narrative about how lies are weaponized by states, armies, and individuals. Deception has been a constant instrument of governance and warfare from the beginning of recorded history to the present day. What has changed very little has been the underlying intent—to manipulate by whatever means necessary, whether through new technologies, the pursuit of online dominance, or the shaping of public opinion. The path from the direct, face-to-face rhetoric of ancient city-states, through the mass-produced narratives of the industrial age to the algorithmic chaos of the digital present tells a single story: each new form of information has, in its turn, been surpassed, opening ever wider avenues for outright deception.

Already in the ancient world practical strategy manuals described the utility of deceit and mankind's susceptibility to deception. Thucydides, the historian of the Peloponnesian War, was a founding practitioner of critical history based on the use of empirical observation (history-pelo-war.pdf, n.d.). But at the same time, he made a deep insight that it is in the very nature of human beings to accept as true what they have first heard: "most people take too little trouble in seeking out the truth, but accept the first story they hear" (Evidence on Disinformation & 'fake news', 2018). His research proves how Athenians' awful cognitive bias made them make a series of catastrophic decisions including unfounded claims like plans to take over Sicily.

Meanwhile, at the other end of the world, the Chinese military strategist Sun Tzu codified deception as centre-stage in war in his book The Art of War (ArtOfWar.pdf, n.d., p. 31). Sun Tzu's teachings transcended simple battle tactics and laid out a comprehensive framework for psychological manipulation, advising commanders to feign weakness when able to attack and to appear inactive when using their forces (ArtOfWar.pdf, n.d., p. 32). He went so far as to propose fraud not only on the enemy, but on his own forces as well: a "General" should be able "to mystify" his officers and men by lying to them, keeping everything secret (ArtOfWar.pdf, n.d., p. 103).

The Roman Empire mastered the practice of state-run story-telling when it formalized propaganda to a whole new level. Roman coins were then, as the mass media are today, a common and effective channel of communication (Roman Coinage, n.d.). Inasmuch as they were an unavoidable part of daily life and ubiquitous, they served as a permanent physical reminder of the power and legitimacy of the state itself. The ancestors of living powerful politicians soon appeared on coins as a political weapon which reached its zenith through the figures of Julius Caesar, who became the first living man to appear on a coin and whose actions were even imitated by subsequent emperors. This strategy takes a page directly from the most effective disinformation playbook: embedding a message in an essential, credible, and widely used medium.

During the Middle Ages, disinformation had an important place in political and religious dissidence, especially in a society where deep-rooted prejudice grew up side by side with lack of channels for information (Misinformation in the Middle Ages: Towards understanding conspiracy theories throughout history, 2025). In addition to the written records, visual culture was also weaponized. In politics, rumours and conspiracy theories were a powerful weapon to weaken opponents. One of the most disruptive rumours in early fifteenth-century England claimed that the deposed King Richard II was still alive and would return to reclaim his throne. The rumour gained traction when Scotland harboured a pretender claiming to be Richard, using the story to weaken England politically (Misinformation in the Middle Ages: Towards understanding conspiracy theories throughout history, 2025). Those attempts were successful because they preyed on existing beliefs and fears in the public. It shows how an old core principle of disinformation works, one that has gone back centuries: more often than not, disinformation functions best not by inventing new lies but by weaponizing already existing social divisions and prejudices.

The creation of the Gutenberg press in the fifteenth century revolutionized how information was distributed, breaking the informational monopoly held by the Church and its attendant nobles. It made the first genuine mass-media campaign possible by making books and pamphlets cheap and easy to distribute (Mark, 2022). This new instrument gave the reformers, like Martin Luther, a way to circumvent the traditional gatekeepers and reach an enormous audience directly. Luther himself made the most of this opportunity, having hundreds of his works published between 1517 and 1525 and thus becoming an "early modern bestseller" (Mark, 2022). But the printing press also democratized disinformation. Although it gave a voice to those who previously had none, it also spread political libels and enabled mass hoaxes.

The propaganda of war took a giant leap forward with the industrial age. During World War I, Allied propaganda relied heavily on emotionally charged atrocity stories to demonize the German enemy and mobilize public outrage. Horrific stories of German soldiers bayoneting Belgian babies and stories that the Germans made soap from bodies of Allied troops were commonly told, though with little or no basis in fact (The legacy of wartime propaganda Part 2|PROV, n.d.). A general scepticism arose in the post-war years, when it was discovered that most of these stories were not true. Such post-war disillusionment was also so potent that in the post-war era a "counter myth" began to emerge of the war's origin having been nothing more than government lies, according to which it had all been sold to people through mass-deception (Propaganda at home and abroad, 2017). That incredulity came with a tragic cost years later. True reports of the atrocities of Nazi Germany, when they started coming out during World War II, were likely to be dismissed as lies since people had been told that the atrocity stories of the previous war were all fabrications. This is a pretty direct through line: disinformation in one era opened up society's immune system to disbelieving the truth in another.

World War II saw the full development of a new, total type of propaganda in Nazi Germany's Josef Goebbels. Goebbels did more than just lie, he set up a whole state apparatus of psychological and political control, the basic principles which were centralization of all propaganda in one agency, emphasis on what would now be called emotional rather than rational appeal, and reliance on pre-packaged short slogans and stereotyped images (Posetti and Matthews, n.d., p. 3). One strategy was to focus on a particular enemy—say, Jews or Communists—and demonize it utterly, making it the perennial object of hatred. A guiding dictum of Goebbels was that "credibility alone must determine whether propaganda output should be true or false" (Propaganda—Goebbels' Principles, 1950). It shows that lies were never the object, control was. If the Axis powers refined a total system of propaganda, however, the Allies had their own model of disinformation as an essential military strategy. The most well-known being Operation Bodyguard, the strategic deception plan executed to deceive the German High Command about the details of the D-Day invasion. The operation's name was derived from Winston Churchill's quote: "In war-time, truth is so precious that she should always be attended by a bodyguard of lies" (Remarks before the Nazi War Criminals Interagency Working Group, 2016).

The Cold War made disinformation a permanent, systemic feature of geopolitics. The Soviet Union institutionalized a diversified range of political warfare activities, referred to as "active measures", inside the KGB (Soviet "Active Measures" Forgery, Disinformation, Political Operations, n.d.). These consisted in more than mere propaganda, and extended to fabrications or support for specific medializations, political subversion (Active Measures: Russia's Covert Geopolitical Operations | George C. Marshall European Center For Security Studies, 2019). The clear aim was to weaken the West, to drive a wedge in the Western community alliances and so to sow discord among allies. A particularly infamous example is Operation Infection, a KGB campaign to spread the fabricated claim that HIV/AIDS was created by the United States as a biological weapon in a military laboratory at Fort Detrick, Maryland. The campaign started with a fabricated letter from an alleged "American scientist" published in an Indian pro-Soviet newspaper. This fictional source was then echoed by friendly media, enabling Soviet state-controlled outlets to "cite foreign sources" for the lie and claim some level of credibility.

The post-Cold War optimism that accesses to free information is inherently catalytic of democracy appears misplaced. With the advent of the Internet, the cost of distributing content went to almost zero, and falsehoods started spreading as never before, reaching an unimaginable scale (What's the real cost of disinformation for corporations?, 2025). True news tends to travel differently than false news, which often spreads quickly and easily online. Researchers have found that stories are more likely to go viral when they inspire strong emotions, regardless of whether those reactions are positive or negative. This new information ecology has had enormous economic and social costs, including billions of dollars in stock market losses driven by fake news and deepfakes (Del Vicario et al., 2016). Social media platforms in particular have brought a new, systemic challenge: algorithmic amplification. Algorithms are created and tuned to optimize user engagement by promoting content like the type that reinforces current bias (i.e., creating an "echo chamber" or "filter bubble") (Chung, 2024). That creates a new vulnerability, the fact that disinformation is no longer a human act but a computational one. The deficiency of "algorithmic literacy" experienced by users—the inability to navigate how opaque these systems' function—limits their ability to critically analyse information, and as a result exposes them more easily to disinformation. That modern democracy is vulnerable to this new digital ecology was made glaringly apparent by Russia's interference in the 2016 U.S. presidential election. The effort, carried out mostly by the Internet Research Agency (IRA), was not a typical propaganda push, but rather a systematic attempt to undermine digital tools that many hoped would unite people: social media. The key tactics included Russian trolls posing as American individuals to sow division by targeting both the political left and right simultaneously, creating "us vs. them" narratives around sensitive "wedge issues" such as race, immigration, and gun control. The aim was to stoke anger, hostility and a state of constant confusion and distrust.

> The post-Cold War optimism that accesses to free information is inherently catalytic of democracy appears misplaced. With the advent of the Internet, the cost of distributing content went to almost zero, and falsehoods started spreading as never before, reaching an unimaginable scale.

2.2 Russian Propaganda Aimed at Ukraine

> By 2022, when Russian full-scale invasion was launched, these well-worn narratives laid down the ideological basis for aggression. Among the central themes were the attempt to delegitimize Ukrainian nationhood by representing Ukrainians and Russians as "one people", the charge that Ukraine was led by "neo-Nazis", and allegations that Kyiv was perpetrating a "genocide" against Russian speakers. All these story lines were old news, having been developed and reinforced over the long haul to build up animus toward Ukraine and motivation for support at home in Russia, as well as confusion or ambivalence beyond.

For Ukraine, disinformation has not been a tangential issue but rather an enduring and existential threat. Russian propaganda aimed at Ukraine has a history predating the 2014 occupation of Crimea and originates in Soviet information policies that systematically ignored Ukrainian statehood and identity. After the restoration of Ukraine's independence in 1991, Moscow consistently promoted narratives about Ukraine as a failed state or an artificial entity to discredit its sovereignty and keep it from becoming integrated into Euro-Atlantic structures. The turning point was the intensification of Russia's aggression in 2014, when these narratives were weaponized and enhanced through traditional and digital media. Russian state media, proxy outlets and coordinated online networks worked to delegitimize Ukraine's government by characterizing it as "fascist", and at the same time cast a war in Donbas not as foreign aggression. This was not a campaign merely for internal consumption in Russia and Ukraine—but also one directed at an international audience, in hopes of undermining support for the Ukrainian government in Europe and beyond.

By 2022, when Russian full-scale invasion was launched, these well-worn narratives laid down the ideological basis for aggression. Among the central themes were the attempt to delegitimize Ukrainian nationhood by representing Ukrainians and Russians as "one people", the charge that Ukraine was led by "neo-Nazis", and allegations that Kyiv was perpetrating a "genocide" against Russian speakers. All these story lines were old news, having been developed and reinforced over the long haul to build up animus toward Ukraine and motivation for support at home in Russia, as well as confusion or ambivalence beyond.

Ukraine responded with a combination of defensive and offensive measures. The establishment of the Center for Countering Disinformation (CCD) has been an institutionalization of the response to the search, detection, and counteraction of the adversary's propaganda (Decree of the President of Ukraine No. 106, 2021). In parallel, there are investments by Ukraine in strategic communications (Cabinet of Ministers of Ukraine—Center for Strategic Communications & Information Security presented, 2021) to build a strong domestic resilience and maintain international solidarity. Stories of national unity, resistance and heroic action have become vitally important to the mobilization of society and the generation of global support.

The Ukrainian case demonstrates how disinformation is now inextricable from modern warfare. Information operations are not just an afterthought to military campaigns but a vital part of them: they help justify aggression, try to demoralize the enemy and influence how international partners view events. For Ukraine, combating disinformation is not just a question of communication policy, but also an issue of national defense.

Thus, from antiquity until today, disinformation has long served as a primary weapon for those aiming to rise in power and dominance. Local radio, the Roman coin, medieval rumor or state-run broadcasting: the aim has always been to control the narrative, delegitimize opponents and shape public will. The success of these efforts has always been based on the exploitation of basic human cognitive biases and preexisting social divisions. But the tools of disinformation have never ceased to evolve. The physical, decentralized mediums of the past have been replaced by a global, instantaneous, and algorithmically-driven information ecosystem. This is a crucial distinction. Disinformation used to be a weapon deployed with intent by humans against competing humans, but in the digital era information itself has become an undirected attack vector. This is a new, systemic problem in which untruths are not merely human false statements but computational constructs that can underpin systems operated by hostile actors. The stakes are just a lot higher today. Where historical disinformation was intended to tilt wars or control governments, digital age disinformation undermines the very fabric of the trust that undergirds society. By eroding the very possibility of shared facts and a common reality, it puts at risk not just policy debates but the building blocks of democratic society. The fight is no longer about competing ideas but competing realities, which is a much deeper and more existential threat.

> The Ukrainian case demonstrates how disinformation is now inextricable from modern warfare. Information operations are not just an afterthought to military campaigns but a vital part of them: they help justify aggression, try to demoralize the enemy and influence how international partners view events. For Ukraine, combating disinformation is not just a question of communication policy, but also an issue of national defense.

2.3 Comparative Legislation

> Comparative law suggests there's no one-size-fits-all approach for tackling disinformation. The EU stresses systemic accountability, Germany prioritizes speed but struggle with rights, the U.S. defers to expression protection, Singapore emphasizes state control. What underpins these disparate efforts is the growing awareness that disinformation challenges trust and sovereignty.

If history suggests a continuous human impulse to deceive, however, modern lawmaking shows an unpredictable and contested effort by states to police disinformation according to law. These legal structures are not just technical rules, they also embed a society's more profound political judgments about how to reconcile the requirements of security with the fundamental right to freedom of expression and how much power to give private digital platforms versus the state itself. As we compare the varied legislative ecology, a global typology of response is playing out, each with its own priorities and struggles against constant technological development.

Today, the European Union has become the most ambitious democratic regulator, shifting from a reactive, content-by-content response to an attempt to govern the information architecture itself. This model has been gradually intensified with the foundation of "soft law". One early initiative was the establishment in 2015 of East StratCom Task Force, whose project EUvsDisinfo acted as an "early warning system" to identify and de-mystify pro-Kremlin disinformation campaigns (Questions and Answers about the East StratCom Task Force | EEAS, 2021; EUvsDisinfo | Detecting, analysing, and raising awareness about disinformation, 2025). The latter resulted in the voluntary Code of Practice on Disinformation that was first agreed in 2018 and substantially reinforced in 2022 to take account of the Digital Services Act (DSA). The revised Code includes 44 commitments and 128 specific measures, among which we find steps to reduce the financial incentives that concern those disseminating disinformation (i.e., by demonetizing them) and measures increasing the transparency of political advertising (EU Code of Practice on Disinformation, 2022). And it also enables researchers and fact checkers to have greater access to data, with compliance backed by rigorous SLIs (Service Level Indicators) and third-party audits. The EU's flagship initiative is the DSA, which applies to Very Large Online Platforms (VLOPs) and Very Large Online Search Engines (VLOSEs), entered into force in August 2023, with a full applicability across the EU as of February 2024. The DSA creates a series of legally enforceable responsibilities for VLOPs—defined as any service with more than 45 million users in the EU. These online platforms are also subject to compulsory annual systemic risk assessments, which must identify, analyze and take appropriate actions to tackle risks emanating from their services, such as illegal content spreading or adverse effects on fundamental rights and freedoms, civic participation and the functioning of democratic processes.

Some European countries chose a starker, punitive approach earlier on. Germany set in place a law, the Network Enforcement Act (NetzDG), in 2017 that gave social media platforms just 24 h to delete posts containing "manifestly unlawful content" after receiving a complaint. The law, which covered far more content already criminalized under Germany's criminal code, was supposed to prompt platforms to become more expeditious addressing online hate speech and illicit material. Failing to comply could result in severe penalties of up to €50 million (Tworek & Leerssen, n.d.). Although the legislation has proven effective in prompting platforms to become more aggressive in moderating content, it has come under criticism from scholars and human rights organizations for incentivizing "overblocking" and "collateral censorship." This is because the onerous timescales and high fines force companies to take down legal but controversial speech to steer clear of liability. Later, it was the European Union's DSA that took over from the NetzDG (Mixed feelings: Digital Services Act replaces NetzDG—HateAid, 2024).

The United States is marked by significant influence of the First Amendment to the United States Constitution on its disposition toward disinformation, which preserves wide latitude for freedom of speech and some types of false speech (Hwang, 2025). In the U.S., the government may not serve as an "arbiter of truth", and there are strong limitations on direct censorship (Mccaul et al., 2023, p. 12). Rather than legislating takedown duties, the law relies on a free and vigorous public debate in which truth will eventually emerge from the clash of views. In order to prevail on a defamation claim—and this is even more true when the plaintiff is a public figure—the plaintiff must show "actual malice," or that the speaker had knowledge of its falsity, said it with "reckless disregard of whether it was false or not" (Actual Malice, 2025). With these constitutional limitations and a focus on free speech protection in mind, the use of soft power tools has prevailed as the U.S. model, avoiding regulatory steps for the most part. Created in 2016, one of the main functions of the Global Engagement Center (GEC) was to counter foreign disinformation operations, notably by Russia and China (About Us—Global Engagement Center, 2024). The GEC was defunded in December 2024 by the GOP-led Congress that refused to reauthorize its funding, and so too was its successor the Counter Foreign Information Manipulation and Interference Office

(R/FIMI) (Scherling, 2025). These shutdowns underscore legal obstacles in any American government attempt to fight disinformation head-on. Instead, the U.S. depends on voluntary commitments by platforms and public–private partnerships as a principle that emphasizes freedom of expression.

Unlike in the U.S., in several Asian countries, this model leans toward centralizing the control of information in a state-run authority. For instance, Singapore's Protection from Online Falsehoods and Manipulation Act (POFMA) of 2019 allows government ministers to mandate the correction or removal of any statement of fact that is found "false" (Singapore: "Fake News" Law Curtails Speech | Human Rights Watch, 2021). Nevertheless, the law has been repeatedly condemned by human rights groups and opposition for giving disproportionate power to the executive, and being used to silence opposition leaders.

Internationally, multilateral agencies have for the most part concentrated on formulating principles to guide that countermeasure will not violate human rights. The Council of Europe insists that restrictions on freedom of expression must be lawful, necessary, and proportionate. It also calls on states to prioritize transparency, media pluralism and resilience rather than punitive censorship (Member states should enforce standards to combat online disinformation while protecting human rights for all—Portal—www.coe.int, 2025). Similarly, UNESCO conceptualizes disinformation as a governance and structural threat to democratic discourse stressing that solutions must manage trade-offs between the need to curtail abusive manipulation while ensuring protective measures for independent journalism, fact-checking and media literacy initiatives (Balancing Act: Countering Digital Disinformation While Respecting Freedom of Expression-executive summary, n.d.).

NATO meanwhile takes a doctrinal stance towards disinformation. Disinformation is listed within the larger category of information threats in the Strategic Concept 2022, which embrace both disruptive information campaigns and coordinated cyber-sphere and PSYOPs (NATO's approach to counter information threats, 2025). Countering disinformation is integrated into NATO's cyber defense policies, hybrid defense strategies, and strategic communications frameworks. NATO doctrines are not (like laws in a nation-state) legally binding. But they set norms and principles that, to be sure, member states are obliged to take into account in the elaboration of their own security policies. One significant institutional node is the NATO Strategic Communications Centre of Excellence (StratCom COE) in Riga. The Centre is conducting research of tactics used in information operations, methods of disinformation identification and offering recommendations on the use of legal, technical and communicational solutions in national strategies. It bridges the gap between policy doctrines and practical execution allowing member states to gain access to training, researching paper and crisis scenario simulations (Decoding the Information Environment: NATO's Strategic Communications Centre of Excellence, 2024).

Comparative law suggests there's no one-size-fits-all approach for tackling disinformation. The EU stresses systemic accountability, Germany prioritizes speed but struggle with rights, the U.S. defers to expression protection, Singapore emphasizes state control. What underpins these disparate efforts is the growing awareness that disinformation challenges trust and sovereignty. What separates them is the age-old political and philosophical debate over how to balance freedom and security in a rapidly changing digital world. The regulation of disinformation goes far beyond the relative comparison of laws, and in fact it begs profound questions about democracy and the nature of information within a functioning society. An especially alarming trend is the use of anti-disinformation laws by authoritarian governments to legitimize censorship. For instance, Russia's 2022 law on "fake news" has been weaponized to prosecute true reporting about Russia's war against Ukraine, with journalists facing severe penalties, including years in prison, for challenging the official state narrative. This illustrates the trade-offs that are necessary if laws are to be tailored to deal with disinformation, without facilitating censorship of free speech and points more broadly toward implications for democratic governance and the health of public discourse.

Of particular note is the rise of generative AI, which has elevated these threats to an unprecedented magnitude. AI can produce highly realistic "deepfakes" at low cost, which can be used to create chaos and disrupt democratic processes, as exemplified by the audio deepfakes deployed during the 2023 Slovak election (Meaker, 2023). Despite legislative efforts to mandate labeling (such as those outlined in the EU's AI Act), deepfakes illustrate a case in which technology evolves more rapidly than regulation (EU AI Act: first regulation on artificial intelligence, 2023).

In the end, counter-disinformation policy is not merely about controlling speech, but about shaping the democratic space itself. Insufficient action leaves societies vulnerable to foreign manipulation and internal division, while excessive intervention risks sliding toward authoritarianism. The most sustainable path forward appears to be a holistic approach that combines proportional, rights-respecting legal frameworks with renewed investment in public trust, media literacy, and civic resilience. This is because a healthy democracy is sustained not only by laws, but also by an informed and critically engaged citizenry.

References

About Us—Global Engagement Center.(2024). United States Department of State. Available at https://2021-2025.state.gov/about-us-global-engagement-center-2/. Accessed 1 November 2025.

Active Measures: Russia's Covert Geopolitical Operations | George C. Marshall European Center for Security Studies. (2019). Available at https://www.marshallcenter.org/en/publications/security-insights/active-measures-russias-covert-geopolitical-operations-0. Accessed 1 November 2025.

Actual Malice. (2025). The Free Speech Center. Available at https://firstamendment.mtsu.edu/article/actual-malice/. Accessed 1 November 2025.

ArtOfWar.pdf. (n.d.). Available at https://dn790006.ca.archive.org/0/items/TheArtOfWarBySunTzu/ArtOfWar.pdf. Accessed 1 November 2025.

Cabinet of Ministers of Ukraine—Center for Strategic Communications and Information Security presented (2021). Available at https://www.kmu.gov.ua/news/prezentovano-centr-strategichnih-komunikacij-ta-informacijnoyi-bezpeki. Accessed 1 November 2025.

Chung, M. (2024). Want to fight misinformation? Teach people how algorithms work. Nieman Lab. Available at https://www.niemanlab.org/2024/09/want-to-fight-misinformation-teach-people-how-algorithms-work/. Accessed: 1 November 2025.

Decoding the Information Environment: NATO's Strategic Communications Centre of Excellence. (2024). NATO's ACT, 18 September. Available at https://www.act.nato.int/article/stratcom-coe-2024/. Accessed 1 November 2025.

Decree of the President of Ukraine No. 106/2021. (2021). Official Internet representation of the President of Ukraine. Available at https://www.president.gov.ua/documents/1062021-37421. Accessed 1 November 2025.

Del Vicario, M., et al. (2016). The spreading of misinformation online. *Proceedings of the National Academy of Sciences, 113*(3), 554–559. https://doi.org/10.1073/pnas.1517441113

EU Code of Practice on Disinformation. (2022). Brookings. Available at https://www.brookings.edu/articles/eu-code-of-practice-on-disinformation/ Accessed 1 November 2025.

EU AI Act: first regulation on artificial intelligence. (2023). Topics | European Parliament. Available at https://www.europarl.europa.eu/topics/en/article/20230601STO93804/eu-ai-act-first-regulation-on-artificial-intelligence. Accessed 1 November 2025.

EUvsDisinfo | Detecting, analysing, and raising awareness about disinformation. (2025). EUvsDisinfo. Available at https://euvsdisinfo.eu/. Accessed 1 November 2025.

Evidence on Disinformation and 'fake news'. (2018). Available at https://committees.parliament.uk/writtenevidence/90842/html/. Accessed 1 November 2025.

History-pelo-war.pdf. (n.d.). Available at https://antilogicalism.com/wp-content/uploads/2017/07/history-pelo-war.pdf. Accessed 1 November 2025.

Hwang, L. (2025). Regulation of misinformation in the digital age: First amendment rights and government's role in social media. *Critical Debates in Humanities, Science and Global Justice, 5*(2), 103–113. Available at https://criticaldebateshsgj.scholasticahq.com/article/137214-regulation-of-misinformation-in-the-digital-age-first-amendment-rights-and-government-s-role-in-social-media. Accessed 1 November 2025.

Mark, J. J. (2022). The printing press and the protestant reformation. World History Encyclopedia. Available at https://www.worldhistory.org/article/2039/the-printing-press--the-protestant-reformation/. Accessed 1 November 2025.

Mccaul, M. T., et al. (2023). Committee on homeland security.

Meaker, M. (2023). Slovakia's election deepfakes show AI is a danger to democracy. Wired. Available at https://www.wired.com/story/slovakias-election-deepfakes-show-ai-is-a-danger-to-democracy/. Accessed 1 November 2025.

Member states should enforce standards to combat online disinformation while protecting human rights for all—Portal—www.coe.int. (2025). Portal. Available at https://www.coe.int/en/web/portal/-/member-states-should-enforce-standards-to-combat-online-disinformation-while-protecting-human-rights-for-all. Accessed 1 November 2025.

Misinformation in the Middle Ages: Towards understanding conspiracy theories throughout history. (2025). The British Academy. Available at https://www.thebritishacademy.ac.uk/blog/misinformation-in-the-middle-ages-towards-understanding-conspiracy-theories-throughout-history/. Accessed 1 November 2025.

Mixed feelings: Digital Services Act replaces NetzDG—HateAid. (2024). Available at https://hateaid.org/en/mixed-feelings-digital-services-act-replaces-netzdg/. Accessed 1 November 2025.

NATO's approach to counter information threats (2025). Available at https://www.nato.int/cps/en/natohq/topics_219728.htm. Accessed 1 November 2025.

Propaganda—Goebbels' Principles (1950). Available at https://www.physics.smu.edu/pseudo/Propaganda/goebbels.html. Accessed 1 November 2025.

Propaganda at home and abroad. (2017). Available at https://encyclopedia.1914-1918-online.net/article/propaganda-at-home-and-abroad-1-1/. Accessed 1 November 2025.

Questions and Answers about the East StratCom Task Force | EEAS. (2021). Available at https://www.eeas.europa.eu/eeas/questions-and-answers-about-east-stratcom-task-force_en. Accessed: 1 November 2025.

Remarks before the Nazi War Criminals Interagency Working Group. (2016). National Archives. Available at https://www.archives.gov/iwg/research-papers/weitzman-remarks-june-1999.html. Accessed 1 November 2025.

Roman Coinage. (n.d.). American Numismatic Association. Available at https://www.money.org/money-museum/virtual-exhibits-hom-case3/. Accessed: 1 November 2025.

Scherling, L. (2025). *The downfall of the global engagement center and disappearing guardrails against disinformation*. TechPolicy.Press, Tech Policy Press. Available at https://techpolicy.press/the-downfall-of-the-global-engagement-center-and-disappearing-guardrails-against-disinformation. Accessed 1 November 2025.

Singapore: "Fake News" Law Curtails Speech | Human Rights Watch. (2021, 13 January). Available at https://www.hrw.org/news/2021/01/13/singapore-fake-news-law-curtails-speech. Accessed 1 November 2025.

Soviet "Active Measures" Forgery, Disinformation, Political Operations. (n.d.). Available at https://www.govinfo.gov/content/pkg/GOVPUB-S-PURL-gpo90452/pdf/GOVPUB-S-PURL-gpo90452.pdf. Accessed 1 November 2025.

What's the real cost of disinformation for corporations? (2025). World Economic Forum. Available at https://www.weforum.org/stories/2025/07/financial-impact-of-disinformation-on-corporations/. Accessed: 1 November 2025.

3 Center for Countering Disinformation: Activities and Lessons Learned

One of the primary battlespaces of the twenty-first century has become the information space. For Ukraine, this is not a theoretical but an existential truth. Since 2014, when the Russian Federation forcibly seized Crimea and began its hybrid aggression in the Donetsk and Luhansk region, disinformation has been used as a method of warfare. It has worked to delegitimize Ukraine's sovereignty, fracture its alliances, destabilize its democracy and increase its vulnerability to make it easier to attack on the world stage.

By the time the full-scale invasion began in February 2022, Ukraine was already recognized as one of the world's most targeted countries by foreign disinformation operations. The Kremlin's approach was methodical: to flood the information space with false narratives, obscure accountability for its aggression, deny atrocities, and erode confidence in Ukrainian institutions and international partners. In response, Ukraine understood that it needed more than ad hoc communication—it required a permanent, institutionalized structure to safeguard its information integrity.

This awareness resulted in the formation of the Center for Countering Disinformation (CCD) in March 2021 by Presidential Decree №106/2021 under the National Security and Defence Council of Ukraine (NSDC) (Decree of the President of Ukraine No. 106, 2021). Its establishment reflected two insights. First, disinformation is a strategic weapon like any other—or at least it has strategic impact equivalent to a conventional weapon. Second, resilience needs to be institution-backed—not just crisis response.

The CCD's mission is broad in scope: to analyse and counter disinformation, coordinate efforts across government, inform the public, and cooperate with international partners. In practical terms, this involves challenging hostile narratives and advising the President and the NSDC, supporting ministries where appropriate, strengthening societal resilience, and contributing to global counter-disinformation

A. Marushchak et al., *Counter Disinformation System Development in Ukraine*,
Terrorism, Security, and Computation, https://doi.org/10.1007/978-3-032-24731-5_3

efforts (About Center for Countering Disinformartion | Center for Countering Disinformation, 2021). In essence, Ukraine's CCD is not merely a fact-checking body, it is a national security institution and a liaison that bridges intelligence, diplomacy, civil society, and international partners.

Placing the CCD under the NSDC has been a strategic and meaningful decision. The NSDC, chaired by the President, is the highest decision-making body on national security. This positioning ensures that information security is treated not as an afterthought, but as a core component of strategic defense. At the same time, it allows the CCD to feed its analysis directly into high-level policy formulation. Unlike many of its Western counterparts, which operate within foreign ministries or as independent regulators, the CCD occupies a central role within Ukraine's national security architecture.

3.1 Core Activities of the CCD

The CCD's organization mirrors its two-fold mission to analyse and communicate. While analysts monitor media and digital platforms, trace hostile campaigns, and produce reports, communication specialists ensure that these findings are translated into outputs for the general public: daily bulletins, infographics, press briefings, pre-bunking campaigns.

It is through its practical activities that the CCD's institutional structure confers authority. Since 2021, the Center has been actively engaged in monitoring, communications, international cooperation, engagement with digital platforms, and providing policy support.

Monitoring disinformation lies at the heart of the CCD's mission. Analysts employ OSINT tools, social media listening, and manual review, combining quantitative data collection with qualitative analysis. The goal is not merely to identify falsehoods, but to map the entire disinformation landscape and trace how narratives emerge, spread, or fade. This approach enables the detection of both coordinated campaigns and subtler amplification by influencers or anonymous accounts. For example, Russian campaigns repeatedly recycle the same thematic clusters: portraying Ukraine as a "failed state," NATO as an "aggressor," and Western aid as "pointless." These narratives are subsequently disseminated through multiple channels, creating an illusion of consensus and inevitability.

So CCD's weekly and periodic reports provide not just isolated debunks, but comprehensive taxonomies of propaganda—revealing how Kremlin agitprop mutates and migrates across social media, state TV, and foreign outlets. By identifying patterns early, the CCD affords policymakers crucial lead time, enabling them to anticipate potential escalations in the information domain and adjust communication strategies accordingly. These reports also serve as accessible resources for civil society organizations, media, and international partners. In this way, the CCD functions both as an early-warning system and as a conduit for knowledge transfer, linking national security imperatives with the broader goals of democratic resilience.

The CCD works closely with Ukraine's security services to ensure that its analyses are actionable. When the CCD's monitoring identifies disinformation or hostile influence, the findings are shared with the Security Service of Ukraine to aid in actor identification and the attribution of coordinated networks. In addition, the CCD provides Ukraine's Defence Intelligence with open-source analytical support, including contributions to the War & Sanctions portal, which publicly lists individuals and entities involved in supporting Russian aggression and information operations (The main portal about sponsors and supporters of the aggression, n.d.). This analysis-to-action pipeline strengthens Ukraine's sanctions regime and international advocacy, while maintaining clear division of roles: the CCD focuses on attribution and transparency, whereas competent authorities decide on remedial measures. In this way, the CCD contributes to broader national security outcomes while preserving its civilian and advisory mandate.

The CCD's organization mirrors its two-fold mission to analyse and communicate. While analysts monitor media and digital platforms, trace hostile campaigns, and produce reports, communication specialists ensure that these findings are translated into outputs for the general public: daily bulletins, infographics, press briefings, pre-bunking campaigns. Monitoring would be meaningless if it remained internal. By turning analysis into clear communication, the CCD explains ongoing threats and strengthens public resilience. During the first months of the full-scale invasion, such outputs proved vital in countering panic and sustaining trust.

The CCD also pioneered the concept of pre-bunking—anticipating falsehoods before they spread and equipping the public with tools to recognize them. For example, prior to Russian missile strikes on Ukrainian cities, the CCD warned that Russia would deny civilian casualties and shift blame onto Ukrainian air defences (Telegram: View @CenterCounteringDisinformation, n.d. a). This type of anticipatory communication helps audiences dismiss fake news, mitigates the shock effect of adversarial narratives, and pre-empts mental distress. Thus, pre-bunking has been employed not only to counter military propaganda but also to address economic and political manipulations, such as claims that Western support is "crumbling" or social unrest is "inevitable." By setting expectations in advance, the CCD narrows the window of opportunity for disinformation to take hold and influence public debate.

Another key aspect of the CCD's work is its educational mission, aimed at making media literacy a fundamental civic skill. The Center develops media literacy campaigns, produces youth-targeted explainer videos and classroom modules, and delivers public lectures. For example, in 2022, the CCD, in collaboration with the NACP Integrity Office, supported the creation and dissemination of the animated series Dobrochesnist Online ("Integrity Online"), through which children and youth learn to identify manipulation and prevent disinformation in the digital space (The Integrity Online Project, 2022). The CCD has also partnered with NGOs to teach young people how to pre-bunk. This focus stems from the recognition that societal resilience today cannot rely solely on state institutions; it requires citizens who can think critically and evaluate the information they encounter.

The CCD is embedded in an international counter-disinformation network and collaborates with similar organizations, such as the EU East StratCom Task Force, NATO StratCom COE, the G7 Rapid Response Mechanism, and major technology companies. It shares information with allied entities engaged in information security and strategic communications. Ukraine has even co-authored an analytical report with NATO PDD IEA – an unprecedented partnership for a non-NATO country. Beyond governmental relations, the CCD works with international NGOs, think tanks, and academic institutions, including universities and research centers across Europe, to undertake joint projects that combine diplomacy with the dissemination of Ukraine's expertise. These partnerships enable a two-way exchange of knowledge: Ukraine shares frontline observations on Russian operations, while partners provide comparative data and methodological support. In this dual capacity as both a recipient and provider of expertise, the CCD is firmly established within the global counter-disinformation landscape.

In today's information ecosystem, collaboration with Big Tech is a critical component of any effective counter-disinformation strategy. Major technology platforms play a dual role: while they can be exploited to spread disinformation, they are also invaluable partners in efforts to combat it. The CCD maintains direct operational relationships with TikTok, YouTube, and Meta, enabling active information exchange and an anticipatory approach to emerging threats. Analysts monitor for anomalies, flag coordinated inauthentic activity, and identify Kremlin-linked networks, providing recommendations for the timely removal of content that violates platform rules. This partnership allows the CCD not only to counter hostile narratives but also to help design and implement platform-specific detection tools and reporting mechanisms. Moreover, these collaborations facilitate the exchange of knowledge, as platforms continue to learn about emerging hybrid information campaign tactics and contribute to the broader global effort to safeguard the integrity of the digital information space.

At the same time, the CCD advocates for structural transparency, including clearer labelling of state-affiliated media, disclosure of algorithmic risks, and access to platform data for independent researchers. By promoting these reforms, the CCD aims to make information ecosystems more transparent and resilient against covert manipulation. The CCD also supports educational initiatives in collaboration with platforms—for example, working with YouTube to amplify verified Ukrainian channels and with TikTok to develop pre-bunking content tailored to young audiences. These efforts not only elevate trusted sources of information but also provide users with practical tools to recognize and reject disinformation. Through this dual approach, the CCD seeks to strengthen the integrity of digital platforms while simultaneously enhancing the media literacy of citizens.

In today's information ecosystem, collaboration with Big Tech is a critical component of any effective counter-disinformation strategy. Major technology platforms play a dual role: while they can be exploited to spread disinformation, they are also invaluable partners in efforts to combat it. The CCD maintains direct operational relationships with TikTok, YouTube, and Meta, enabling active information exchange and an anticipatory approach to emerging threats.

3.2 Case Studies of CCD Activity

The "UkrLeaks" case has highlighted how disinformation has become a globalized, industrial-scale operation in which individual falsehoods are incorporated into vast, complex multiplatform ecosystems. Successful mitigation therefore requires a multipronged strategy, including rapid action against operators, international cooperation, coordinated engagement with platforms, and civic education. The CCD's approach to the case provides a clear example of how rigorous analysis, attribution, and strategic communication can be used together to disrupt sophisticated disinformation networks.

Instead of focusing on what the Center for Countering Disinformation (CCD) will do in the abstract, it is better to look at how such an institution responds to actual campaigns and crises. The case studies illuminate both the evolution of Russia's information warfare tactics and the CCD's adaptive practices in countering them. They offer a road map: from spotting coordinated propaganda and exposing deepfakes to anticipating the spread of disinformation tied to military operations. Based on the work of CCD, we can see that addressing disinformation effectively calls for more than solid analysis: response and strategic communication must be equally rapid.

One of the first major disinformation campaigns addressed by the CCD was "Black Hole," which erupted in late 2022 ('Analytical research based on the results of the revealed disinformation campaign the "Black hole" of the Russian federation aimed at discrediting Ukraine and President Zelensky | Center for Countering Disinformation', 2023). Russian propagandists sought to portray President Volodymyr Zelenskyy, and, by extension, Ukraine, as a "bottomless pit" for Western aid. What made this campaign distinctive was its multi-layered construction: a seemingly simple metaphor planted on Telegram evolved into a coordinated operation involving fabricated videos, falsified U.S. news broadcasts, fake magazine covers, and even doctored graffiti. Russian state and proxy media subsequently amplified these materials across Western platforms through bot networks and sympathetic fringe outlets.

In recording and exposing this operation, the CCD demonstrated remarkable agility, showing not just the falsity of individual pieces of content but also the patterned strategy behind them. Analysts mapped the information flow, identified key actors, and examined the techniques employed to promote credibility and dissemination. The case underscored a basic lesson: disinformation is most potent when it becomes multi-platform, gradual and strategically layered, and in turn demands equally comprehensive responses. In addition to rapid debunking, the intervention of CCD involved proactive dialogue with media partners and public advisories as well as liaison with social media platforms to minimize amplification. The "Black Hole" case therefore illustrates CCD's practice of technical investigation, story analysis and strategic engagement in service of information integrity as well as public trust.

A different kind of challenge was provided by the "UkrLeaks" network which CCD exposed in 2024. In contrast to the "Black Hole" campaign, "UkrLeaks" demonstrated a high degree of planning and coordination (Analytical report «The network of Russian propaganda resources «Ukrleaks» | Center for Countering Disinformation, 2024). Dozens of interconnected accounts cross-posting in several languages made for a sophisticated ecosystem designed to amplify reach and influence. The narratives are varied and harrowing, from claims that "Ukraine is a terrorist state" to grotesque allegations of organ and child trafficking. The CCD's response was more than a reactive debunking. Analysts meticulously detailed the structure of the network, followed the flow of content and attributed its operation to a sanctioned figure, Vasyl Prozorov. The CCD demonstrated how stories were methodically recast and carried out in translation for targeted audiences throughout Europe and Asia.

The "UkrLeaks" case has highlighted how disinformation has become a globalized, industrial-scale operation in which individual falsehoods are incorporated into vast, complex multiplatform ecosystems. Successful mitigation therefore requires a multipronged strategy, including rapid action against operators, international cooperation, coordinated engagement with platforms, and civic education. The CCD's approach to the case provides a clear example of how rigorous analysis, attribution, and strategic communication can be used together to disrupt sophisticated disinformation networks.

If "UkrLeaks" is about scale, the "clandestine transplantation" narrative proved staying power. A grotesque conspiracy theory alleging the trafficking of human organs, which has circulated in Ukraine since the 1990s, was weaponized during the Revolution of Dignity in 2014 and resurfaced after 2022 (Analytical research of the information space regarding the issue of «Clandestine transplantation» | Center for Countering Disinformation, 2023). Its persistence is a reminder that certain myths are too emotionally charged ever to die out and can be reactivated in times of crisis. The CCD tracked the evolution of this narrative from falsified testimonies in Donbas, to attacks on healthcare reforms during the tenure of former Minister of Health of Ukraine Ulana Suprun, and finally to post-2022 fabrications accusing Red Cross personnel of involvement in organ trafficking. And the release of RT's documentary "Tanks for kidneys" demonstrated how a long-exposed falsehood can be reinvented as the latest in investigative reporting. In addressing this case, the CCD highlighted a crucial insight: some disinformation cannot be entirely removed and must instead be managed and inoculated against, so that any recurrence encounters an audience already sceptical.

The "information alibi" tactic represents perhaps the most sinister pattern identified by the CCD. In this approach, Russia not only lies after committing mass atrocities but also pre-accuses Ukraine of the very crimes it plans to commit. Prior to the March 2022 bombing of the Mariupol Drama Theater, pro-Kremlin Telegram channels circulated warnings of a supposed Ukrainian "provocation," anticipating Russia's later effort to disclaim responsibility for the attack. Russian forces then bombed the theatre, killing a large number of civilians who had taken refuge inside. In a similar pattern, Russian outlets warned civilians to stay away from trains before the missile strike on Kramatorsk railway station. Comparable tactics preceded the explosion in the Olenivka prison, the discovery of mass graves in Izium, and even threats to Ukraine's hydroelectric dams (Analytical report «The

Use Of Information Alibis By Russian Resources» | Center for Countering Disinformation, 2024). The aim was obvious: to create the conditions for plausible deniability and to preemptively poison international discourse before facts were established. With an account of this pattern, the CCD reframed all these incidents not as one-off propaganda moments but as integral elements of military strategy, demonstrating that disinformation is not a separate war, but part of the war itself.

Together, these cases illustrate the scope and complexity of the CCD's work. Its domain includes episodic crisis response, as seen in the "Black Hole" campaign; systemic mapping and disruption of coordinated disinformation ecosystems, such as "UkrLeaks"; management of persistent and historically rooted conspiracies, for example the "Clandestine transplantation" narrative; and forward-looking exposure of blame-shifting tactics, exemplified by the pattern labelled "information alibi." What unites these diverse initiatives is the recognition that societal resilience requires a sustained and coordinated approach, that combines continuous monitoring and timely public communication, strategic collaboration with law enforcement and security authorities, and joint efforts with the international community.

The CCD must negotiate its way through this high-stakes terrain under conditions of scarce resources. With a small staff and limited technical capabilities, it frequently functions simultaneously as an analytical center, a communication hub and something like a quasi-diplomatic mission. But underfunding information defense during wartime has proved as dangerous as neglecting air defense, a lesson many democracies watching Ukraine's experience from the sidelines come to appreciate only when it is too late to avoid the consequences.

At the core of the problem is a balancing between speed and accuracy. Disinformation travels at digital speed: narratives are planted and amplified within minutes, while the truth must be carefully verified and corroborated before being presented. The tragedies that unfolded in Bucha, Mariupol and Olenivka are cases in point. And those who hesitated to communicate evidence permitted disinformation to gain the narrative, whereas premature disclosure can undermine public trust. The asymmetry is structural: disinformation enjoys a first-mover advantage, exploiting the very processes that give truth its authority.

Even when evidence is strong, another tension remains: trust and legitimacy. A state institution calling material "false" will always be charged with censorship or political bias. Rather than attempting to impose its authority, the CCD avoids such rigidities and relies instead upon transparency as the foundation of its operations. Its guiding principle is that legitimacy must be earned rather than simply imposed, and that public trust depends as much on the transparency and honesty of communication as it does on the factual evidence itself.

Technology has further compounded the complexity. The emergence of deepfakes, synthetic audio, and algorithm-driven amplification has created a fast-shifting battlefield, where states may find themselves confronting threats with tools they neither own nor fully understand. This asymmetry highlights one of the deepest problems with digital sovereignty: for all governments' efforts to protect their citizens from information aggression, they must operate within infrastructures conceived and controlled elsewhere.

In addition to institutional and technological obstacles, there is the human factor. After years of hybrid warfare, Ukrainian society began to show signs of what might be called "truth fatigue." Faced with a constant barrage of competing claims, citizens risked slipping into nihilism – believing nothing rather than everything. In this context, media literacy and pre-bunking are not merely educational initiatives, they are acts of self-preservation. They work more slowly than a viral lie, but they are essential to developing long-term resilience.

As a whole, these experiences provide more than an account of Ukraine's fight against disinformation. They provide lessons for democracies everywhere. The Ukrainian case shows that it is possible to defend truth without claiming ownership of it, to act rapidly without compromising credibility, to work effectively without coercion, and to find resources of resilience against burn-out. Disinformation, in this sense, is not just a distant or adversarial problem. It is about defending the epistemic conditions that make democratic legitimacy possible in an age when information itself has become a form of warfare.

> At the core of the problem is a balancing between speed and accuracy. Dis-information travels at digital speed: narratives are planted and amplified with-in minutes, while the truth must be carefully verified and corroborated before being presented. The tragedies that unfolded in Bucha, Mariupol and Olenivka are cases in point. And those who hesitated to communicate evidence per-mitted disinformation to gain the narrative, whereas premature disclosure can undermine public trust. The asymmetry is structural: disinformation enjoys a first-mover advantage, exploiting the very processes that give truth its authority.
>
> The Ukrainian case shows that it is possible to defend truth without claiming ownership of it, to act rapidly without compromising credibility, to work effectively without coercion, and to find resources of resilience against burn-out.

3.3 Lessons Learned by CCD

> The CCD's work with NATO StratCom COE, the EU East StratCom Task Force, and the G7 Rapid Response Mechanism exemplifies the materialization of a shared cognitive defense. In an era when disinformation travels across borders as swiftly as bullets, national resilience depends on collective vigilance, joint research, and coordinated actions.

If challenges reveal the limitations of counter-disinformation, lessons likewise highlight its potential. A set of insights can be drawn from Ukraine's experience with the CCD—not as prescriptive technical solutions, but as strategic guidance for democracies confronting hybrid threats.

First, institutions matter. Resilience cannot be built on ad hoc initiatives or temporary task forces. The formal institutionalization of the CCD under Ukraine's National Security and Defence Council represents more than a bureaucratic milestone. It sends a clear signal that disinformation is treated as a strategic threat alongside cyberattacks or conventional military aggression. The lesson is evident: durable institutions, well-defined missions, and long-term commitment are essential to sustaining defence against information threats.

Just as important is the principle that whole-of-government approaches are more than just rhetoric. The role of the CCD in coordinating among ministries, agencies, and security services exemplifies both the necessity and the fragility of such strategies. Successful coordination is not about telling people what to do, it is a form of composition—sounding off, dialogic and transparent cooperation that transforms separate actors into a unified system of defence.

Transparency becomes a strategic asset. In democracies, openness turns credibility into resilience. And when Russia tries to discredit Ukraine by accusing it of lying, clear evidence, international data, and visibly transparent partnership serve as shields. The CCD's reliance on an open verification process and its global coordination shows that truth defended openly is truth strengthened.

Alliances also spread the defensive perimeter. The CCD's work with NATO StratCom COE, the EU East StratCom Task Force, and the G7 Rapid Response Mechanism exemplifies the materialization of a shared cognitive defense. In an era when disinformation travels across borders as swiftly as bullets, national resilience depends on collective vigilance, joint research, and coordinated actions.

The first line of defence is society itself. This is not simply a matter of civic programming, media literacy or activities for children, but the national-security infrastructure we need. When critical thinking is effectively planted, it grows into a resilient shield against manipulation and propaganda, placing ordinary citizens on the front lines of national defence.

When critical thinking is effectively planted, it grows into a resilient shield against manipulation and propaganda, placing ordinary citizens on the front lines of national defence.

And, last but not least, being flexible and proactive are keys to survival. Disinformation evolves rapidly, and so must the responses. The CCD has demonstrated flexibility—moving from conventional campaigns to TikTok outreach, and from monitoring to collaborative NATO-supported research. Yet adaptability alone is insufficient. Proactivity is just as important: anticipating narratives, pre-bunking lies, and shaping public expectations before falsehoods can proliferate. The best defence often lies in staying a step ahead.

Analytically, these lessons situate the CCD not only as a Ukrainian institution, but as a laboratory of democratic resilience. Its history affirms that, despite their exposure to disinformation, democracies possess attributes that authoritarian systems cannot replicate: they are transparent, alliance-based, fuelled by citizens with critical thinking, strategically adaptable, and act proactively. The objective isn't to eliminate disinformation—an impossible goal—but to foster resilience: the ability to absorb lies without losing faith, to repel propaganda without sacrificing freedom, and to act in defence of truth before truth itself is weaponized. In doing so, the CCD provides a model for how democracies can stand up for truth under assault, safeguarding both security and the principles they embody.

The CCD is a matter of necessity and a laboratory of innovation. Forged in the crucible of war, it integrates monitoring, strategic communication, international partnerships, and cooperation with security institutions into a single mission: safeguarding Ukraine's information space while sharing its lessons globally. For Ukraine, the CCD is the shield that backs up the military defence with cognitive resilience. And as a model for the international community, it demonstrates that a democracy whose survival is on the line can experiment with new ideas and even instruct others how to defend truth in the digital era.

What's crucial is that the experience of the CCD shows us that resilience cannot and should not be based solely on a response to hostile narratives. While reactivity is important, proactivity is equally essential. Anticipating Russian falsehoods, prebunking foreign intentions, and managing public expectations before manipulation takes hold reduces the effectiveness of disinformation operations while reinforcing trust in democratic institutions. This proactive approach rests on a simple but powerful principle: in the information domain, as in military defence, prevention is frequently worth more than a cure.

Being flexible and proactive are keys to survival. Disinformation evolves rapidly, and so must the responses. The CCD has demonstrated flexibility – moving from conventional campaigns to TikTok outreach, and from monitoring to collaborative NATO-supported research. Yet adaptability alone is insufficient.

References

About Center for Countering Disinformartion | Center for Countering Disinformation. (2021, 22 December). Available at https://cpd.gov.ua/en/docs/about-center-for-countering-disinformartion/. Accessed 1 November 2025.

Analytical research based on the results of the revealed disinformation campaign the "Black hole" of the russian federation aimed at discrediting Ukraine and President Zelensky | Center for Countering Disinformation. (2023, 7 June). Available at https://cpd.gov.ua/en/report/analytical/. Accessed: 1 November 2025).

Analytical report «The network of Russian propaganda resources «Ukrleaks» | Center for Countering Disinformation. (2024, 5 December). Available at https://cpd.gov.ua/en/report/analytical-reportthe-network-of-russian-propaganda-resources-ukrleaks/. Accessed 1 November 2025.

Analytical Report «The Use of Information Alibis by Russian Resources» | Center for Countering Disinformation. (2024, 23 July). Available at https://cpd.gov.ua/en/report/analytical-report-the-use-of-information-alibis-by-russian-resources/. Accessed 1 November 2025.

Analytical research of the information space regarding the issue of «Clandestine transplantation» | Center for Countering Disinformation. (2023). Available at https://cpd.gov.ua/en/report/transplantation/. Accessed 1 November 2025.

Decree of the President of Ukraine No. 106/2021. (2021). Official Internet representation of the President of Ukraine. Available at https://www.president.gov.ua/documents/1062021-37421. Accessed 1 November 2025.

Telegram: View @CenterCounteringDisinformation. (n.d.). Available at https://t.me/CenterCounteringDisinformation/11045. Accessed: 1 November 2025.

The Integrity Online Project. (2022). Available at https://www.youtube.com/watch?v=9mmV2888_KA. Accessed 1 November 2025.
The main portal about sponsors and supporters of the aggression. (n.d.). War & Sanctions. Available at https://war-sanctions.gur.gov.ua/en/. Accessed 1 November 2025.

4 Center for Strategic Communication and Information Security to Reduce the Impact of Disinformation

4.1 Introduction and Context

Since 2014, Ukraine has faced a concerted campaign of Russian disinformation and information warfare aimed at undermining its sovereignty and social cohesion. The Kremlin's use of propaganda to support its military aggression—from the 2014 annexation of Crimea to the full-scale invasion launched in 2022—exposed critical vulnerabilities in Ukraine's information space. In response, Ukraine embarked on building institutional capacity to resist malign information influence. A major step was the creation of dedicated strategic communications and counter-disinformation bodies to coordinate government efforts and leverage civil society expertise.

The Centre for Strategic Communication and Information Security (CSC) was established under the then Ministry of Culture and Information Policy (MCIP) in March 2021 as one such mechanism for strengthening national resilience and countering information threats in partnership with public institutions, civil society, and international allies. It was part of a broader strategy—including a new Information Security Strategy adopted in 2021—to fortify Ukraine's informational sovereignty amid unprecedented hybrid warfare.

4.2 Establishment and Legal Basis of the CSC

The Center's founding mission was to build national resilience to information threats and disinformation through close collaboration with relevant state bodies, the media sector, NGOs, and international partners. It was conceived as a central hub for strategic communications—effectively, Ukraine's governmental fact-checking and strategic messaging organization, aimed at ensuring the integrity of the information environment and countering hostile influence operations.

A. Marushchak et al., *Counter Disinformation System Development in Ukraine*, Terrorism, Security, and Computation, https://doi.org/10.1007/978-3-032-24731-5_4

The Centre for Strategic Communication and Information Security (often abbreviated as CSC or simply "the Center for Strategic Communications") was formally established on March 31, 2021, by order of then the Ministry of Culture and Information Policy. Its creation was driven by recognition of a critical gap in Ukraine's institutional landscape for fighting disinformation. After Russia's initial aggression in 2014, Ukraine's civil society had developed substantial expertise in exposing and debunking propaganda, while government communications remained comparatively uncoordinated and under-resourced. To bridge this divide, then-Minister of Culture and Information Policy Oleksandr Tkachenko announced a new center that would foster a "whole-of-society" response to information threats, uniting governmental and non-governmental efforts (Countering disinformation: Tkachenko spoke about cooperation with the center at the National Security and Defense Council, 2021). The Center's founding mission was to build national resilience to information threats and disinformation through close collaboration with relevant state bodies, the media sector, NGOs, and international partners. It was conceived as a central hub for strategic communications—effectively, Ukraine's governmental fact-checking and strategic messaging organization, aimed at ensuring the integrity of the information environment and countering hostile influence operations.

The legal basis for CSC's activities is grounded in Ukrainian national security strategy documents. In late 2021, the President approved a new Information Security Strategy (Presidential Decree No. 685/2021) (On the decision of the National Security & Defense Council of Ukraine of October15, 2021 'On the Information Security Strategy', 2021) which explicitly highlighted the need for dedicated institutions to counter disinformation. The establishment of the CSC under MCIP (and a parallel Center for Countering Disinformation (CCD) under the National Security and Defense Council) (Mission of the Center for Countering Disinformation, 2021) that year was cited as a key step toward implementing this strategy. The Deputy Minister of MCIP emphasized that standing up the CSC was an "institutional component" of combating propaganda—creating a professional team to work on disinformation countermeasures, media literacy promotion, strategic communications, and related information security tasks (The Center's publication on the information war was created not only for historical purposes but also for law enforcement agencies, says Ihor Solovei, 2024a).

The CSC team is structurally integrated within the national news agency Ukrinform—a setup intended to amplify the Center's messaging reach via state media channels (Ukrinform—Ukrainian National News Agency, n.d.). International donors also supported the Center's formation: for example, a USAID-funded consultancy in 2021 provided best-practice input into designing the CSC's functions and workflow. In sum, the CSC was established as a government entity to fulfil objectives set by Ukraine's information security policies, with a charter empowering it to coordinate across ministries and engage external partners in pursuit of a more resilient information space.

4.3 Mission and Strategic Goals

> By understanding both the content of propaganda and the demographics it targets, CSC aims to provide an evidence-based foundation for response. This analytic function is essentially the "early warning system"—tracking hostile influence activities in real time.

> CSC strives to implement a "One Voice" policy across ministries in the in-formation domain, so that Ukraine projects a consistent and fact-based narrative in the face of propaganda.

The core mission of the CSC is to ensure the integrity of Ukraine's information environment and strengthen societal resilience against misinformation and propaganda. In public-facing terms, the Center's mission is building information integrity by raising awareness about informational threats, empowering civil society to take action, and building public resilience. This succinct statement captures the dual emphasis on defensive measures (protecting the information sphere from malign influence) and proactive capacity-building (enabling citizens and institutions to withstand and counter falsehoods). The CSC explicitly positions itself as a bridge between the government, civil society, and the public, facilitating a unified nationwide response to disinformation (About the Stratcom Centre, 2023). As such, its mission goes beyond government communications alone—it seeks to mobilize and coordinate the whole of society in confronting information threats. This approach reflects lessons learned since 2014: Ukraine's vibrant civil society and independent media had led many counter-disinformation initiatives, so the new Center aimed to integrate and amplify these efforts at the state level rather than supplant them.

Strategic Goals and Functions: To operationalize its mission, the CSC focuses on several strategic goals, often articulated as four core functions:

1. Monitoring and Analyzing the Information Environment: The Center continuously monitors media and online platforms to detect disinformation narratives, influence operations, and emerging information threats. It conducts analysis of these narratives and also researches the vulnerabilities of different audiences. By understanding both the content of propaganda and the demographics it targets, CSC aims to provide an evidence-based foundation for response. This analytic function is essentially the "early warning system"—tracking hostile influence activities in real time.
2. Raising Awareness of Information Threats: A major goal is to inform and educate the public (and media partners) about disinformation tactics and specific false narratives so that Ukrainians are less susceptible to them. The Center produces explainer content, fact-checks, and investigative reports to debunk fake stories. It also organizes press conferences, public discussions, and media campaigns highlighting the nature of information warfare. The objective is to keep society alert to propaganda and to inoculate audiences against manipulation through timely, credible information.

3. Supporting Government Strategic Communications: The CSC works to improve the government's own communication capabilities and coherence in responding to disinformation. This includes developing a rapid response communication system—for example, issuing daily "message boxes" or recommended talking points to align key officials' responses to prominent disinformation themes. It also involves training civil servants in communication skills and counter-disinformation techniques, thereby strengthening the government's institutional resilience against info attacks. In essence, CSC strives to implement a "One Voice" policy across ministries in the information domain, so that Ukraine projects a consistent and fact-based narrative in the face of propaganda.
4. Building Resilience of Vulnerable Audiences: Recognizing that certain segments of the population are more exposed or susceptible to malign information (such as communities in frontline regions, Russian-speaking citizens, or groups with low trust in institutions), the Center runs targeted outreach and education programs to bolster these audiences' resilience. This includes public awareness campaigns, distribution of informational handbooks, and partnering with local organizations to reach at-risk communities. By addressing specific fears or falsehoods circulating among vulnerable groups (e.g. rumours about mobilization or refugees), the CSC aims to preempt wedge issues that adversaries seek to exploit (About the Stratcom Centre, 2023).

Additionally, the CSC contributes to developing Ukraine's overall strategic communications system and policy framework. It advises on terminology and doctrine for information security, and it coordinates multi-stakeholder activities to institutionalize best practices in StratCom. For example, the Center played a lead role in organizing the Kyiv StratCom Forum, which convened dozens of Ukrainian and international experts to discuss building national resilience to information threats. The strategic vision is long-term: to ensure Ukraine's information space remains robust and unified not only during the current conflict but as a permanent component of national security.

By addressing specific fears or falsehoods circulating among vulnerable groups (e.g. rumours about mobilization or refugees), the CSC aims to preempt wedge issues that adversaries seek to exploit.

4.4 Kyiv StratCom Forum (2021–2025)—Annual Strategic Communications Conference

Discussions focused on whole-of-government and whole-of-society strategies – for example, how state institutions could work with media, NGOs, and citizens to counter malign information influence and propaganda.

One of the flagship initiatives of the CSC is the Kyiv StratCom Forum, an annual international conference dedicated to strengthening Ukraine's information resilience. Launched in 2021, this two-day forum brings together officials, experts, and civil society leaders from Ukraine and partner countries to share experiences in countering disinformation and building strategic communications (Kyiv StratCom Forum, n.d.). Over the years, it has grown into Ukraine's largest international platform on information security and strategic communications, organized by the Centre in partnership with government ministries and supported by the EU, NATO, UNDP and other partners (Mykola Tochytskyi officially opened the Kyiv StratCom Forum 2025, 2025). Each forum centers on panel discussions and workshops that address evolving information threats, fostering a "*whole-of-society*" approach to information warfare in line with CSC's mission. Below is an overview of the Forum's development from 2021 through 2025, highlighting its key themes, notable speakers, conclusions, and growing impact.

2021—Inaugural Forum: Building National Resilience to Disinformation
The first Kyiv StratCom Forum was held online on December 7–8, 2021, soon after CSC was founded. It convened 32 Ukrainian and international experts in strategic communications, including high-level officials such as Vice Prime Minister Olha Stefanyshyna and Minister of Culture and Information Policy Oleksandr Tkachenko, alongside NATO and EU representatives like Baiba BraŽe, NATO's Assistant Secretary General for Public Diplomacy (Kyiv StratCom Forum, n.d.). The forum's goal was to coordinate government and civil society efforts to build national resilience against information threats and disinformation. Discussions focused on whole-of-government and whole-of-society strategies—for example, how state institutions could work with media, NGOs, and citizens to counter malign information influence and propaganda. This inaugural event established a foundation for Ukraine's strategic communications community, underlining that fostering cooperation across society is essential to defending the information space. The success of the first forum set the stage for it to become an annual platform for sharing best practices in information security.

2022—Adapting Amid Invasion: No Forum, but Heightened StratCom Efforts
In 2022, the outbreak of Russia's full-scale invasion dramatically shifted the information environment. The Kyiv StratCom Forum planned for that year was put on hold as urgent wartime communication took priority. Instead of convening a formal conference, CSC became intensely focused on real-time strategic communications to support Ukraine's defense. Indeed, after the February 2022 invasion, the Centre evolved into one of the leading channels of official communication about the war, countering Russian disinformation on a daily basis. The lessons and networks from the 2021 forum proved immediately valuable as CSC and its partners worked to inform the public, debunk fakes, and rally international support under crisis conditions. Although an annual forum could not be held in 2022, the year underscored why a coordinated information strategy is critical during conflict, reinforcing the long-term vision behind the StratCom Forum. These wartime experiences would directly inform the next forum's agenda when the event resumed in 2023.

2023—Second Forum: Ukrainian Experience of Strategic Communications in War

The Kyiv StratCom Forum returned in March 2023 as the "Second International Forum on Strategic Communications in Ukraine," now taking stock of a year of war. The 2023 forum (held online) was themed "Ukrainian experience of strategic communications in times of war," reflecting how Ukraine had become a frontline laboratory for counter-disinformation. Ukrainian officials and international partners gathered to analyze how information warfare had evolved since the invasion and to share Ukraine's hard-earned insights with the world. Key discussion themes included:

- Unified Wartime Messaging: How to maintain a *"unified voice"* of the state during war, through coordination among the military, government, and digital sectors. Leaders from the Ministry of Defense, Presidential Office, and Ministry of Digital Transformation discussed their experience aligning communications across agencies in wartime.
- Allied Support on the Information Front: How Western partners (EU, NATO, and individual allies) have been helping Ukraine *"support resilience"* against Russian information aggression. This panel featured ambassadors from Canada, the UK, EU, Sweden and NATO's public diplomacy leadership, focusing on international assistance in counter-propaganda efforts.
- Global Information Warfare Trends: The *global dimension of the information war*—how EU and NATO approaches to disinformation had changed since February 24, 2022. Experts from NATO StratCom COE and the EU's East StratCom Task Force discussed adaptive strategies in a new era of hybrid threats.
- "Information Ramstein" Coalition: Proposals for a united international coalition in the information domain—an "*information Ramstein*" (alluding to the military aid coordination) to synchronize communications strategy among Ukraine and its partners (Already in the first months it was obvious that Ukraine was winning the information war,—Minister Tkachenko—Center for Strategic Communication and Information Security, 2023). Ukrainian ministers and renowned information warfare researchers (like Peter Pomerantsev) deliberated on forging a permanent coalition to fight disinformation.
- Accountability for Propaganda: Whether and how to criminalize Russian propaganda and hold *information war criminals* to account. This novel discussion, led by experts from NATO StratCom and Ukrainian media watchdogs, explored legal mechanisms to prosecute those orchestrating malign information campaigns.

Notable speakers in 2023 included Minister Oleksandr Tkachenko, Presidential advisor Mykhailo Podoliak, Deputy Defense Minister Andriy Shevchenko, and advisors from Ukraine's security agencies—alongside Western figures like British Ambassador Melinda Simmons, Canadian Ambassador Larisa Galadza, EU Chargé d'Affaires Rémi Duflot, and NATO Deputy ASG Carmen Romero. A major conclusion of the 2023 forum was the importance of internationalizing Ukraine's fight against disinformation: Ukraine's representatives urged closer cooperation with allies to mirror the military coalition in the information sphere, and highlighted that Russia's propagandists should face global scrutiny for fueling aggression. The forum also affirmed that Ukraine's experience in strategic communications under fire has valuable lessons for NATO and EU partners («It's time for the world to hear Ukrainian voices": the main points about the EU's approaches to information warfare from the Center's forum—Center for Strategic Communication and Information Security, 2023). Overall, the second StratCom Forum solidified Ukraine's role as a key contributor to the international "*information defense*" dialogue, while reinforcing the need for a unified strategic narrative at home and abroad during the war.

2024—Third Forum: Communicating New Challenges and the Future

Held on March 27–28, 2024 in Kyiv, the third Kyiv StratCom Forum shifted focus toward the future. Titled "How to Communicate New Challenges to Ukraine and the World (Strategy for the Future)", the 2024 forum addressed how Ukraine should project its narrative looking forward, even as the war continued. Acting Minister of Culture and Information Policy Rostyslav Karandieiev opened the event by emphasizing that strategic communications are vital to sustain international solidarity: global leaders and publics *"must realize that Ukraine needs international support in fighting Russian aggression,"* and telling Ukraine's story effectively—including its struggles and successes—is key to securing weapons, funds, and humanitarian aid (*kicks off*, 2024).

Over two days, stratcom experts from Ukraine, the EU, and the U.S. discussed emerging challenges in the information war and how to keep the world engaged as attention to Ukraine's war risks fading. Participants examined questions such as: *How can Ukraine communicate the "new challenges" of 2024—from war fatigue to reconstruction—both domestically and internationally?* Panels delved into forward-looking topics. For example, one session showcased successful Ukrainian communication case studies from the past year and how these could inform future strategies. Another key theme was the "single information front": Ukrainian and Western participants discussed ways to create a unified information front against Russian propaganda going forward (Mykhailo Fedorov: 'We need to offer the world a new agenda on how to counter disinformation', 2024). Throughout the forum, there was an emphasis on innovation and adaptation in messaging—training officials in new stratcom skills, leveraging digital tools, and anticipating the narratives of the coming year.

The breadth of participants in 2024 demonstrated the forum's growing scope: *"high-ranking officials, communication experts, journalists, TV presenters, sociologists, and diplomats"* all took part (Kyiv StratCom Forum, 2024 kicks off, 2024). This cross-sector presence underscored that strategic communications is not just a government endeavor but a society-wide effort. A notable outcome of the 2024 forum was a shared understanding that Ukraine's communications strategy must transition from purely wartime messaging to a forward-looking narrative. The forum's discussions helped chart how Ukraine could talk about recovery, reforms, and its future in a way that keeps global partners invested while countering Kremlin narratives about Ukraine's endurance. In essence, the third StratCom Forum served to bridge the present conflict to Ukraine's post-war aspirations—ensuring that information resilience remains strong in the long term, not just in immediate crisis.

2025—Fourth Forum: Strengthening Information Resilience amid Global Changes

On April 24–25, 2025, the fourth Kyiv StratCom Forum took place in Kyiv (notably hosted at the National Museum of WWII, symbolizing Ukraine's historic resilience). The 2025 forum's theme—"Information Resilience of Ukraine in the Context of Global Changes"—reflected the broadening scope of Ukraine's information security concerns. With the war still ongoing but the global landscape shifting, the forum focused on how to amplify Ukraine's voice worldwide and fortify its information space against both Russian aggression and other emerging challenges. Mykola Tochytskyi, Ukraine's Minister of Culture and Strategic Communications, officially opened the forum, underlining that strategic communications had become a top national priority. He stressed the need to discuss ways to protect the country from information threats and to unite citizens around a common vision for Ukraine's future amid the war. "*Russia will never stop trying to undermine Ukraine and deny our right to exist as a sovereign nation. Defending and asserting this right is the core mission of Ukraine's strategic communications system,*" Minister Tochytskyi declared, framing the forum's significance (Mykola Tochytskyi officially opened the Kyiv StratCom Forum 2025, 2025). This statement highlighted that information defense is as critical as military defense in safeguarding Ukraine's sovereignty.

By 2025, the StratCom Forum had evolved into a major international gathering, with diplomats, government representatives, military communicators, journalists, and civil society leaders all in attendance. The agenda addressed both Ukraine's internal communication strategy and its coordination with allies. Notable panels and sessions in 2025 focused on: Ukraine's wartime communications strategy and lessons learned; "United Front" allied cooperation in strategic comms (bringing together NATO, EU, and Ukrainian officials to enhance multilateral coordination); the coordination of multi-layered defense in information warfare (how to align efforts from the tactical frontline to the cyber domain); and the challenges of communications on the frontline and in temporarily occupied territories, where participants discussed innovative solutions for reaching populations under duress. There was also strong emphasis on practical capacity-building, with workshops on improving communicators' skills and focused meetings to plan joint initiatives. Throughout these discussions, a recurring theme was resilience—both societal resilience, by inoculating the public against propaganda, and institutional resilience, by improving coordination mechanisms with international partners.

By the forum's conclusion, participants reinforced commitments to deepen international cooperation in StratCom, integrate Ukraine's insights into Western practices, and continuously adapt to new threats such as foreign "information manipulation and interference (FIMI)" in democratic societies ("A resilient Ukraine is important for a resilient Europe." Kyiv StratCom Forum 2025 has begun in Kyiv, 2025). The impact of the 2025 forum was evident in how institutionalized Ukraine's approach had become: strategic communications now have dedicated ministry oversight, regular high-level forums, and an international coalition of supporters. The Kyiv StratCom Forum at this stage was widely recognized as "Ukraine's largest international forum focused on information security, countering foreign interference, and advancing strategic communications" (Mykola Tochytskyi officially opened the Kyiv StratCom Forum 2025, 2025), underlining its importance as a permanent element of Ukraine's national security architecture.

Impact and Long-Term Vision: Across 2021–2025, the Kyiv StratCom Forum series has markedly advanced Ukraine's strategic communications capacity and international collaboration. Each year's forum built on the last—from establishing basic cooperation frameworks in 2021, through the wartime innovations shared in 2023, to the forward-looking strategies of 2024–2025—thereby institutionalizing best practices in counter-disinformation work. Crucially, the forum has embodied CSC's mission to foster a sustained response to disinformation at the level of society as a whole. By convening government, military, media, and NGO stakeholders in one space, the Centre uses the forum to coordinate multi-stakeholder activities for information security (as mandated in its charter) (Centre for Strategic Communication and Information Security, 2025). The strategic vision behind these efforts is unmistakably long-term: to ensure Ukraine's information space remains robust and unified not only during the current conflict, but as a permanent component of national security. The Kyiv StratCom Forum, now an annual institution, plays a lead role in realizing that vision—helping Ukraine and its allies to stay ahead of information threats through unity, shared knowledge, and proactive communication strategies.

> Participants reinforced commitments to deepen international cooperation in StratCom, integrate Ukraine's insights into Western practices, and continuously adapt to new threats such as foreign "information manipulation and interference (FIMI)" in democratic societies.

4.5 The CSC's Organizational Structure and Resources

The internal structure of CSC is organized around its core functional areas. There are dedicated teams for: Monitoring & Analysis, Content/Digital Communications, Strategic Projects/Campaigns, and Capacity-Building (Training). Each team comprises specialists with relevant skills—for example, the Monitoring & Analysis unit includes media monitoring experts, data analysts, and researchers; the Digital Communications unit has editors, copywriters, social media managers, videographers, and designers producing multimedia content. The Projects team leads initiatives like the Dovidka.info handbook and other campaigns, while the Capacity-Building team organizes training programs for officials. A small support staff (for administration, coordination, and MEL—monitoring, evaluation, learning—functions) underpins these teams.

The CSC operates with a degree of autonomy in its day-to-day functions (especially editorial output), but it is subject to the oversight of MCIP's leadership and aligns with government policy on information security. Importantly, the Center's content-production arm till February 2025 was embedded in Ukrinform, the state-owned news agency. This arrangement means that CSC analysts can leverage Ukrinform's distribution channels to reach wide audiences, while maintaining the Center's distinct branding (such as the "Spravdi" website, which serves as CSC's public portal). The Spravdi portal and associated social media accounts are a primary vehicle for the Center's public communications, marked as official materials of the CSC.

The Center is led by a Head (Director) appointed by the Minister of Culture and Information Policy of Ukraine. The first head of the CSC was Liubov Tsybulska, a seasoned expert on hybrid warfare, who took charge at inception in spring 2021 (Cabinet of Ministers of Ukraine—Center for Strategic Communications & Information Security presented, 2021). In September 2021, Ihor Solovey, a journalist and information policy expert, assumed leadership of the Center and continues to serve as Head as of 2025 (The Center for Strategic Communications and Information Security has a new head, 2021).

The internal structure of CSC is organized around its core functional areas. There are dedicated teams for: Monitoring & Analysis, Content/Digital Communications, Strategic Projects/Campaigns, and Capacity-Building (Training). Each team comprises specialists with relevant skills—for example, the Monitoring & Analysis unit includes media monitoring experts, data analysts, and researchers; the Digital Communications unit has editors, copywriters, social media managers, videographers, and designers producing multimedia content. The Projects team leads initiatives like the Dovidka.info handbook and other campaigns, while the Capacity-Building team organizes training programs for officials. A small support staff (for administration, coordination, and MEL—monitoring, evaluation, learning—functions) underpins these teams.

In total, the CSC staff numbered a few dozen as of 2023, reflecting a relatively lean organization. This human capital has been augmented by external expertise and partnerships. The Center routinely collaborates with civil society organizations, academic researchers, and volunteers who contribute to its projects or share data/insights. For instance, Ukrainian fact-checking NGOs and think tanks often coordinate with CSC analysts on research studies and debunking efforts, effectively extending the Center's network beyond its formal staff. International advisers have also assisted—the initial roadmap was developed with input from Western StratCom practitioners, and Western governments have provided training opportunities to CSC personnel.

While the CSC itself is relatively small, it functions as a coordinator within a larger ecosystem. Internally, it coordinates with MCIP's other departments (e.g. those handling media development or international cultural diplomacy). Externally, it liaises with the National Security and Defense Council (which oversees the Center for Countering Disinformation), with the Ministry of Defense and military StratCom units, with the security services, and with regional authorities. To formalize civil society cooperation, the CSC set up a Civil Society Cooperation Framework—essentially a platform for regular information exchange and joint planning with NGOs, media, and fact-checking initiatives. This whole-of-society coordination mandate is a defining feature of its structure. Deputy Minister Taras Shevchenko of MCIP noted that beyond creating the Center as an institution, another key pillar of Ukraine's approach was an "information security strategy encompassing counteraction to disinformation, media literacy, strategic communication," and legal protections—indicating that CSC is one node in a broader interagency and public–private network addressing these tasks (The Center's publication on the information war was created not only for historical purposes but also for law enforcement agencies, says Ihor Solovei, 2024a). The Center also serves as a point of contact for international cooperation on counter-disinformation: it represents Ukraine in various multilateral forums and liaises with the EU StratCom units, NATO centers, and partner governments' communications teams.

4.6 The CSC's Core Activities and Operational Practices

The CSC executes a wide array of activities in pursuit of its mission, ranging from daily media monitoring to nationwide public campaigns. These activities align with the core functional areas outlined earlier. In this section, we examine each major category of the Center's operations—illustrating how the CSC works on a practical level and highlighting notable initiatives under each category.

4.6.1 Monitoring and Threat Analysis

> The Center's Project Library includes studies like "The Main Myth of Russian Propaganda: An Analysis of the Narrative of 'Ukrainian Fascism'" (2025) and "Kremlin's Anti-European Narratives: A Map of Information Threats to Ukraine" (2025), among many others.

The starting point for effective counter-disinformation is situational awareness. The CSC operates a Monitoring & Analysis unit that keeps a constant pulse on the information environment. This team employs both automated tools and manual analysis to track print, broadcast, online, and social media for emerging disinformation narratives. Special focus is given to Russian state media and proxy outlets, as well as popular social networks like Facebook and Telegram where false stories may spread. For example, the Center's analysts monitor Telegram channels (including Russian and collaborator-run channels targeting Ukrainian audiences) and identify key propaganda themes on a daily and weekly basis. Due to technical and legal limitations (e.g., data access restrictions on certain platforms), the Center also relies on crowd-sourced inputs—notably the "Spravdi Bot," a chatbot launched to allow citizens to report suspected disinformation they encounter. Tips from the public via the Spravdi Bot are processed and cross-checked by analysts, enhancing the Center's coverage of the information battlefield.

The Monitoring unit produces analytical bulletins and alerts on disinformation trends. During the full-scale war, the CSC moved to a 24/7 monitoring cycle, issuing *daily propaganda digests* that summarized prominent Russian lies of the day and provided context for why those narratives were being pushed (The Center's publication on the information war was created not only for historical purposes but also for law enforcement agencies, says Ihor Solovei, 2024b). These daily reports not only informed government decision-makers but have now been compiled into a comprehensive publication How the Russian information ship sank (How the Russian Information Ship Went To..., n.d.). This volume is a longitudinal reconstruction and analysis of Russia's information war against Ukraine during the first 21 months of the full-scale invasion. The book is based on a curated selection of the Centre's daily digests of Russian disinformation and propaganda. It covers the period from 24 February 2022 to the end of November 2023, presenting a day-by-day chronicle of key messages, narratives and information operations targeting Ukraine, its partners, and occupied territories.

Empirically, the collection functions as a dense primary source corpus. It documents how, within the first two months of the invasion, the Kremlin deployed almost the full spectrum of its "toxic narratives", and how subsequent information activity consisted largely of re-activating and recycling already familiar themes. The material allows researchers to trace both the thematic "backbone" of Russian propaganda and its dynamics over time: the shift from euphoria and expectations of a rapid victory, through attempts to rationalize military failures, to increasingly desperate efforts to maintain domestic control and intimidate external audiences.

Analytically, the book foregrounds several interlocking dimensions of Russia's information warfare:

- Novomova and euphemisms. A substantial section dissects the regime's specific vocabulary ("special military operation" instead of "war", "regrouping", "gesture of goodwill", "education of military activity"), showing how language is used to normalise aggression, erase Ukrainian agency and mask defeats. This "newspeak" is read as a deliberate strategy to manipulate emotional perception and suppress the political meaning of events.
- Master narratives and recurring techniques. Across the chronicle the reader sees the consistent deployment of core narratives: inevitability of Russian victory; dehumanisation and demonisation of Ukrainian defenders; systematic attacks on Ukrainian leadership as "incompetent", "corrupt" and "controlled from abroad"; delegitimisation of Western support; and extensive mirror-propaganda that projects Russian war crimes onto Ukraine. The text provides numerous instances where Russia blames Ukrainian air defence for civilian casualties or stages shelling of occupied cities to obscure its own attacks.

- Information control on temporarily occupied territories. The book outlines a typical sequence of measures: creating an information vacuum; monopolising access to news; spreading disinformation about the fall of Kyiv and collapse of Ukrainian governance; constructing dependency through controlled "humanitarian aid"; and then moving to de-Ukrainisation via destruction of Ukrainian symbols, forced passportisation, pseudo-referenda and staged "elections". Particular attention is paid to the targeting of children and youth, including indoctrination in schools and deportations, situating propaganda within a broader system of occupation practices.
- Actors and ecosystem of the propaganda machine. Rather than reducing propaganda to a single institution, the volume shows it as an integrated feature of the Russian political system. It maps roles across levels—from Putin's "programmatic" speeches that set the frame, through church leaders, senior officials and diplomats, to television show hosts, "war correspondents", "experts", foreign amplifiers and collaborators. The book also highlights tensions within this ecosystem, such as the rise and subsequent disciplining of "war correspondents" and figures like Yevgeny Prigozhin.

A distinctive contribution of the volume is its periodization of the information war into seven phases, synchronized with major military and political developments: the initial offensive and failed blitzkrieg; the shift to attrition warfare in the east; Ukrainian counter-offensives in Kharkiv and Kherson; the campaign against Ukraine's energy infrastructure; the emergence of armed Russian anti-Kremlin formations; Prigozhi's mutiny and internal destabilisation; and the opening of additional crises (e.g. the Hamas attack on Israel) that Russia attempts to exploit. For each phase, the book shows how propaganda narratives are adjusted to explain away setbacks, maintain the illusion of control, and reframe defeats as tactical maneuvers.

At the same time, the authors insists that this should not obscure the legal and criminological dimension. By systematically documenting statements, themes and calls to violence, it positions the collection as a resource for law-enforcement bodies and international justice mechanisms investigating Russian information crimes, incitement, and justification of aggression and genocide.

For researchers of propaganda, information operations, and contemporary Russian–Ukrainian relations, the volume offers:

- a structured, time-stamped empirical base for narrative analysis;
- an inside view of how a state StratCom body monitored, classified and interpreted hostile information activities in real time;
- a bridge between discourse analysis (lexicon, metaphors, symbols such as the "Z") and the material effects of occupation, deportation and terror.

In sum, it is both a chronicle and an analytical guide to Russia's information warfare playbook in 2022–2023: how narratives are constructed, tested, stabilized and weaponized—and how they interact with kinetic operations, occupation policies and global crises.

In addition to such digests, the CSC analysts author in-depth research reports dissecting specific influence campaigns. For instance, the Center's Project Library includes studies like "The Main Myth of Russian Propaganda: An Analysis of the Narrative of 'Ukrainian Fascism'" (2025) and "Kremlin's Anti-European Narratives: A Map of Information Threats to Ukraine" (2025), among many others (Project Library, 2025). These reports compile data and examples of recurring falsehoods (e.g., the trope that Ukraine is a "Nazi" state) and examine their evolution and impact. By publishing such analyses, the CSC aims to raise awareness among policymakers, journalists, and the public of the tactics, themes, and objectives of Russian information operations.

4.6.2 Public Communication and Awareness Campaigns

The reach of Dovidka's multimedia content grew impressively: as of the end of 2023, Dovidka.info expert videos on YouTube had accumulated 8.6 million views in 2023 alone, and over 24.7 million total views since the project's start. These videos were not confined to the internet—they were also broadcast on national television (e.g. via the United News marathon), on public transit media (digital screens in the Kharkiv metro system and on Intercity trains), and through regional media partnerships. Such distribution ensured that Dovidka's guidance could reach even those without constant internet access, exemplifying an adaptive communication strategy that bridged digital and traditional channels.

A central pillar of CSC activity is its outward-facing communication to inform and inoculate the public. The Center runs a multi-platform content operation under the banner "Spravdi" (meaning "In Truth" in Ukrainian). This includes an official website (spravdi.gov.ua, with Ukrainian and English content sections) and active accounts on Facebook, Twitter (X), Instagram, YouTube, Telegram, and Viber. Through these channels, the CSC disseminates a steady stream of content: debunkings of fake news, fact-check explainers, infographics, situation updates, and positive narratives about Ukraine's resilience. For example, the Center's "Debunking Fake" section might take a viral false claim (such as a fabricated story about Ukrainian leadership or the military) and publish a short article explaining the truth of the matter and the likely origin of the fake (Project Library, 2025). The tone of these communications is kept professional and evidence-driven to build trust; as an official government outlet, Spravdi must carefully distinguish itself from propaganda.

The Center also engages in long-form content to deepen public understanding of the information war. It has published books and manuals, such as *"Russia's Hybrid War against Ukraine: How to Win on the Information Front"* (June 2023) (Project Library, 2025). This particular manual compiles lessons learned and guidance for both officials and citizens on countering Russian propaganda, reflecting the CSC's role in documenting best practices.

Dovidka.info

Another notable product is the Dovidka.info emerged as a core initiative of CSC in 2021. The project's foundation was laid with an informational brochure titled "In Case of Emergency or War", presented in Kyiv in June 2021 as the first public product of the newly formed Centre. According to CSC head Liubov Tsybulska, this brochure was inspired by Sweden's civil defense handbook tradition—exemplified by Sweden's famous *If Crisis or War Comes* guide—and aimed to condense survival instructions into simple, accessible language (rather than a dense 500-page manual) (An information brochure "In case of emergency or war" was presented in Kyiv—ArmyInform, 2021). Developed in cooperation with Ukraine's Ministry of Defence, General Staff, State Emergency Service and expert NGOs, the brochure provided basic recommendations that citizens could quickly read during imminent danger, with a dedicated section on information hygiene and countering disinformation. Media experts in Ukraine immediately recognized this effort as only a "first step" toward protecting the public from the pervasive influence of hostile propaganda, noting that Russian "disinformation troops" operate relentlessly and that counter-measures must be systematic and sustained. In this context, the Dovidka project was envisioned as a means to build societal resilience by educating and preparing the civilian population for both physical emergencies and the information war. Following Russia's military buildup and hybrid threats in 2021, the Centre expanded the brochure into a comprehensive digital platform. The Dovidka.info website officially went live on 23 February 2022, exactly one day before the full-scale invasion of Ukraine, as a publicly accessible "safety handbook" for wartime (EU Project to Help Ukrainians with Adaptation in Wartime, 2022). The timing was strategic—anticipating the invasion and the consequent surge in public demand for reliable guidance. At launch, Dovidka.info aggregated the crucial content of the earlier brochure (civil defense instructions and tips to counter disinformation) and was poised to update citizens in real-time as the crisis unfolded. Indeed, once the war began, the Dovidka.info team began daily updates of instructions covering an expanding range of scenarios—from how to behave under artillery shelling or occupation, to cyber hygiene and coping with stress (EU Project to Help Ukrainians with Adaptation in Wartime, 2022). The platform's core purpose was defined as promptly providing citizens with verified, life-saving information across "a wide range of issues connected with Russia's full-scale invasion". In essence, Dovidka.info transformed the static 2021 brochure into a living, multimedia hub for civil defense knowledge, directly addressing the unprecedented challenges Ukrainians faced after February 2022.

From its inception as a website, Dovidka.info rapidly evolved into a multi-platform civil defence tool, expanding its formats and outreach channels through 2022 and 2023. The core website—available in Ukrainian, Russian and English versions—serves as a repository of practical instructions, organized by thematic sections (e.g. what to do "*during shelling*," "*under occupation*," "*in evacuation*," etc.). All content is developed in collaboration with subject-matter experts from relevant state agencies to ensure accuracy (for example, guidance on nuclear safety comes from the State Nuclear Regulatory Inspectorate, while medical tips involve the Ministry of Health). Notably, the instructions are presented in clear, concise language for broad accessibility. To cater to different preferences and reach citizens who may not frequently visit websites, the Dovidka project grew a presence on multiple popular platforms:

- Chatbots and Messengers: The Centre launched Dovidka chatbots on Telegram and Viber that replicate the website's tips in an interactive format. Users can obtain instant answers by querying these bots, which became especially valuable when web access was limited or when quick, on-the-go advice was needed. By late 2022, over 400,000 people had used the Dovidka chatbots on messaging apps (EU Project to Help Ukrainians with Adaptation in Wartime, 2022). Moreover, an official Dovidka Viber public channel was created, which by 2023 accrued 64,000 subscribers and was featured in Viber's "Useful" channels section to improve discoverability. These chatbots and channels effectively allowed Dovidka's guidance to "live" inside the apps Ukrainians were already using daily, constituting a form of real-time, conversational civil defense aid.
- Social Media and Video Content: Given the diverse media consumption habits of the public, Dovidka.info also extended into social networks and video platforms. The Centre's YouTube channel began hosting a dedicated series of Dovidka.info video explainers, where trusted experts (such as psychologists, medics, legal advisors, etc.) provided advice on surviving and organizing life during war. In cooperation with the European Union, a series of video instructions was produced throughout late 2022—with three new expert videos released each week on the SPRAVDI YouTube channel and cross-posted on social media. By November 2022, 51 such Dovidka video episodes had been published, covering topics from coping with grief to restarting a small business in wartime. This EU-supported video campaign (running through mid-2023) complemented the static web text with engaging, adaptive video content, allowing viewers to absorb guidance audibly and visually. The reach of Dovidka's multimedia content grew impressively: as of the end of 2023, Dovidka.info expert videos on YouTube had accumulated 8.6 million views in 2023 alone, and over 24.7 million total views since the project's start. These videos were not confined to the internet—they were also broadcast on national television (e.g. via the United News marathon), on public transit media (digital screens in the Kharkiv metro system and on Intercity trains), and through regional media partnerships. Such distribution ensured that Dovidka's guidance could reach even those without constant internet access, exemplifying an adaptive communication strategy that bridged digital and traditional channels.
- Social Networks Presence: Dovidka's team leveraged popular social platforms to disseminate tips in more bite-sized and visual forms. In all cases, the messaging was tailored to fit the medium—for example, concise graphical posts on Instagram, or subtitled vertical videos for TikTok—reflecting a multi-platform content adaptation approach. By diversifying across these networks, Dovidka.info established an omnipresent voice in the digital information

space, actively pushing authoritative information to citizens and countering the cacophony of rumors on social media.

- Offline and Print Extensions: While primarily a digital initiative, Dovidka.info also recognized the importance of offline reach, especially in regions with infrastructural challenges. The core advice from the site was compiled into a printed handbook (brochure) that was distributed across Ukraine, with special focus on front-line and occupied areas. As the RAND Corporation noted, Dovidka.info essentially functions as an *"online brochure"* that was also disseminated in print form to ensure even those without internet could access its life-saving tips (Ukrainian Resistance to Russian Disinformation: Lessons for Future Conflict, 2024). Additionally, in 2023 the Centre launched "Dovidka.info Resistance"—a regional outreach program bringing trainings, printed leaflets and posters to communities in liberated or high-risk areas. For example, posters with QR codes linking to Dovidka's website and YouTube were placed in all Ukrainian Railways (Ukrzaliznytsia) train carriages, providing passengers with easy access to the guidance on their smartphones. Short Dovidka audio clips (public service announcements with safety tips) were also aired on popular radio stations (HIT FM, Lux FM, etc.), collectively broadcast over 1500 times in the second half of 2023 (Centre for Strategic Communication: Results of 2023, 2023). This integration of Dovidka content into physical and traditional media environments underscores the project's expansion from a single website into a ubiquitous civil defence information ecosystem.

The audience reach of Dovidka.info grew correspondingly with its expansion. Within the first 9 months of the full-scale war, the Dovidka.info website had been visited by more than 1.5 million unique readers seeking guidance. By the end of 2023, the site's total cumulative reach had climbed to 12.7 million views since launch (Centre for Strategic Communication: Results of 2023, 2023). Such figures are remarkable for a governmental informational site, reflecting the public's continued reliance on Dovidka for trustworthy advice amid ongoing crises. This breadth of subject matter, combined with the multi-channel delivery, made Dovidka.info an essential part of daily life for many Ukrainians in 2022–2023. The project's importance was further cemented by high-profile support: it was funded in part by the European Union's "Support to Strategic Communication in Ukraine" initiative, and its success was cited by officials as evidence of Ukraine's resilience. For instance, EU representative Martin Schroeder praised Dovidka.info for giving hope and helping people navigate unprecedented challenges, noting that "Ukrainians have already experienced the first waves of emotions… however, there is a long way to go to overcome the consequences… This project aims to help people take this path and give hope" (EU Project to Help Ukrainians with Adaptation in Wartime, 2022).

Dovidka.info's effectiveness is not only due to its content, but also its emphasis on technical accessibility and real-time responsiveness. A few innovative features illustrate this aspect:

1. Real-Time Updates: The platform functions as a dynamic crisis-response tool, with the team updating instructions as new threats emerge or situations change on the ground. For example, when Russia began targeting Ukraine's energy infrastructure in late 2022, Dovidka.info quickly added guides on enduring long power outages and maintaining communications during blackouts. In 2023, as reports spread of Russian attempts to recruit Ukrainian teenagers for sabotage, Dovidka published detailed explainers for parents on how to recognize and prevent such recruitment tactics. This agility—posting verified information within hours of new developments—helped pre-empt misinformation and provided citizens with actionable advice in near real-time. The content is also curated in multiple formats (text articles, infographics, short FAQ answers) to suit different levels of internet bandwidth and user needs. The Centre intentionally kept the website lightweight and even provided a text-only "lite" option through chatbots, mindful of conditions where connectivity might be limited (About us—Dovidka.info, n.d.).
2. Chatbot Integration: As mentioned, Dovidka's Telegram and Viber chatbots were key technical solutions to deliver content interactively. These chatbots use simple menu-driven interfaces so that users can quickly navigate to the topic of concern (e.g. "*What to do if under artillery fire*" or "*How to filter fake news*") without browsing a website. By offloading the content to messaging apps, the information becomes available even when users have only intermittent or slow mobile internet, since text from a chatbot is low-bandwidth. The chatbot system effectively turned Dovidka's static articles into a query-response knowledge base, accessible on basic smartphones. This approach reflects Ukraine's wider trend of digital governance (such as the Diia app for government services) focusing on user-centric, chatbot-accessible design. Indeed, the Dovidka team worked with the Ministry of Digital Transformation and the cyber police to ensure authenticity and security of such bot-based services. A "Botchecker" tool was developed and embedded on Dovidka.info to allow citizens to verify any Telegram chatbot claiming to be an official service. This database of verified bots (and known imposters) addresses a specific threat: Russian actors have created fake Telegram bots mimicking Ukrainian official services to phish for citizens' data. With Botchecker, users can input a bot's name and immediately see if it is genuine, who its creator is, and how many clone fakes exist. This feature—a collaborative effort of CSC with the Cyber Police, State Special Communications Service, and Ministry of Digital Transformation—illustrates Dovidka's technical adaptability in the face of hybrid threats. By spring 2023, the Centre reported processing thousands of user reports of suspicious bots via this system, leading to the removal of many hostile bots (Centre for Strategic Communication: Results of 2023, 2023).
3. Multimedia and Adaptive Content: Dovidka.info invested in producing content in formats optimized for various platforms and audiences—an approach sometimes termed "adaptive content" in strategic communications. For instance, the team created animated explainer videos (with subtitles and minimal text) that were suitable for broadcasting on public screens like those in the subway or

trains. These animations conveyed essential tips (such as rights to access bomb shelters, or basic first aid) in a visually engaging way that transcended language barriers and could be understood even with audio off. Dovidka also tailored its visuals to age groups: in cooperation with Ukraine's Special Communications Service, it made short cartoon videos on cybersecurity for children, recognizing that children too were exposed to online threats and needed age-appropriate guidance. Likewise, social media content was localized—e.g., Instagram posts often used illustrative carousels that could be swiped, while Telegram posts were succinct bullet points, acknowledging that Telegram audiences often forward messages quickly. The underlying strategy was to meet citizens where they already consume information and package the guidance in the most digestible form possible for that context. This technical flexibility greatly boosted the content's uptake—evidenced by the high engagement numbers on each platform (millions of views and interactions as noted above).

In summary, Dovidka.info's technological and multimedia choices—chatbots for low-bandwidth access, continuous updates, and cross-platform content adaptation—have been pivotal in scaling its reach and impact. These innovations ensured that critical guidance was accessible to all segments of the population in real time, whether through a smartphone chat, a radio PSA, or an on-demand YouTube tutorial. The success of this approach is now cited as a model for digital civil defense: in one study, experts described Dovidka.info as a prime example of how to digitally equip the civilian population to behave during crises. Ukrainian officials likewise emphasize that such tools are an integral part of Ukraine's modern information strategy, complementing kinetic defense with a "digital home front" for citizens.

From the outset, a central objective of Dovidka.info has been to inoculate the public against Russian disinformation and psychological warfare, thereby strengthening Ukraine's societal resilience. This aligns with the broader mandate of the Centre for Strategic Communication to counter enemy information operations. Dovidka's contributions in this realm can be seen on several levels:

- Preempting and Debunking False Narratives: Many of the instructions on Dovidka.info explicitly address common falsehoods circulated by Russian propaganda, correcting them with facts and official positions. For example, Dovidka's advice pages urge citizens "*not to believe reports of the Ukrainian army surrendering*", explaining that such messages are a classic attempt to demoralize the population. They also warn against credence in claims that Ukrainian forces deliberately shell civilians, clarifying how the aggressor uses such lies to erode trust in Ukraine's defenders. By publishing these counters (often in a Q&A or myth-vs-fact format), Dovidka functions as a myth-busting resource parallel to real-time events. During mass bombardment campaigns, for instance, the site featured guidance on how to identify and ignore panic-inducing fake news about electricity outages or "betrayals," which Russian info-ops tried to spread on social media. The content encourages readers to verify alarming news via independent sources or official channels before reacting, essentially teaching media literacy. In doing so, Dovidka reinforces a habit of skepticism toward unverified reports—a critical defense against disinformation. Empirical research by the RAND Corporation in 2023 noted that Ukraine's communication strategy heavily leveraged such public guidance to blunt the effect of Russian psychological tactics, and it cited Dovidka.info as an important medium providing *"practical tips... to protect Ukraine from Russian disinformation"* to the populace (Ukrainian Resistance to Russian Disinformation: Lessons for Future Conflict, 2024).

- Psychological Resilience and Public Morale: Beyond factual corrections, Dovidka.info has a pronounced focus on mental resilience—helping Ukrainians cope with fear, stress, and attempts at intimidation. The inclusion of a dedicated section on "how to stay calm" and manage anxiety in crisis situations is one example (Centre for Strategic Communication: Results of 2023, 2023). Early in the war, the Centre deliberately added content to *give people hope and confidence* amidst the chaos. A special module titled "Ukraine's Defensive Capabilities" was prepared with military experts, aimed at reassuring citizens of the strength and readiness of Ukraine's Armed Forces. *"The main task is to calm people, to give them hope and confidence that the Ukrainian army is capable of protecting them,"* explained a Ministry of Defence official about this initiative armyinform.com.ua. By publishing positive facts about Ukraine's defenses and unity, Dovidka counteracts the intended effect of enemy propaganda (which often seeks to instill panic and helplessness). It also celebrates stories of Ukrainian resilience—for instance, featuring real narratives of volunteers and survivors—to reinforce national morale. This aligns with the concept of *"strategic communications as morale management"* during war. Indeed, the Centre's leadership has espoused a "one voice" policy, meaning all official channels (including Dovidka) present a consistent narrative of determination and stability foi.se. The evident success of this approach is reflected in Ukraine's sustained civilian resolve. Surveys and studies have observed that Ukrainians largely trust official information and have not succumbed to mass panic, despite Russia's intense information onslaught ran d.org. Dovidka.info's trusted guidance can be credited as a contributing factor—by reducing uncertainty, it reduced the psychological impact of enemy misinformation.
- Education in Information Hygiene: Dovidka serves not just to debunk individual fake stories, but to educate citizens in the broader *skills of media discernment*. Several Dovidka articles function as tutorials on detecting propaganda techniques and avoiding manipulation. For example, it provides checklists for verifying sources and instructs readers not to share any unconfirmed reports of military movements or strikes on social media. It details how to configure apps and devices to secure personal data against spying, thus thwarting another angle of information warfare. In partnership with platforms like Rakuten Viber, Dovidka even issued community guidelines for neighborhood group chats—advising Ukrainians how to maintain "communication hygiene"

in local Telegram/Viber groups by filtering out suspicious posts, refraining from heated arguments that could be exploited, and appointing moderators dovidka. info. These seemingly simple tips help close off channels that Russian operatives might use to seed falsehoods or sow discord at the grassroots level. In essence, Dovidka empowers citizens to become active defenders in the information space, complementing the state's counter-disinformation operations. This community-centric resilience—teaching millions of individuals how to be more critical consumers and distributors of information—has been a force multiplier in Ukraine's information war. It reflects a whole-of-society approach where every citizen contributes to psychological defense, something NATO experts have highlighted as vital in modern conflicts nato.int.

- Reinforcing Civic Responsibility and Unity: By providing clear instructions on what to do (and what not to do) in crises, Dovidka.info also strengthens civic responsibility. For instance, the guidance not to post photos of missile strike sites or troop movements is repeated often dovidka.info—framing it as a patriotic duty to deny the enemy any intelligence. The platform encourages collective actions such as volunteering, donating blood, or assisting neighbors during evacuations, thereby fostering social cohesion under stress. This narrative of "Invincibility through unity", promoted in Dovidka materials and related campaigns, directly counters Russian attempts to fracture Ukrainian society along regional or linguistic lines spravdi.gov.ua. By highlighting shared struggles and shared solutions (every Ukrainian civilian can follow the same air-raid survival steps or digital safety tips), Dovidka.info helps cement a national sense of empowerment and agency in the face of aggression. Academic observers have pointed out that Ukraine's strategic communications during the invasion succeeded largely because of this mobilization of the populace into a unified communications effort—essentially a "*whole-of-society information front*" foi.se. Dovidka.info epitomizes that principle, acting as the civil linchpin of Ukraine's information front.

Between 2021 and 2025, Dovidka.info evolved from a basic informational brochure into a comprehensive, multi-platform instrument of civil resilience, demonstrating the strategic significance of communication in modern national defence. Managed by the Centre for Strategic Communication and Information Security, the platform addressed the challenges of Russia's full-scale invasion through the continuous delivery of verified, accessible, and psychologically stabilizing information rather than through coercive information control.

By integrating a website, chatbots, social media channels, video explainers, radio broadcasts, and print materials, Dovidka.info ensured that essential guidance reached diverse audiences under conditions of acute stress. This approach enhanced civilian capacity to act appropriately during missile attacks, displacement, occupation, and infrastructure disruption, while simultaneously reducing vulnerability to disinformation. Through the systematic provision of credible content, the platform cultivated a form of digital resilience, reinforcing public trust, media literacy, and collective stability.

The project's agility was central to its effectiveness. As the conflict evolved, Dovidka.info rapidly updated its thematic priorities, incorporating new guidance on humanitarian, cyber, and psychological challenges. In doing so, it functioned as a force multiplier for broader defence efforts, strengthening societal cohesion and supporting informed decision-making at scale.

Beyond digital content, the Center carries out offline outreach and events. It hosts community roundtables, trainings, and the aforementioned annual Kyiv Strat-Com Forum which brings together stakeholders to share insights on countering disinformation. The CSC has organized press briefings at Ukraine Media Center and other venues to present its research findings (for instance, releasing studies on Russian information crimes, which also serve to inform allied countries and international media) spravdi.gov.uaspravdi.gov.ua. Campaigns have been run in partnership with other agencies—an example being the "Unbreakable When United" campaign in 2023, where CSC joined with the Ukrainian World Congress to promote national unity narratives in the face of Russian aggression spravdi.gov.ua. In such campaigns, the Center often provides the analytical background and messaging strategy, while partner organizations help with on-the-ground activation and amplification. The success of CSC's public communications is reflected in its growing audience reach—by early 2024, its daily digital content was reaching hundreds of thousands of followers across all major social media platforms, indicating significant public trust in the Center as a source of truthful information. High engagement levels (shares, comments, participation in quizzes and polls the Center runs) suggest that CSC has managed to establish itself as a go-to hub for factual information and debunking during the war.

Tyvukraini.com

Tyvukraini.com (Ukrainian for "You Are in Ukraine")—a Digital Lifeline for Ukrainians Under Occupation Platform Overview and Purpose—is a secure online platform created specifically for Ukrainians living in territories temporarily occupied by Russia ("You Are in Ukraine": Security Service Launched for Citizens in Occupied Territories, 2024). Launched in late 2024 by the Yellow Ribbon resistance movement in collaboration with Ukraine's Center for Strategic Communications (via the Dovidka.info project), it aims to help people in occupied Crimea and parts of Donetsk, Luhansk, Zaporizhzhia, and Kherson "stay with Ukraine" despite isolation (The resistance movement 'Yellow Ribbon' launched a VPN service for residents of the TOT region of Ukraine, 2024). In practice, this means providing tools and guidance so that citizens under occupation can safely access truthful information, maintain contact with the rest of the country, and even participate in peaceful resistance. The site explicitly offers support to ensure that "you are not forgotten" and that one's home "was and is [your] home", reinforcing hope and national identity (About the project|You are in Ukraine, 2025).

At its core, Tyvukraini addresses the strategic objective of the occupier: isolating the civilian population from their state, controlling all channels of communication, suppressing Ukrainian identity, and creating a coerced informational "ghetto." Russia systematically blocks Ukrainian websites, surveils online activity, forces residents onto Russian SIM cards and ".ru" digital services, and deploys the portal "Ya v Rossii" for digital passportization, data capture, and narrative control. This combination of infrastructure control, censorship, intimidation, and propaganda forms an integral part of Russia's hybrid warfare doctrine in occupied areas.

Tyvukraini functions as a counter-infrastructure, enabling people in TOT to quietly re-enter Ukraine's information space. Its two technological pillars—a secure browser and free VPN—allow users to bypass surveillance and censorship, access Ukrainian news, keep contact with relatives, and avoid becoming dependent on Russian digital services. The platform is deliberately designed for high-risk environments: all content emphasizes operational security, anonymity, and safe usage under conditions of monitoring and physical threat.

Beyond technical protection, Tyvukraini provides cognitive and psychological resilience. Its sections on safety during occupation, countering disinformation, digital hygiene, and recognizing manipulation help mitigate the effects of Russian psychological operations. Yellow Ribbon and StratCom experts also supply guidance on nonviolent resistance—such as symbolic acts, safe communication, and community-level information activism—offering civilians a sense of agency even under strict control. Importantly, the platform incorporates Ukrainian language learning, enabling cultural continuity and countering Russification efforts in schools and public life. By mid-2025, hundreds of adults and children were studying Ukrainian through the platform, showing the demand for cultural self-maintenance even in captivity.

Tyvukraini also illustrates an important hybrid governance model in information defense: synergy between civil society operating inside occupied territories and state strategic communication bodies operating outside. Yellow Ribbon contributes situational awareness, trust networks, and an understanding of the risks people face. This partnership allows rapid adaptation when occupiers attempt to block services, and it ensures that content is attuned both to user safety and to broader national strategic communication goals.

Tyvukraini demonstrates how digital platforms can become strategic bridges across lines of occupation, mitigating cognitive isolation, preserving national identity, and enabling covert civic engagement. The platform is a practical example of a targeted, audience-specific communication ecosystem designed for contested environments—one that integrates security tools, information provision, psychological support, cultural programming, and resistance guidance into a single coherent experience.

Ultimately, Tyvukraini shows that in modern hybrid conflict, battles over connectivity, identity, and truth are as central as battles over territory.

4.6.3 Government Communications Support ("One Voice" Coordination)

The CSC invests in capacity-building for government communicators through its Public Servants School program. This is a systematic training initiative targeting public officials at national, regional, and local levels.

Another critical sphere of CSC operations is enhancing the coherence and effectiveness of government messaging. In practice, this has involved setting up mechanisms for rapid inter-agency communication in response to disinformation incidents. Every day, the Center's analysts distill the top hostile narratives circulating in the information space and prepare briefing notes with recommended responses. These "daily messaging guidance" documents (often called "message boxes") are shared with a network of government communicators—including ministry press secretaries, military public affairs officers, and even proactive civil society communicators and journalists. The guidance typically identifies false or misleading claims gaining traction and suggests fact-based counter-arguments or key points for officials to emphasize. For example, if a Russian disinformation theme claims Ukrainian leadership is about to capitulate, the message box would provide the actual situation and quote authoritative sources to refute the claim, enabling all Ukrainian spokespeople to stay on the same page. This system has been likened to establishing a "One Voice" policy for strategic communications during the war ('FIMI as part of Russian war machine: Ukraine's fight', 2024). While Ukraine's decentralized governance and political pluralism make full synchronization challenging, the CSC's efforts have significantly improved coordination. A representative of Ukraine's military StratCom noted that the unity of purpose between government and civil society communicators—facilitated by platforms like the CSC—has been invaluable in achieving consistent messaging.

In addition to written guidance, the Center convenes weekly (or ad hoc) coordination meetings among government communication officials. The CSC's "nominally independent" status (sitting in a civilian ministry rather than directly in the Cabinet or President's Office) has paradoxically helped it foster trust—civil society actors see it as a slightly arm's-length partner, while government bodies see it as an impartial coordinator rather than a competitor. This positioning enabled CSC to become a bridge for information-sharing between government and NGOs, something that had been lacking pre-2021. During the two years of full-scale war, the Center has regularly brought together officials and independent experts in joint workshops to develop communication strategies on specific issues (for instance, countering disinformation about Ukrainian refugees in Europe, or narratives aiming to erode Western aid). CSC helps orchestrate the messaging by coordinating with the Office of the President and relevant ministries, ensuring prompt and unified public information is released to preempt rumors. Ukrainian officials have credited the "one voice" approach in counter-propaganda with debunking and preventing the spread of most Russian fakes before they gain traction domestically and internationally (The Center's publication on the information war was created not only for historical purposes but also for law enforcement agencies, says Ihor Solovei, 2024b). This is a testament to improved agility—a far cry from 2014 when Ukraine often struggled to rapidly refute falsehoods.

Furthermore, the CSC invests in capacity-building for government communicators through its Public Servants School program. This is a systematic training initiative targeting public officials at national, regional, and local levels. Since 2021, the Center has organized hundreds of training sessions and workshops covering topics like strategic communications principles, how to counter common disinformation techniques, crisis press briefing skills, and social media best practices. Training curricula are tailored for different audiences—from central ministry spokespersons to regional military-civil administration staff—and delivered in various formats (in-person seminars, online courses, and even Telegram-based micro-learning modules). By 2023, the CSC had also developed an online training platform and a series of handbooks for public servants to use as reference in their daily work. The goal of these efforts is not only to impart skills but to instill a mindset that effective communication is a part of defense. As the Roadmap 2.0 describes, the trainings give officials "the motivation and confidence to counter disinformation, build campaigns, and communicate more effectively during crises", thereby helping build a sustainable system for strategic communications in Ukraine. The impact of this can be seen in practice—for example, local government press officers in frontline regions, once left on their own, are now part of a network that can tap into CSC resources and expertise when confronting rumours or panic in their communities. These local "first responders" in the information sphere have been trained to recognize emerging Russian narratives and to respond credibly to their communities, an approach that has strengthened grassroots resilience.

4.6.4 Targeted Resilience and Outreach Projects

> The Center provides ad hoc support to Ukraine's partners by sharing its expertise and content. For instance, CSC has collaborated with Polish authorities on joint debunking efforts when Russian narratives attempt to sow discord between Ukrainians and Poles. It also translates and publishes some of its analytical materials in key foreign languages (English, Russian, and even Chinese or Spanish), to ensure global audiences—especially in the Global South—have access to facts about Russian disinformation and war crimes.

The CSC runs or supports several special projects aimed at directly engaging vulnerable groups and countering specific strands of malign influence. One flagship project, already discussed, is Dovidka.info, focused on frontline and at-risk civilian communities with life-saving info and myth-busting. The Center has also been involved in projects addressing disinformation in occupied territories. Communicating with Ukrainians under Russian occupation is extremely challenging (due to enemy censorship and propaganda dominance). Ukraine attempted tactics like distributing "radio in a box" devices (portable FM transmitters with pre-packaged broadcasts) to villages near front lines. A CSC representative noted that such methods had limited success because Russia aggressively jams signals and saturates occupied areas with its own information, from radio to billboards. A lesson learned is that new solutions are needed to penetrate the "sealed" information bubble in occupied zones—an area where the Center is researching alternative approaches (potentially leveraging satellite broadcasts, guerrilla leaflet campaigns, or digital tools).

The CSC also contributes to international information campaigns. It cooperates with Ukrainian diplomats and partner governments to expose Russian disinformation globally. An initiative nicknamed "Information Ramstein" has been proposed by Ukrainian officials, including Ihor Solovey, envisioning a coalition of Western and allied countries pooling resources to counter Kremlin propaganda, analogous to the military aid coordination platform (FIMI as part of Russian war machine: Ukraine's fight, 2024).

In the interim, the Center provides ad hoc support to Ukraine's partners by sharing its expertise and content. For instance, CSC has collaborated with Polish authorities on joint debunking efforts when Russian narratives attempt to sow discord between Ukrainians and Poles. It also translates and publishes some of its analytical materials in key foreign languages (English, Russian, and even Chinese or Spanish), to ensure global audiences—especially in the Global South—have access to facts about Russian disinformation and war crimes (The Center's publication on the information war was created not only for historical purposes but also for law enforcement agencies, says Ihor Solovei, 2024b). This outward-facing role aligns with Ukraine's broader strategy to win the information war internationally, not just at home.

In summary, the CSC's operations span from micro-level actions (a single tweet debunking a fake, a training session for village officials) to strategic initiatives (nationwide campaigns, international coordination proposals). Through monitoring and analysis, it identifies threats; through public communications it directly counters falsehoods; through coordination and training it amplifies the capacity of others (government or civil society) to respond; and through special projects it targets gaps in resilience. This multifaceted approach reflects the Center's understanding that combating disinformation is not a narrow PR task, but a holistic effort involving security, education, communication, and community engagement. Those objectives are continually measured via surveys, feedback, and metrics like the number of user reports to the Spravdi bot—which serve as indicators of public trust and vigilance.

4.7 Achievements and Impact of the CSC

After the invasion, the CSC quickly became one of the leading channels for official information about the war, especially for countering Russian falsehoods. Its Spravdi portal and social feeds gained a wide following among Ukrainian citizens seeking factual news amidst the chaos. The Center's ability to produce rapid responses and debunking had tangible effects.

Over its relatively short existence, the CSC has made significant contributions to Ukraine's information defense and garnered a track record of achievements. Some of the most salient accomplishments and impacts include:

- Improved National Readiness and Prebunking Before the Full-Scale War: In the months leading up to February 2022, the CSC played a role in preparing the population for potential conflict. This meant that when the full-scale attack came, many Ukrainians had already seen guidance on, for example, how to distinguish official messages from fake ones, or how to behave under shelling. Additionally, Ukrainian authorities, with input from CSC and others, undertook an intelligence-driven "prebunk" in January–February 2022 by publicly warning that Russia would try to fabricate a pretext for invasion (like a false flag attack). Exposing that plan in advance blunted its effectiveness. While that particular effort was led by intelligence services, it was part of the broader culture of strategic communication that Ukraine had started to embrace—a culture to which CSC contributed by stressing proactive disclosure of the truth. President Zelenskyy's administration and government spokespeople entered the war with a more unified and confident communications posture than in 2014, thanks in part to the mechanisms and training established in 2021–22 (for which CSC was a key facilitator) (FIMI as part of Russian war machine: Ukraine's fight, 2024). As one RAND report puts it, Ukraine's counter-disinformation campaign benefitted from "shaping operations" before the war—including the building of institutions like the CSC to coordinate efforts and the unique step of stopping the flow of Russian propaganda into the country via bans on Russian media and platforms. The CSC was both a product of and contributor to this improved state of readiness.
- Serving as a War Communications Hub: After the invasion, the CSC quickly became one of the leading channels for official information about the war, especially for countering Russian falsehoods. Its Spravdi portal and social feeds gained a wide following among Ukrainian citizens seeking factual news amidst the chaos. The Center's ability to produce rapid responses and debunking had tangible effects. One example noted was when a fake story emerged in fall 2023 alleging that First Lady Olena Zelenska had spent $1.1 million of aid money on a shopping spree. The CCD and CSC together rapidly verified her actual whereabouts and debunked the story before it spread widely. This prevented potential damage to Ukraine's image at a sensitive time. More broadly, senior officials credit the collective "single voice" communications (to which CSC was central) with forestalling the success of Russia's primary information warfare goals. Ihor Solovey observed in February 2024 that "the main tasks of Russian propaganda at the beginning of the full-scale invasion have not been fulfilled"—Ukrainians did not panic or surrender en masse, society was not split apart, and Western support was not cut off (The Center's publication on the information war was created not only for historical purposes but also for law enforcement agencies, says Ihor Solovei, 2024b). While many factors contributed to this outcome (patriotic resolve, effective military resistance, Western

media efforts, etc.), Ukraine's internal information strategy was crucial. By consistently debunking lies (like "Kyiv has fallen" in the war's early hours, or later the recurrent nuclear and biolab conspiracy tropes), Ukrainian communicators maintained public morale and denied the Kremlin easy victories in the cognitive domain. The CSC, as the coordinator and source of much of these debunk efforts, can be credited with helping Ukraine *"fight back and win against the enemy's disinformation attacks"* to a remarkable degree (The Center's publication on the information war was created not only for historical purposes but also for law enforcement agencies, says Ihor Solovei, 2024b).

- Empowering Civil Society and a "Whole-of-Society" Response: One of the CSC's biggest achievements is institutionalizing collaboration with civil society in the fight against disinformation. Several observers have highlighted that the Center's close working relationship with Ukraine's vibrant civil society sector is a notable feature that distinguishes it from many other countries' approaches. The CSC created formal and informal channels for NGOs, fact-checkers, and independent media to feed in their insights and receive support. For example, civil society groups approach the CSC with ideas for research or proposals for counter-narratives, and the CSC helps with data or coordination. During the war, this synergy meant that initiatives like StopFake, Detector Media, VoxCheck, Internews Ukraine and others were not operating in silos but were part of a broader ecosystem with the CSC. A representative of the EEAS Stratcom unit noted that Ukraine's ability to interface government with civil society in this space "proved invaluable" in achieving unity of purpose. Indeed, a CSC representative reflected that from day one they saw civil society as their "biggest partner," implementing a "whole-of-society response" model. The fruits of this can be seen in joint campaigns (like media literacy projects co-run by government and NGOs) and in an overall pluralistic yet coordinated information environment. Unlike a top-down propaganda ministry, the CSC fostered a networked, participatory approach—sometimes described metaphorically as a "swarm of StratCom bees" moving in the same direction. This model, while somewhat chaotic, has been effective for Ukraine and is now studied as a strength. Western analysts have suggested that creating an institution like the CSC that can leverage civil society is a lesson for other nations looking to bolster their defenses against disinformation. In other words, the CSC has provided a template of how to integrate non-government actors into national strategic communications without compromising their independence.
- Building Capacity and a Cadre of Trained Communicators: Through its training and educational initiatives, the CSC has by mid-2025 equipped a significant number of officials and journalists with the skills to detect and counter false information. The Public Servants School run by the Center has trained over 1000 public officials in subjects ranging from crisis communication to OSINT (open-source intelligence) for debunking fakes. Many of these trainees have since put their knowledge to use at various levels of government. For example, regional administrations in Odesa, Mykolaiv, Kherson and others now have personnel who have gone through CSC workshops and subsequently established

local monitoring groups to watch for disinformation in their communities. These local "information first responders" have proven crucial in areas targeted by intense Russian influence attempts—they can quickly relay what falsehoods are circulating on the ground to the Center, and equally quickly push out corrections or truthful narratives that resonate locally. This decentralization of capacity means Ukraine's information defense is not solely run from Kyiv, but has a broad base. Additionally, by producing handbooks (like a guide on strategic communications for public servants) and online courses, the Center has created reference materials that will benefit future cadres of civil servants beyond the current conflict. While some fragmentation remains (each ministry still has its own comms unit and political priorities), the general awareness of information security across government is at an all-time high. Officials speak of being "motivated" and "confident" in addressing disinformation thanks to the CSC's influence. This is a stark change from earlier years when responses were often ad hoc.

- Concrete Outputs and International Recognition: Numerically, the CSC can point to many outputs: dozens of research publications, hundreds of news analyses and fake debunkings on Spravdi, multiple campaigns and events, and the establishment of enduring platforms like Dovidka.info and the StratCom forum (Project Library, 2025). Its publications have not only domestic impact but are being used abroad. The comprehensive volume on Russian propaganda narratives (covering 2022–2023) that the Center published in early 2024 is being translated into English and other languages for foreign audiences and for use in holding Russian propagandists accountable (The Center's publication on the information war was created not only for historical purposes but also for law enforcement agencies, says Ihor Solovei, 2024b). Law enforcement bodies in Ukraine, such as the Prosecutor General's office, have utilized CSC analysis when preparing files on incitement and propaganda as war crimes. Furthermore, the Center's work has gained international recognition in the policy community. The RAND Corporation's 2024 report on Ukrainian resistance to disinformation devoted attention to the CSC as a case study and highlighted its model of civil society collaboration and pre-war preparation as key lessons (Ukrainian Resistance to Russian Disinformation: Lessons for Future Conflict, 2024). The NATO Strategic Communications Centre of Excellence has engaged with CSC experts in exercises and conferences, underscoring the respect Ukraine's experience commands among allies (Decoding the Information Environment: NATO's Strategic Communications Centre of Excellence, 2024). Ukraine's successful information defense—to which CSC is central—has arguably reshaped how the world views counter-disinformation: proving that even against a massive propaganda machine, a nimble, truth-focused strategy can prevail.
- In sum, the CSC's achievements can be seen in Ukraine's maintained unity and resilience under the most intense information onslaught in modern European history. By no means can the Center claim sole credit for this resilience (it is one part of a broader societal effort), but its contributions have been pivotal in orchestrating and amplifying that effort. As one Ukrainian security official

put it, having a *"one voice in countering Russian propaganda"*—embodied by institutions like the CSC—has been a crucial component in debunking and preventing the spread of most fakes and ensuring they *"do not gain traction among Ukrainians"* (The Center's publication on the information war was created not only for historical purposes but also for law enforcement agencies, says Ihor Solovei, 2024b). This is perhaps the ultimate measure of success for the Center's mission.

The RAND Corporation's 2024 report on Ukrainian resistance to disinformation devoted attention to the CSC as a case study and highlighted its model of civil society collaboration and pre-war preparation as key lessons

4.8 The CSC's Challenges and Limitations

The CSC must ensure it targets disinformation, not legitimate dissent or critical journalism. Thus far, it appears to have navigated this well, sticking to refuting provable falsehoods and not straying into political commentary (its content library is largely about Russian lies and how to debunk them). Still, as Ukraine remains a pluralistic society even during war, the Center's role could be scrutinized.

Despite its successes, the Center for Strategic Communication and Information Security faces a number of challenges, both inherent to its mission and arising from Ukraine's complex information landscape. Understanding these challenges provides a balanced view of the CSC's performance and areas needing improvement or caution:

1. Balancing Security and Freedom of Speech: In fighting "fake news", the CSC operates within a democratic context and must be careful not to overreach in ways that could be viewed as censorship or propaganda itself. Early in its existence, some Ukrainian media observers were skeptical of any government-led initiative in the information sphere, fearing it might morph into a Ministry of Truth. The Center has had to earn trust by being as transparent and factual as possible. It avoids engagement in political domestic messaging, focusing strictly on countering falsehoods from hostile sources. Nonetheless, there is always a risk that the lines blur—especially when disinformation narratives dovetail with internal opposition rhetoric or controversial topics. The CSC must ensure it targets disinformation, not legitimate dissent or critical journalism. Thus far, it appears to have navigated this well, sticking to refuting provable falsehoods and not straying into political commentary (its content library is largely about Russian lies and how to debunk them). Still, as Ukraine remains a pluralistic society even during war, the Center's role could be scrutinized. This challenge is about maintaining credibility: if the public ever perceived the CSC as just churning out government propaganda, its effectiveness would evaporate. By anchoring everything in evidence and citing sources (often directly linking to

where a fake was debunked), the Center has maintained a reputation for reliability. Continuing that will be vital, especially in the post-war period where media freedoms will fully normalize and any government messaging will be under tighter scrutiny.

2. Adapting to Evolving Tactics (e.g., Telegram and other social media): The information environment is dynamic, and the adversary adapts. One serious challenge noted is the rise of Telegram as a primary news source for over 70% of Ukrainians. Telegram is a platform favored by Russian propagandists and intelligence for its anonymity and reach. The CSC can monitor open Telegram channels, but countering disinformation on Telegram is tricky—there's no algorithmic content moderation to flag falsehoods, and many official Ukrainian entities themselves use Telegram for communications, inadvertently lending credibility to the platform. The Prism Ua analysis highlighted the "uncontrolled use" of Telegram as a serious threat, and while Ukraine's cybersecurity bodies took steps to restrict its use in government networks (FIMI as part of Russian war machine: Ukraine's fight, 2024), the general populace remains exposed. The CSC must find ways to *engage audiences on Telegram without boosting adversarial content*. They have created official Telegram channels and bots, but getting users to subscribe to those over sensationalist anonymous channels is an uphill battle. Similarly, emerging technologies like deepfakes and AI-generated propaganda pose new challenges. By 2023, Russians began deploying deepfake videos of Ukrainian officials (e.g., a fake surrender speech by President Zelenskyy in March 2022). The Center had to scramble to issue instant warnings about these deepfakes. Keeping up with the speed and sophistication of such tactics will require continual tech upgrades and perhaps an AI-assisted alert system—areas where the Center is not yet fully equipped. Another aspect is countering propaganda in the Global South online spaces, where different languages and narratives (often Russian-friendly) proliferate. The CSC's mandate is primarily domestic, but as it steps into international messaging, it faces the resource and skill challenge of multilingual influence.
3. Reaching Occupied and Information-Isolated Populations: As noted earlier, penetrating the information bubble in Russian-occupied territories or areas with little internet is extremely difficult. Traditional methods (TV, radio broadcasts from Ukraine-controlled areas) are often jammed or shut out by the occupiers. While the CSC and partners have tried creative means—from guerilla journalism to sending SIM cards with Ukrainian networks into occupied zones—these efforts see limited success against a determined censor. This reality is a frustrating challenge: there are Ukrainians under occupation whose only media are Russian channels painting Kyiv as the enemy. The CSC cannot easily service those audiences, meaning the information war in those areas is essentially lost for now. This has humanitarian implications (people believing dangerous disinformation about evacuation routes or relief supplies, etc.) and post-liberation implications (needing to reintegrate citizens who were subjected to intensive propaganda). The challenge for the Center is planning for how to rapidly fill the information void in liberated areas when the time comes, and how to

counteract years of enemy indoctrination. This is something that will require coordination with psychological services and local authorities—a complex, resource-intensive undertaking.

4. Strategic Coherence and Long-Term Strategy: Finally, a macro-level challenge is ensuring that all these efforts—by CSC and the myriad other actors—add up to a cohesive long-term strategy. Some experts have noted that Ukraine's response, while successful, can seem improvised and loosely organized ("bottom-up polyphony"). The lack of a single hierarchy or doctrine guiding the entire information campaign means that success has partly relied on individual initiative and creativity (which Ukraine has in abundance). However, over the long run, institutionalizing lessons in formal doctrine and strategy is necessary. The CSC has contributed to drafting such strategies (the Information Security Strategy, sections of the Military StratCom doctrine, etc.), but implementation across government remains uneven. Moreover, legislative gaps—like the absence (until recently) of clear legal definitions for terms like "disinformation" or penalties for engaging in information warfare—need addressing to empower agencies like the CSC. Efforts are underway (e.g., Ukraine's new Media Law of 2023 aligns with EU standards and strengthens the regulatory framework for online platforms) (FIMI as part of Russian war machine: Ukraine's fight, 2024). The Center must continue advocating for policies that fill these gaps, such as frameworks for dealing with hostile use of social media or clarifying the roles of various agencies in a crisis.

Another aspect is countering propaganda in the Global South online spaces, where different languages and narratives (often Russian-friendly) proliferate. The CSC's mandate is primarily domestic, but as it steps into international messaging, it faces the resource and skill challenge of multilingual influence.

4.9 Conclusion

The CSC has reinforced Ukraine's national security by protecting the country's information space and thus its societal cohesion—something that has proven as important as tanks and missiles in this conflict. It has also become a key node in the international fight against disinformation, with Ukraine emerging as a leader in this domain.

The establishment and operations of the Center for Strategic Communication and Information Security have had profound implications for Ukraine's national security and its engagement with international counter-disinformation efforts.

The Russian full-scale invasion cemented the understanding that information security is a pillar of national security. The CSC, though a civilian institution, became in effect a non-kinetic arm of Ukraine's defense. By fortifying the information domain, it indirectly bolsters the physical domains of warfare. For example, when Russia's forces tried to demoralize Ukrainian soldiers and citizens through SMS campaigns and social media (such as sending mass texts urging surrender in early 2022), Ukraine's information defenders countered by exposing these as fake and highlighting Russian atrocities to stiffen resolve. This coordination between CSC, military StratCom, and civil society narratives contributed to Ukrainians' remarkably high will to resist. A RAND study concluded that Ukraine's information campaign (of which CSC is a key part) provides a unique case of how a nation can counter disinformation during conflict and maintain unity. Indeed, in the "three theaters" of Russia's information war—domestic Russian audience, international audience, and Ukrainian audience—Ukraine has largely prevented Russia from achieving its objectives in the Ukrainian theater, which is crucial for national survival. The CSC's role as a central node in organizing this defense means it is now considered an integral component of Ukraine's security sector, even though it is formally under a culture ministry. It works alongside the Armed Forces StratCom (which handles military psychological operations and operational security), and the intelligence community, thereby embedding information considerations into broader strategic planning.

Furthermore, CSC's emphasis on societal resilience (educating the public, debunking in real time, promoting media literacy) has increased the population's "immunity" to psychological operations. Sociologically, this contributes to what is often called "civil resilience"—a public that can withstand panic and divide-and-rule tactics. For example, when Russia attempted to spread narratives about Ukraine's government abandoning citizens or about ethnic divisions, these found little fertile ground, partly because years of factual public communication and myth-busting by entities like NGO project StopFake (and later CSC) had inoculated people to such classic propaganda tropes. Surveys in Ukraine have shown consistently high distrust of Russian media sources and high confidence in Ukraine's own information channels as the war progressed, indicating successful resilience-building. This is a stark contrast to 2014, when Russian TV disinformation did influence segments of the population in the Donbas and Crimea; the spread of that was curtailed in subsequent years by cutting retransmission and by raising awareness (Alexandra Wiktorek Sarlo, 2017; FIMI as part of Russian war machine: Ukraine's fight, 2024). The CSC can be seen as the culmination of that trajectory—putting an institutional stamp on resilience efforts that were previously ad hoc. In essence, the CSC contributes to deterrence: Russia knows that simply flooding Ukraine with false narratives will not lead to collapse or chaos easily, as Ukrainians are primed to question and verify. This does not stop Russia from trying, but it raises their costs and lowers their effectiveness, which is exactly what you want from a national security standpoint. Each democratic state needs frameworks like CSC in place before a crisis, which Ukraine fortunately did by early 2022. That preparatory value is now proven and will likely be institutionalized permanently.

In conclusion, the CSC has reinforced Ukraine's national security by protecting the country's information space and thus its societal cohesion—something that has proven as important as tanks and missiles in this conflict. It has also become a key node in the international fight against disinformation, with Ukraine emerging as a leader in this domain. The integration of CSC into global efforts underscores a broader recognition: in the twenty-first century, effective strategic communications and counter-disinformation are fundamental to national resilience and alliance solidarity. Ukraine's struggle and the CSC's work have driven that lesson home, likely influencing how other nations structure their defenses. As academic and policy observers study the case of CSC, it stands alongside institutions like the EEAS StratCom, Sweden's MPF, and Baltic StratCom initiatives as part of a growing architecture dedicated to safeguarding truth and trust in the face of falsehood and hostility.

In summary, the CSC operates in an exceptionally complex environment where its mission inevitably encounters structural, technological, and ethical constraints. These challenges—balancing security with free expression, adapting to evolving platforms like Telegram, reaching isolated populations, ensuring institutional coherence, and sustaining limited resources—underscore both the fragility and importance of Ukraine's information defense ecosystem. Yet, the Center's ability to maintain credibility, learn quickly, and adjust within a democratic framework suggests that its limitations are not signs of weakness but of an evolving institution under pressure.

References

"A resilient Ukraine is important for a resilient Europe." Kyiv StratCom Forum 2025 has begun in Kyiv (2025). *detector.media*. Available at https://detector.media/infospace/article/240284/2025-04-24-stiyka-ukraina-vazhlyva-dlya-stiykoi-ievropy-u-kyievi-rozpochavsya-kyiv-stratcom-forum-2025/. Accessed 27 December 2025.

About the Stratcom Centre. (2023). Center for Strategic Communication and Information Security. Available at https://spravdi.org/en/about-us/. Accessed 27 December 2025.

About the Project|You are in Ukraine. (2025). Available at https://tyvukraini.com/about. Accessed 28 December 2025.

About Us—Dovidka.info (n.d.). Available at https://dovidka.info/en/about-us/. Accessed 28 December 2025.

Alexandra Wiktorek Sarlo. (2017). Fighting Disinformation in the Baltic States—Foreign Policy Research Institute. Available at https://www.fpri.org/article/2017/07/fighting-disinformation-baltic-states/. Accessed 1 January 2026.

Already in the first months it was obvious that Ukraine was winning the information war,—Minister Tkachenko—Center for Strategic Communication and Information Security (2023). Available at https://spravdi.org/uzhe-v-pershi-misyaczi-bulo-ochevydno-shho-ukrayina-peremagaye-v-informaczijnij-vijni-ministr-tkachenko/. Accessed 27 December 2025.

An information brochure "In case of emergency or war" was presented in Kyiv—ArmyInform (2021). Available at https://armyinform.com.ua/2021/06/23/u-kyyevi-prezentuvaly-informaczijnu-broshuru-u-razi-nadzvychajnoyi-sytuacziyi-abo-vijny/. Accessed 28 December 2025.

Cabinet of Ministers of Ukraine—Center for Strategic Communications and Information Security presented. (2021). Available at https://www.kmu.gov.ua/news/prezentovano-centr-strategichnih-komunikacij-ta-informacijnoyi-bezpeki. Accessed 1 November 2025.

Centre for Strategic Communication: Results of 2023. (2023). Available at https://spravdi.org/en/centre-for-strategic-communication-results-of-2023/. Accessed 28 December 2025.

Centre for Strategic Communication and Information Security. (2025). *Wikipedia*. Available at https://en.wikipedia.org/w/index.php?title=Centre_for_Strategic_Communication_and_Information_Security&oldid=1274548184. Accessed 27 December 2025.

Countering disinformation: Tkachenko spoke about cooperation with the center at the National Security and Defense Council (2021). Available at https://www.ukrinform.ua/rubric-antifake/3218981-protidia-dezinformacii-tkacenko-rozpoviv-pro-spivpracu-z-centrom-pri-rnbo.html. Accessed 7 December 2025.

Decoding the Information Environment: NATO's Strategic Communications Centre of Excellence. (2024). *NATO's ACT*, 18 September. Available at https://www.act.nato.int/article/stratcom-coe-2024/. Accessed 1 November 2025.

EU Project to Help Ukrainians with Adaptation in Wartime. (2022). *Center for Strategic Communication and Information Security*. Available at https://spravdi.org/en/eu-project-to-help-ukrainians-with-adaptation-in-wartime/. Accessed 28 December 2025.

FIMI as part of Russian war machine: Ukraine's fight. (2024). *Prism Ua*, 8 October. Available at https://prismua.org/en/english-fimi-as-part-of-russian-war-machine-ukraines-fight/. Accessed 30 December 2025.

How the Russian information ship went to.... (n.d.). Available at https://spravdi.org/wp-content/uploads/2024/02/yak-rosijskyj-informaczijnyj-korabel-pishov-na%E2%80%A6-naratyvy-propagandy-pid-chas-povnomasshtabnoyi-vijny.pdf. Accessed 27 December 2025.

"It's time for the world to hear Ukrainian voices": the main points about the EU's approaches to information warfare from the Center's forum—Center for Strategic Communication and Information Security (2023). Available at https://spravdi.org/nastav-chas-svitovi-pochuty-ukrayinski-golosy-golovne-pro-pidhody-yes-do-informaczijnoyi-vijny-z-forumu-czentru/. Accessed 27 December 2025.

Kyiv StratCom Forum 2024 kicks off (2024). Available at https://www.ukrinform.net/rubric-polytics/3845528-kyiv-stratcom-forum-2024-kicks-off.html. Accessed 27 December 2025.

Kyiv StratCom Forum. (n.d.). Center for Strategic Communication and Information Security. Available at https://spravdi.org/en/kyiv-stratcom-forum-all/. Accessed 27 December 2025.

Mission of the Center for Countering Disinformation. (2021). *Official web portal of the Parliament of Ukraine*. Available at https://zakon.rada.gov.ua/go/187/2021. Accessed 10 November 2025.

Mykhailo Fedorov: "We need to offer the world a new agenda on how to counter disinformation". (2024). *detector.media*. Available at https://detector.media/infospace/article/224694/2024-03-27-mykhaylo-fedorov-nam-potribno-zaproponuvaty-svitu-novu-adzhendu-yak-borotysya-z-dezinformatsiieyu/. Accessed 27 December 2025.

Mykola Tochytskyi officially opened the Kyiv StratCom Forum 2025. (2025). *Ministry of Culture of Ukraine*, 24 April. Available at https://mcsc.gov.ua/en/news/mykola-tochytskyi-officially-opened-the-kyiv-stratcom-forum-2025/. Accessed 27 December 2025.

On the decision of the National Security and Defense Council of Ukraine of October 15, 2021 'On the Information Security Strategy'. (2021). Official web portal of the Parliament of Ukraine. Available at https://zakon.rada.gov.ua/go/685/2021. Accessed 7 December 2025.

Project Library. (2025). Center for Strategic Communication and Information Security. Available at https://spravdi.org/en/research-and-analytics/project-library/. Accessed 27 December 2025.

The Center for Strategic Communications and Information Security has a new head. (2021). Institute of Mass Information, 8 September. Available at https://imi.org.ua/news/tsentr-strategichnyh-komunikatsij-ta-informatsijnoyi-bezpeky-otrymav-novogo-kerivnyka-i41124. Accessed 27 December 2025.

The Center's publication on the information war was created not only for historical purposes but also for law enforcement agencies, says Ihor Solovei. (2024a). Center for Strategic Communication and Information Security. Available at https://spravdi.org/en/the-centers-publication-on-the-information-war-was-created-not-only-for-historical-purposes-but-also-for-law-enforcement-agencies-says-ihor-solovei/. Accessed 7 December 2025.

The Center's publication on the information war was created not only for historical purposes but also for law enforcement agencies, says Ihor Solovei. (2024b). Center for Strategic Communication and Information Security. Available at https://spravdi.org/en/the-centers-publication-on-the-information-war-was-created-not-only-for-historical-purposes-but-also-for-law-enforcement-agencies-says-ihor-solovei/. Accessed 27 December 2025.

The resistance movement 'Yellow Ribbon' launched a VPN service for residents of the TOT region of Ukraine (2024). Suspilne|News. Available at https://suspilne.media/zaporizhzhia/847341-ruh-sprotivu-zovta-stricka-zapustili-servis-dla-bezpecnogo-koristuvanna-internetom-na-tot-ukraini/. Accessed 28 December 2025.

Ukrainian Resistance to Russian Disinformation: Lessons for Future Conflict. (2024). RAND Corporation. https://doi.org/10.7249/RRA2771-1

Ukrinform—Ukrainian National News Agency. (n.d.). Available at https://www.ukrinform.net/. Accessed 7 December 2025.

"You Are in Ukraine": Security Service Launched for Citizens in Occupied Territories. (2024). *Mission of the President of Ukraine in the Autonomous Republic of Crimea.* Available at https://ppu.gov.ua/en/press-center/ty-v-ukraini-stvoreno-servis-pro-bezpeku-dlia-ukrainskykh-hromadian-na-okupovanykh-terytoriiakh/. Accessed 28 December 2025.

5 Other Governmental Bodies Involved in Counter Disinformation in Ukraine

Ukraine's struggle against disinformation is not the responsibility of a single institution. It involves a network of governmental bodies that collectively form the state's defensive architecture against hybrid threats. Each institution contributes a unique perspective: some approach disinformation as a matter of national security, others as law enforcement, regulation, diplomacy, or education. This ecosystem of institutions demonstrates that the fight against disinformation is not only about debunking falsehoods but about mobilizing the entire state apparatus in defense of sovereignty and democratic legitimacy.

Since the beginning of Russia's hybrid aggression in 2014, Ukraine has gradually institutionalized its responses. Early efforts were often fragmented, with individual ministries and agencies reacting independently. Over time, however, a more integrated, multi-agency architecture emerged, reflecting the recognition that disinformation is not merely a media issue but a matter of national security. This model provides a powerful and agile response to dynamic threats. At the same time, this system reveals the complexities of democratic governance in wartime. Coordination among agencies is both necessary and challenging. Overlaps can lead to friction, while gaps can be exploited by hostile actors. The Ukrainian case therefore provides valuable lessons for democracies: defending the information space requires multi-agency cooperation, clear mandates, adaptability, and a proactive strategy.

5.1 Security, Defence and Intelligence Bodies

The Ministry of Defence actively contributes to countering disinformation through a combination of operational communication, intelligence, and coordination with international partners. Briefings from the MoD provide verified updates on battlefield developments,

A. Marushchak et al., *Counter Disinformation System Development in Ukraine*,
Terrorism, Security, and Computation, https://doi.org/10.1007/978-3-032-24731-5_5

helping to pre-empt Russian attempts to distort events or mislead domestic and international audiences.

In the face of Russia's ongoing hybrid war, the Ministry of Defence (MoD) and the Armed Forces of Ukraine (AFU) play a crucial role not only in defending the country's territory but also in safeguarding its information space. These institutions are engaged in more than traditional military operations—they actively counter disinformation, prevent hostile narratives from spreading, and work to maintain public trust at home while preserving credibility abroad. In modern conflict, where propaganda and disinformation are used as strategic tools, this dual responsibility has become essential.

The MoD actively contributes to countering disinformation through a combination of operational communication, intelligence, and coordination with international partners. Briefings from the MoD provide verified updates on battlefield developments, helping to pre-empt Russian attempts to distort events or mislead domestic and international audiences. In addition, the MoD responds rapidly to false military narratives. Coordination with allies further amplifies these efforts: by sharing intelligence with NATO and EU partners, the MoD ensures that consistent, evidence-based accounts of Russian war crimes circulate internationally, supporting a unified narrative on the conflict.

This work is reinforced by close collaboration with the CCD. For instance, Russian propagandists circulated an image of an allegedly official MoD letter claiming that compensation for the families of fallen soldiers was denied due to "the inability to establish the circumstances of death". The CCD verified the information directly with the MoD and confirmed that the document was a forgery. The letter's format did not meet any official ministry standards, and it contained numerous errors in wording and layout, highlighting how Russian disinformation seeks to undermine trust and morale even through falsified official documents.

Analytically, the MoD and AFU embody the operational dimension of counter-disinformation. Unlike regulators or diplomats, they operate in real time, navigating both physical and informational battlefields. Their credibility is a major strength—Ukrainian citizens and international observers alike consistently rank the armed forces among the most trusted institutions. Yet, the challenge remains in balancing transparency with operational security, ensuring enough information is shared to counter propaganda without compromising military effectiveness.

Within this broader effort, specialized units such as the Main Intelligence Directorate (HUR) operate as part of the MoD, providing intelligence, monitoring adversary information campaigns, and carrying out targeted actions to disrupt Russian disinformation. The HUR, historically focused on traditional military intelligence, has significantly expanded its mandate in response to the evolving nature of war. Recognizing that modern warfare extends beyond the battlefield, the HUR now actively addresses information operations and influence campaigns designed to shape public perception, undermine trust in Ukrainian institutions, and amplify hostile narratives abroad. Today, the HUR plays a central role in countering disinformation through two complementary approaches: tracking disinformation actors operating internationally, supporting sanctions and accountability by systematically documenting individuals and entities involved in hostile propaganda. These efforts reflect an understanding that intelligence work must integrate both operational and informational dimensions to effectively defend national sovereignty.

In this context, the HUR continues to employ asymmetric measures to counter the operations and strategic plans of the adversary. In the ongoing war, Russia has increasingly leveraged not only sports but also media and propaganda networks as strategic instruments for disinformation, sanctions evasion, and the expansion of its global influence. International competitions, sports institutions, prominent athletes, and state-aligned propagandists have been systematically manipulated to project a favourable image of Russia, obscure the realities of the war, legitimize its actions abroad, and shape international public opinion in Moscow's favour. The systematic exploitation of both cultural and informational channels highlights the sophisticated, multi-layered character of Russia's hybrid warfare, demonstrating that influence operations now extend beyond traditional military and political arenas into social, cultural, and media spaces, where they are used to distort narratives and consolidate strategic advantages. In response to these multifaceted threats, the HUR has taken concrete measures to translate intelligence insights into actionable tools for countering disinformation.

To counter these tactics, the HUR launched the War & Sanctions platform in June 2024 as a publicly accessible tool to document individuals and entities complicit in Russian aggression (WAR&SANCTIONS: DIU organises international hackathon for OSINT investigators, 2025). In collaboration with the CCD, the HUR subsequently developed two specialized sections within the platform: "Champions of terror" and "Kremlin Mouthpieces." "Champions of Terror" documents Russian athletes, coaches, and sports officials who participate in international competitions to whitewash Russia's image, disseminate disinformation, legitimize aggression against Ukraine, and assist in circumventing sanctions, often functioning as instruments of Russian intelligence abroad (Champions of terror, n.d.). "Kremlin Mouthpieces" complements this by identifying Russian propagandists and media managers who justify the war against Ukraine, incite hatred, glorify war criminals, and amplify hostile narratives to international audiences (Kremlin Mouthpieces, n.d.). These initiatives transform intelligence gathering into a tool for public diplomacy and international advocacy, providing governments, NGOs, and the global public with actionable data to reinforce sanctions, limit malign influence, and hold individuals accountable for their roles in Russia's hybrid operations.

Ukraine's security and intelligence institutions form the backbone of national defense in the information and security domain. Within this framework, the Security Service of Ukraine (SBU) has historically served as the country's principal counterintelligence body, with a broad mandate covering espionage, terrorism, cyber threats, and information warfare. Since 2014 the SBU has expanded its focus beyond conventional counterintelligence to addressing hybrid threats.

The SBU's work is critical for protecting Ukraine's digital sovereignty, it has consistently repelled massive attacks on government resources, critical infrastructure, and telecommunications companies. The SBU's role in this fight is built on three main pillars: attributing hostile actors by identifying those behind online networks and troll farms; disrupting their infrastructure by shutting down bot farms, seizing servers, and blocking financial flows; and pursuing criminal prosecution.

A prime example of this operational power is the SBU's work since the full-scale invasion began, when, in coordinated operations with the National Police, the SBU shut down two bot farms in the Kyiv and Odesa regions that were used to create fake accounts on social networks and messaging apps in order to sow panic within Ukrainian society (SSU shuts down 2 bot farms that spread destructive content in Ukraine, 2022). It was later reported that the SBU blocked the activities of 76 bot farms with a combined capacity of over 3 million fake accounts, which were used to spread pro-Russian narratives within Ukraine (SBU blocks 76 bot farms with 3 mln fake accounts since start of full-scale war, 2023). The scale of these operations illustrates how disinformation has become industrialized, with entire networks working around the clock to manipulate perceptions. It also underscores the importance of coupling technical expertise with legal authority—ensuring that dismantling bot farms is followed by criminal investigations to bring perpetrators to justice.

In 2024, the CCD, working jointly with the SBU's Cybersecurity Department, expanded this approach by introducing proactive measures to strengthen societal resilience. Beyond merely exposing hostile networks, they developed and published lists of verified and trustworthy information channels, offering citizens a reliable guide amid the noise of competing narratives (List of secure channels for obtaining information|Center for Countering Disinformation, 2024). At the same time, they uncovered and mapped coordinated networks of accounts operating on platforms such as TikTok, which were used to spread falsehoods targeting younger audiences, and compiled a list of hostile accounts on X that consistently promoted Russian propaganda and manipulative content (List of TikTok channels spreading hostile propaganda|Center for Countering Disinformation, 2024; List of channels for spreading hostile propaganda on social media X|Center for Countering Disinformation, 2024). These efforts sought to shift the information balance by not only removing malign influence but also promoting credible alternatives. The initiative immediately attracted attention from Russian propagandists, who launched smear campaigns against the CCD and the SBU, attempting to delegitimize the lists. This backlash revealed both the effectiveness of the Ukrainian approach and the sensitivity of disinformation actors to measures that disrupt their ability to reach and influence audiences.

The SBU embodies the security dimension of counter-disinformation: it treats information attacks as part of hostile statecraft. Its strength lies in its capacity for coercive action—seizures, arrests, prosecutions. Yet its challenge is to maintain legitimacy in a democracy, avoiding accusations of censorship or political bias. This requires transparency, judicial oversight, and cooperation with civil institutions.

The role of the Security Service of Ukraine in this fight is built on three main pillars: attributing hostile actors by identifying those behind online networks and troll farms; disrupting their infrastructure by shutting down bot farms, seizing servers, and blocking financial flows; and pursuing criminal prosecution.

5.2 Law Enforcement and Regulatory Bodies

In coordination with the CCD, the Ministry of Internal Affairs of Ukraine and National Police have developed a strategic framework to identify and respond to information threats. This collaboration ensures closer interagency coordination in both preventive measures and rapid response operations. For example, the Cyber Police and CCD compiled and published a list of official pages of government institutions, providing citizens with verified sources of information.

The Ministry of Internal Affairs of Ukraine (MIA) and its agencies, particularly the National Police and the Cyber Police Department, have increasingly integrated counter-disinformation efforts into their broader security mandate. While their core mission traditionally centered on maintaining public order and combating crime, these institutions now play a critical role in protecting Ukraine's information environment against hostile influence operations.

In coordination with the CCD, the MIA and National Police have developed a strategic framework to identify and respond to information threats. This collaboration ensures closer interagency coordination in both preventive measures and rapid response operations. For example, the Cyber Police and CCD compiled and published a list of official pages of government institutions, providing citizens with verified sources of information (Cyberpolice and the Center for Countering Disinformation have prepared a list of official pages of government bodies: only reliable and verified information—Cyberpolice Department, 2024). This measure helps the public avoid falling victim to propaganda or criminal schemes, reducing the spread of disinformation by encouraging users to follow official communication channels.

The Cyber Police Department also contributes to national resilience by promoting cyber hygiene and digital literacy among law enforcement personnel. Its training programs enhance officers' ability to identify, document, and respond to hybrid threats effectively. Beyond professional development, the MIA implements the public-oriented project "Cyber BRAMA," which provides all Ukrainian citizens with practical guidance and critical thinking skills to recognize, evaluate, and resist disinformation (Cybersecurity in Wartime|Cyber Brama, n.d.).

Public awareness initiatives extend these efforts to the wider population. The #ШахрайГудбай (Fraud Goodbye) campaign educates citizens on payment fraud schemes that often accompany disinformation campaigns, combining financial security with broader information protection (All-Ukrainian information campaign on payment security #ShakhraiGoodbye is launched, 2025). Operationally, the Cyber Police conducts systematic interventions against bot networks, dismantling coordinated platforms used to amplify hostile narratives and manipulate public discourse.

Collectively, these efforts demonstrate the MIA's and National Police's evolving contribution to Ukraine's national defense. By integrating strategic collaboration, verified communication channels, rapid IPSO response, professional and public education, and targeted cyber operations, they provide a comprehensive and multifaceted approach to countering disinformation. This approach not only disrupts hostile influence operations but also strengthens societal resilience, ensuring that Ukrainian citizens remain informed and resistant to manipulation.

The National Council of Television and Radio Broadcasting of Ukraine (NCTRB) represents the regulatory dimension of counter-disinformation. Since 2014, it has been responsible for defending the country's information space by restricting Russian channels, and monitoring compliance with Ukrainian law. In 2014, the Council banned the retransmission of Russian state channels, citing their role in spreading war propaganda. These bans were expanded after 2022 to cover additional outlets and online transmissions, with the Council justifying its decisions on the basis of national security in wartime. By November 2023, the National Council for Television and Radio Broadcasting had extended the list of media resources forbidden in Ukraine, adding another 16 services affiliated with the aggressor state, justifying the decisions based on specific criteria such as the use of Russian domains, a default Russian interface language, and advertising that targets the aggressor state's audience (Ukraine bans 16 Russian media resources|Ukrainska Pravda, 2023).

In 2023, the CCD and NCTRB launched a joint project, titled "Hatespeech" (Hate speech—a joint project of the National Council and the Center for Countering Disinformation—National Council on Television and Radio Broadcasting of Ukraine, 2025). The goal of this project is to inform a Western, English-speaking audience about the Russian threat by showcasing specific examples of threats made by propagandists, such as "hitting the UK with a nuclear bomb" or "burning Berlin". This initiative highlights how cross-agency cooperation can enhance resilience: the CCD contributes analytical capacity, while the National Council brings regulatory authority and visibility, creating a platform to publicly expose hate-driven narratives and show international partners that the threat is not as distant as it may seem. The Council's strength lies in its legal authority to restrict harmful media, but its challenge is the post-war horizon: how to design media regulation that protects security without creating a precedent for censorship.

The goal of "Hatespeech" project is to inform a Western, English-speaking audience about the Russian threat by showcasing specific examples of threats made by propagandists, such as "hitting the UK with a nuclear bomb" or "burning Berlin".

5.3 Foreign Policy and International Coordination

The Ministry of Foreign Affairs systematically countered Russian falsehoods by presenting visual evidence, survivor testimonies, and reports from NGOs and investigative journalists, ensuring that Russian disinformation did not dominate the international record. These interventions shifted the narrative toward accountability and underscored the role of truth in international diplomacy.

On the international stage, the Ministry of Foreign Affairs (MFA) carries Ukraine's counter-disinformation mission into the global arena, operating at the intersection of diplomacy, communication, and advocacy. Ukrainian embassies are transformed into information outposts, actively countering Russian narratives in their host states. A key part of this strategy is proactive communication rather than merely reactive diplomacy. To this end, the MFA has developed regional communication strategies for Latin America, the Caribbean, and Africa ('ukraine-latin-america-and-the-caribbean-eng-web.pdf', n.d.; 'ctrategiya-afrika-eng.pdf', n.d.). These strategies emphasize Ukraine's fight as a defense of sovereignty, freedom, and the right to choose its own future, presenting narratives that resonate with local audiences and counter hostile messaging more effectively. To implement this, the MFA engages regional media outlets, partners with local opinion leaders, and adapts its messaging to reflect the specific political and cultural context of each region. By doing so, Ukraine ensures that its voice is heard beyond traditional Western platforms, building long-term resilience to Russian propaganda in strategically important information spaces.

This proactive regional engagement is complemented by Ukraine's active counter-disinformation efforts at the United Nations, where Russian falsehoods are systematically challenged. During UN General Assembly debates, Russian representatives have persistently denied atrocities committed in Bucha, Mariupol, and Izium. The MFA systematically countered these falsehoods by presenting visual evidence, survivor testimonies, and reports from NGOs and investigative journalists, ensuring that Russian disinformation did not dominate the international record. These interventions shifted the narrative toward accountability and underscored the role of truth in international diplomacy. A central figure in this effort was Ukraine's former Permanent Representative to the UN, Sergiy Kyslytsya. His speeches—sharp, evidence-based, and rhetorically powerful—reframed disinformation not as mere falsehoods but as active enablers of war crimes. In his April 2022 address to the General Assembly, Kyslytsya directly confronted Russia's lies about Bucha, Irpin and other Ukrainian sites, stressing how disinformation was deliberately used to conceal civilian killings and facilitate impunity for atrocities (Further statement by Permanent Representative of Ukraine to the UN Sergiy Kyslytsya at the UN Security Council meeting, 2022). Through such interventions, Ukrainian diplomacy demonstrated how strategic rhetoric, rooted in legal argumentation, moral clarity, and factual evidence, can effectively undermine propaganda in real time and strengthen the global call for justice.

Building on these proactive efforts, the MFA, in partnership with Estonia, launched the "Nations Against Disinformation" initiative, reflecting a broader strategy to engage international audiences in understanding and resisting Russian information operations (Ministry of Foreign Affairs of Ukraine - Nations Against Disinformation: A New Creative Tool To Counter Disinformation, 2023). At the heart of this campaign is a creative digital tool called "The Distortion

Test," designed to demonstrate in a tangible way how disinformation can gradually distort a person's perception of reality. The tool invites users to upload a personal image and then answer a series of seven questions related to recent disinformation attacks. Based on the accuracy of their responses, the uploaded image becomes visually distorted, providing an immediate and striking illustration of how exposure to false information can warp understanding over time. By combining interactive engagement with educational content, this initiative not only informs users about the mechanics of propaganda but also encourages critical thinking and active discernment of online content. In this way, the campaign serves as both a pedagogical instrument and a public diplomacy tool, helping Ukraine reach global audiences with a compelling, evidence-based counter-narrative to hostile information campaigns.

A further important direction of the MFA's work is cultural and historical diplomacy. In 2025, the MFA launched the educational initiative "Diplomacy of Memory," in partnership with the Babyn Yar National Historical and Memorial Reserve (The Ministry of Foreign Affairs launched an educational project 'Diplomacy of Memory' to counter Russian disinformation, 2025). This project equips Ukrainian diplomats with tools to defend historical truth and counter Russia's manipulation of history as an instrument of hybrid warfare. Through lectures and training sessions diplomats learn to apply historical knowledge in international negotiations, public communications, and responses to disinformation. The project thus transforms memory into both a shield and a tool of international advocacy.

Collectively, these efforts demonstrate how the MFA has internationalized Ukraine's counter-disinformation strategy. By combining proactive campaigns, strategic partnerships, regionally tailored messaging, cultural and historical diplomacy, and high-level advocacy, the Ministry of Foreign Affairs not only disrupts Russian propaganda abroad but also strengthens global solidarity with Ukraine. These initiatives help shape international public opinion, ensuring that foreign governments, media, and civil society actors are better informed about the realities of the war. Moreover, they contribute to building long-term resilience against hostile narratives, empowering audiences to critically assess information and resist manipulation. Through these sustained, multifaceted actions, the MFA reinforces Ukraine's image as a credible, transparent, and resilient democratic state while creating a coordinated international front against disinformation.

In 2025, the MFA launched the educational initiative "Diplomacy of Memory," in partnership with the Babyn Yar National Historical and Memorial Reserve to equips Ukrainian diplomats with tools to defend historical truth and counter Russia's manipulation of history as an instrument of hybrid warfare. Through lectures and training sessions diplomats learn to apply historical knowledge in international negotiations, public communications, and responses to disinformation. The project thus transforms memory into both a shield and a tool of international advocacy.

5.4 Cultural and Educational Bodies

Teacher training remains a central focus of Ukraine's efforts to strengthen media literacy. The "Digital Teacher" online course, developed in partnership with UNESCO and Google.org, helped educators build stronger digital skills and adapt effectively to hybrid and remote learning environments. Beyond technical competencies, the program equipped teachers with strategies to guide students in critically evaluating the information they encounter online. By empowering educators in this way, the initiative enhances class-room instruction and contributes to developing a generation of students who can recognize disinformation and think independently about the content they consume.

Another crucial layer of defense is the cultural and educational front. The Ministry of Education and Science (MoES) plays a pivotal role in fostering an information-resilient society. The Ministry's efforts focus on equipping citizens with the tools to critically evaluate information, combat manipulation, and promote media literacy across various educational platforms.

The MoES integrates media literacy into school curricula, ensuring that students develop the skills to discern credible information from falsehoods. One of the examples of these efforts is the "Learn to Discern" initiative, implemented in collaboration with IREX (Program "Learn and Distinguish: Infomedia Literacy", n.d.). This program is a media literacy initiative designed to give people the tools and skills to critically assess the information they encounter. Rather than telling participants which sources to trust, it focuses on teaching the underlying skills needed to evaluate content, recognize manipulation, and make informed judgments.

Teacher training remains a central focus of Ukraine's efforts to strengthen media literacy. The "Digital Teacher" online course, developed in partnership with UNESCO and Google.org, helped educators build stronger digital skills and adapt effectively to hybrid and remote learning environments (Ukraine: UNESCO trains 50,000 teachers on digital pedagogy|UNESCO, 2023). Beyond technical competencies, the program equipped teachers with strategies to guide students in critically evaluating the information they encounter online. By empowering educators in this way, the initiative enhances classroom instruction and contributes to developing a generation of students who can recognize disinformation and think independently about the content they consume.

Through these multifaceted initiatives, the MoES not only strengthens national security but also fosters a generation of informed citizens capable of critically engaging with information. By embedding media literacy in education, supporting research, and forging strategic partnerships, the Ministry ensures a robust defense against disinformation, safeguarding Ukraine's information ecosystem.

This educational work is complemented by the efforts of the Ministry of Culture (MC). By fostering media literacy, promoting strategic communication, and collaborating with international and domestic partners, the MC has implemented a range of initiatives to counter disinformation and build societal resilience.

The MC has prioritized media literacy as a cornerstone of its strategy to combat disinformation. One of its flagship initiatives is the "Filter" project, launched in

2021 to consolidate the efforts of the state, civil society, and international organizations in strengthening society's resilience to manipulative content (About the Project, 2021). The project seeks to build a culture of critical thinking by equipping citizens with tools and resources that enable them to verify information independently and resist disinformation campaigns. At its core, "Filter" provides a platform where educators, journalists, and ordinary citizens can access practical guides, online trainings, and interactive materials designed to improve media literacy skills. It emphasizes the importance of recognizing manipulative techniques, understanding how propaganda works, and distinguishing credible information sources from deceptive ones.

The MC has been steadily developing international partnerships to strengthen the country's resilience against disinformation. Cooperation with the United Nations Development Programme has focused on advancing media literacy, supporting counter-disinformation initiatives, and ensuring inclusive access to reliable information (Media literacy and countering disinformation: Mykola Tochytskyi and Jaco Cilliers discussed key areas of cooperation between the MC and UNDP, 2024). This collaboration highlights a shared recognition that resilience is not only about protecting institutions, but also about equipping citizens with the skills to navigate the information space critically.

Equally significant is the Ministry's partnership with UNESCO, which has combined cultural preservation with the safeguarding of information integrity (MCSC and UNESCO strengthen strategic partnership in the fields of culture, media and digitalization, 2025). UNESCO has supported the modernization of Ukraine's cultural registries to ensure secure storage and protection of heritage records during wartime, while also engaging in dialogue on emerging challenges such as the regulation of artificial intelligence, the risks of deepfakes, and the need to reinforce local information ecosystems. Together, these initiatives demonstrate that countering disinformation is not solely a national effort but a global responsibility that depends on cooperation and innovation.

Despite challenges, such as resource constraints and the evolving tactics of disinformation campaigns, the MC continues to innovate. Plans to integrate artificial intelligence into disinformation detection and expand media literacy initiatives to broader audiences demonstrate its forward-thinking approach. Through these efforts, the MC not only protects Ukraine's informational space but also fosters a culture of critical thinking and resilience, ensuring that citizens are equipped to navigate and counter disinformation effectively.

One of its flagship initiatives of the Ministry of Culture is the "Filter" project, launched in 2021 to con-solidate the efforts of the state, civil society, and international organizations in strengthening society's resilience to manipulative content. The project seeks to build a culture of critical thinking by equipping citizens with tools and resources that enable them to verify information independently and resist disinformation campaigns. At its core, "Filter" provides a platform where educators, journalists, and ordinary citizens can access practical guides, online trainings, and interactive materials designed to improve media literacy skills. It emphasizes the importance of recognizing manipulative techniques, understanding how propaganda works, and distinguishing credible information sources from deceptive ones.

5.5 Anti-corruption and Integrity Body

> Disinformation thrives in an environment where corruption is hidden and un-addressed, allowing propagandists to amplify suspicions and spread mistrust. By contrast, when corruption is systematically uncovered, investigated, and punished, the state denies the enemy this narrative resource. Thus, the very act of building an effective anticorruption system becomes part of Ukraine's information defense.

In the context of Russia's full-scale war against Ukraine, corruption has become one of the most exploited topics in the enemy's information arsenal. Russian propaganda systematically manipulates the idea of corruption, presenting it as proof of Ukraine's supposed weakness, ungovernability, and lack of prospects for reform. These narratives are aimed both at undermining citizens' trust in their own state and at convincing international partners that supporting Ukraine is "futile". Against this backdrop, the National Agency on Corruption Prevention (NACP) has assumed a role that goes beyond its traditional mandate. It has become a key actor in the wider system of countering disinformation, where the fight against corruption is not only about internal reform but also about strengthening the resilience of society and the credibility of the state in the eyes of the world.

A central framework for this effort is the State Anti-Corruption Program for 2023–2025 (General Information on the Anti-Corruption Strategy and the State Anti-Corruption Program, n.d.). For the first time, this strategic document explicitly connects the prevention of corruption with countering hostile information influence. The program underlines that transparency and accountability are not only tools of good governance but also powerful shields against manipulation. Disinformation thrives in an environment where corruption is hidden and unaddressed, allowing propagandists to amplify suspicions and spread mistrust. By contrast, when corruption is systematically uncovered, investigated, and punished, the state denies the enemy this narrative resource. Thus, the very act of building an effective anti-corruption system becomes part of Ukraine's information defense.

Openness and communication are central to the NACP's approach. The agency deliberately rejects the logic of concealment, choosing instead to emphasize that recognition of problems and consistent punishment of abuses is a sign of resilience, not weakness. This strategy undermines one of the key pillars of Russian disinformation, which portrays Ukraine as a "failed state." By highlighting progress in reforms and pointing to concrete results, the NACP shows that Ukraine is capable of self-renewal even under the most difficult conditions of war. In doing so, it strengthens trust domestically, where citizens increasingly see integrity as a shared value, and internationally, where partners are more inclined to continue their support when they see a functioning system of accountability.

Equally important is the NACP's ability to analyse and anticipate information threats. The agency closely monitors how Russian propaganda weaponizes corruption-related themes, identifying patterns, methods, and target audiences. This analytical work is not done in isolation; it is supported through cooperation with international partners and other Ukrainian institutions, including the CCD. Such monitoring makes it possible to issue timely clarifications and expose manipulative narratives before they gain traction. It also helps Ukrainian society to recognize hostile influence operations and to distinguish between legitimate criticism of corruption and fabricated propaganda designed to weaken morale.

Taken together, these efforts show that the NACP is not limited to technical oversight of compliance and integrity rules. It is an institution that consciously positions transparency and integrity as part of Ukraine's national defense. By turning anti-corruption reform into an element of information resilience, the NACP deprives Russia of one of its favourite propaganda tools and demonstrates that Ukraine can combine resistance on the battlefield with progress in governance. In a modern hybrid war, where the line between military, political, and informational fronts is blurred, this contribution is both unique and indispensable.

The National Agency on Corruption Prevention closely monitors how Russian propaganda weaponizes corruption-related themes, identifying patterns, methods, and target audiences. This analytical work is not done in isolation; it is supported through cooperation with international partners and other Ukrainian institutions, including the CCD. Such monitoring makes it possible to issue timely clarifications and expose manipulative narratives before they gain traction. It also helps Ukrainian society to recognize hostile influence operations and to distinguish between legitimate criticism of corruption and fabricated propaganda designed to weaken morale.

5.6 Inter-agency Coordination

Joint task forces combine operational intelligence, strategic communication, and societal outreach, creating a more comprehensive defense against manipulation.

Disinformation is a multifaceted threat that no single institution can address alone. In Ukraine, hostile narratives span military, political, social, and cultural domains, making inter-agency collaboration essential. The country's experience demonstrates that effective counter-disinformation requires not only coordination but also careful management of overlapping responsibilities and institutional boundaries.

Ukraine's counter-disinformation ecosystem shows that resilience demands a whole-of-state approach, with each institution contributing its unique capacities: the MOD/AFU secure the operational battlefield of truth, the SBU provides coercive enforcement; the HUR supports strategic attribution and international advocacy; the NCTRB regulates media and sets boundaries; the MFA projects Ukraine's truth internationally; the Ministry of Education builds societal immunity; the MC sustains narrative sovereignty; and the NACP counter corruption disinformation.

Several examples illustrate successful mechanisms. Joint task forces, such as those formed by the MFA and SBU, have been crucial in tracing and attributing hostile campaigns abroad. Similarly, the HUR collaborates closely with the CCD on sanction-related initiatives, coordinating efforts to identify individuals and entities involved in hostile activities and support targeted measures. These partnerships combine operational intelligence, strategic communication, and societal outreach, creating a more comprehensive defense against manipulation.

However, coordination is not without its challenges. Overlapping mandates can slow response times, while bureaucratic competition sometimes leads to duplicated efforts. For instance, both the MoE and the MC conduct media literacy programs, requiring careful synchronization to avoid redundancy and ensure consistent messaging. Moreover, there is a delicate balance between coordination and perceived centralization: excessive control can be misinterpreted as propaganda, potentially undermining public trust.

To address these challenges, Ukraine has experimented with whole-of-government approaches, such as inter-agency working groups under the National Security and Defense Council. These groups aim to streamline information sharing, clarify responsibilities, and ensure rapid, evidence-based responses to emerging threats. These experiences underline the democratic dilemma: coordination is essential, but centralization can be misinterpreted as propaganda control.

Overall, Ukraine's inter-agency coordination demonstrates a model for modern information defense. By combining intelligence, regulatory oversight, diplomacy, and civil society engagement, the country has created a dynamic and adaptive framework. This experience underscores that defending the information space is as much about institutional cooperation as it is about technological tools or strategic messaging—it requires sustained effort, flexibility, and a constant commitment to truth.

5.7 Conclusion

Ukraine's experience shows that defending against disinformation is far more complex than simply fact-checking false claims. It requires a whole-of-government approach, where each institution brings its unique strengths to the table. Security services investigate and respond to threats on the ground, intelligence agencies track and expose hostile campaigns, regulators enforce rules and impose sanctions, diplomats advocate Ukraine's position abroad, educators and cultural institutions nurture critical thinking and societal resilience, and the armed forces provide timely, evidence-based updates from the battlefield. Together, these efforts form a protective shield for democracy, each element reinforcing the others.

The crucial insight is that resilience must be both proactive and reactive. It's not enough to respond to disinformation after it spreads—institutions must anticipate emerging narratives, prepare countermeasures, and help society recognize and resist manipulation before it takes hold. Ukraine's approach shows that the strongest defense comes from collaboration: when every branch of government works toward a shared strategy of foresight, coordination, and narrative resilience, the country builds a lasting capacity to withstand information threats. In this way, protecting the information space becomes not just a set of technical measures, but a broader cultural and institutional effort, embedding vigilance, trust, and critical thinking at the heart of democratic governance.

References

About the Project. (2021). Filter—A national media literacy project. Available at https://filter.mcsc.gov.ua/about-us/. Accessed 6 November 2025.

All-Ukrainian information campaign on payment security #ShakhraiGoodbye is launched (2025). Available at https://mvs.gov.ua/news/startuje-vseukrayinska-informaciina-kampaniia-z-platiznoyi-bezpeki-saxraigudbai. Accessed 6 November 2025.

Champions of terror (n.d.) War & Sanctions. Available at https://war-sanctions.gur.gov.ua/en/sport/persons. Accessed 6 November 2025).

ctrategiya-afrika-eng.pdf (n.d.). Available at https://mfa.gov.ua/storage/app/sites/1/ctrategiya-afrika-eng.pdf. Accessed 6 November 2025).

Cyberpolice and the Center for Countering Disinformation have prepared a list of official pages of government bodies: only reliable and verified information—Cyberpolice Department (2024). Available at https://cyberpolice.gov.ua/article/kiberpoliczziya-ta-czentr-protydiyi-dezynformacziyi-pidgotuvaly-perelik-oficzijnyx-storinok-derzhavnyx-organiv-lyshe-dostovirna-i-perevirena-informacziya-7756/. Accessed 6 November 2025.

Cybersecurity in Wartime|Cyber Brama (n.d.). Available at https://stopfraud.gov.ua/en/cybersecurity-in-wartime. Accessed 6 November 2025).

Further statement by Permanent Representative of Ukraine to the UN Sergiy Kyslytsya at the UN Security Council meeting (2022) Permanent Mission of Ukraine to the United Nations. Available at http://ukraineun.org/en/press-center/549-further-statement-by-permanent-representative-of-ukraine-to-the-un-sergiy-kyslytsya-at-the-un-security-council-meeting/. Accessed 6 November 2025.

General information on the anti-corruption strategy and the state anti-corruption program (n.d.). Available at https://dap.nazk.gov.ua/en/general-info/. Accessed 6 November 2025.

Hate speech—a joint project of the National Council and the Center for Countering Disinformation—National Council on Television and Radio Broadcasting of Ukraine' (2025). Available at https://webportal.nrada.gov.ua/en/hate-speech-a-joint-project-of-the-national-council-and-the-center-for-countering-disinformation-63/. Accessed 6 November 2025.

Kremlin Mouthpieces. (n.d.). War & Sanctions. Available at https://war-sanctions.gur.gov.ua/en/propaganda/persons. Accessed 6 November 2025.

List of channels for spreading hostile propaganda on social media X|Center for Countering Disinformation (2024, 14 April). Available at https://cpd.gov.ua/reports/spysok-kanaliv-poshyrennya-vorozhoyi-propagandy-v-soczmerezhi-h/. Accessed 6 November 2025.

List of TikTok channels spreading hostile propaganda|Center for Countering Disinformation (2024, 27 March). Available at https://cpd.gov.ua/announcement/spysok-tiktok-kanaliv-poshyrennya-vorozhoyi-propagandy/. Accessed 6 November 2025.

List of secure channels for obtaining information|Center for Countering Disinformation. (2024, 11 March). Available at https://cpd.gov.ua/announcement/spysok-bezpechnyh-kanaliv-otrymannya-informacziyi/. Accessed 6 November 2025.

MCSC and UNESCO strengthen strategic partnership in the fields of culture, media and digitalization (2025). Ministry of Culture and Strategic Communications, 13 August. Available at https://mcsc.gov.ua/news/mksk-ta-yunesko-posylyuyut-strategichne-partnerstvo-u-sferah-kultury-media-ta-czyfrovizacziyi/. Accessed 6 November 2025.

Media literacy and countering disinformation: Mykola Tochytskyi and Jaco Cilliers discussed key areas of cooperation between the MCSC and UNDP (2024). Ministry of Culture and Strategic Communications, 31 October. Available at https://mcsc.gov.ua/en/news/media-literacy-and-countering-disinformation-mykola-tochytskyi-and-jaco-cilliers-discussed-key-areas-of-cooperation-between-the-mcsc-and-undp/. Accessed 6 November 2025.

Ministry of Foreign Affairs of Ukraine—Nations Against Disinformation: A New Creative Tool To Counter Disinformation (2023). Available at https://mfa.gov.ua/en/news/nations-against-disinformation-zapusk-novogo-kreativnogo-instrumentu-z-protidiyi-dezinformaciyi. Accessed 6 November 2025.

Program "Learn and Distinguish: Infomedia Literacy" (n.d.). Available at https://mon.gov.ua/ministerstvo-2/diyalnist/mizhnarodna-spivpratsya-2/spivpratsya-z-mizhnarodnimi-organizatsiyami/rada-mizhnarodnikh-naukovikh-doslidzhen-ta-obminiv-irex/programa-vivchay-ta-rozriznyay-infomediyna-gramotnist. Accessed 6 November 2025.

SBU blocks 76 bot farms with 3 mln fake accounts since start of full-scale war (2023) Interfax-Ukraine. Available at https://en.interfax.com.ua/news/general/945735.html. Accessed 6 November 2025.

SSU shuts down 2 bot farms that spread destructive content in Ukraine (2022) SSU. Available at https://ssu.gov.ua/en/novyny/sbu-zablokuvala-shche-dvi-botofermy-yaki-rozghanialy-destruktyvnyi-kontent-v-ukraini. Accessed 6 November 2025.

The Ministry of Foreign Affairs launched an educational project "Diplomacy of Memory" to counter Russian disinformation (2025). Available at https://www.ukrinform.ua/rubric-polytics/3995511-u-mzs-zapocatkuvali-osvitnij-proekt-diplomatia-pamati-dla-protidii-rosijskij-dezinformacii.html. Accessed 6 November 2025.

Ukraine bans 16 Russian media resources|Ukrainska Pravda (2023). Available at https://www.pravda.com.ua/eng/news/2023/11/09/7428044/. Accessed 6 November 2025.

Ukraine: UNESCO trains 50,000 teachers on digital pedagogy|UNESCO (2023). Available at https://www.unesco.org/en/articles/ukraine-unesco-trains-50000-teachers-digital-pedagogy. Accessed 6 November 2025.

ukraine-latin-america-and-the-caribbean-eng-web.pdf (n.d.). Available at https://mfa.gov.ua/storage/app/sites/1/ukraine-latin-america-and-the-caribbean-eng-web.pdf. Accessed 6 November 2025.

WAR&SANCTIONS: DIU organises international hackathon for OSINT investigators (2025). Available at https://gur.gov.ua//en/content/warsanctions-hur-mo-ukrainy-orhanizovuie-mizhnarodnyi-khakaton-dlia-osintrozsliduvachiv. Accessed 6 November 2025.

Media Literacy Trainings in Ukraine 6

One of the most pressing challenges for Ukraine amid Russia's full-scale war is media literacy and societal immunity to disinformation. The Ukrainian state faces not only conventional military threats but also a sophisticated system of large-scale influence operations aimed at destabilizing society, undermining trust in institutions, and weakening democratic resilience. In this context, the mission of the Center for Countering Disinformation (CCD) extends beyond observing and analysing hostile narratives to building long-term societal resilience via education and training.

This mission is codified in the Regulation on the CCD, which mandates the Center to foster cooperation between state bodies and civil society in addressing disinformation and destructive information operations (Mission of the Center for Countering Disinformation, 2021). The Regulation also requires the CCD to coordinate and participate in campaigns aimed at promoting media literacy within society. This effectively requires the Center's work to extend beyond the security domain, reaching communities, schools, universities, nongovernmental organizations, and local leaders, creating a unique bridge linking expert-driven national security efforts with civic education.

The CCD transforms analytical knowledge into accessible formats that help citizens understand how disinformation operates and what they can do to protect themselves from manipulations. These initiatives prove that the fight against disinformation is not the sole responsibility of national defense alone, it can succeed only if it becomes a broader societal effort. By prioritizing collaborative education, the CCD fosters the exchange of knowledge and practical tools between government agencies and civil society, ensuring that insights are not confined to a small group of experts. In so doing, Ukraine's battle against disinformation is becoming increasingly community-led and bottom-up, grounded firmly in the resilience of its citizens.

A. Marushchak et al., *Counter Disinformation System Development in Ukraine*,
Terrorism, Security, and Computation, https://doi.org/10.1007/978-3-032-24731-5_6

6.1 Training for Resilience: The CCD's Role

Disinformation cannot be effectively countered solely through reactive measures, such as fact-checking or debunking. While these are essential, long-term resilience depends on equipping decision-makers and practitioners with stronger analytical and critical thinking skills. The needs of national civil servants differ from those of regional authorities or specialized agencies. Cooperation with international organizations helps transfer knowledge and strengthens Ukraine's overall capacity in information security. In the context of war, these trainings are not abstract exercises for posterity but urgent measures aimed at addressing immediate threats.

Over the past years, the CCD has formulated several training programs targeted at diverse audiences. Together, these initiatives represent a holistic educational component of Ukraine's counter-disinformation policy, demonstrating how strategic messaging and information-sharing can be instruments of national defense.

In 2022, the CCD, with support of the NACP Integrity Office, launched its first media literacy initiative: the animated series Dobrochesnist Online ("Integrity Online") (The Integrity Online Project, 2022). With seven episodes, the series was created for children and teenagers, providing them relatable stories on how manipulation and disinformation can spread even in casual online spaces. Rather than relying on abstract lectures, the series uses memorable visuals to show young viewers how to identify manipulation and apply simple, practical strategies to resist it.

Importantly, this work is made possible by the expertise of the CCD's staff—specialists with backgrounds in security analysis, communications, international relations, and education. They are able not only to identify and unpack hostile narratives, but also to translate complex security information into practical guidance for non-experts. This unique combination of analytical skill and pedagogical know-how enables the CCD to produce educational materials and deliver training programs that resonate with diverse audiences, ensuring that everyone, from policymakers to children, receives tools tailored to their needs and role.

Several underlying assumptions shape the logic of the CCD's training programs. First, disinformation cannot be effectively countered solely through reactive measures, such as fact-checking or debunking. While these are essential, long-term resilience depends on equipping decision-makers and practitioners with stronger analytical and critical thinking skills. Second, we need customized approaches to address distinct audiences: the needs of national civil servants differ from those of regional authorities or specialized agencies. Third, cooperation with international organizations helps transfer knowledge and strengthens Ukraine's overall capacity in information security. Finally, in the context of war, these trainings are not abstract exercises for posterity but urgent measures aimed at addressing immediate threats.

Building media literacy and institutional resilience against disinformation must start where decisions are made and where citizens most frequently encounter the authority of the state: among civil servants at both national and regional levels. One of the CCD's important projects in this field is its partnership with the Higher

Corps of Civil Service. In cooperation with the National School for Public Administration, the CCD has developed a crisis management course for senior officials, equipping them with practical tools to counteract and mitigate negative information impact on people. The effort focuses on propaganda and disinformation (The Center conducted a training on crisis management for the Senior Civil Service Commission|Center for Countering Disinformation, 2024). The training serves two purposes. First, it provides participants with actionable strategies for managing crises in an environment of hybrid warfare, where military or political escalations are often accompanied by information operations. Second, it emphasizes the importance of public communication, transparency, and the role of civil servants as trusted messengers in times of crisis. Taking a problem-based approach, working on ways for practitioners to prevent their organisations and peers from being used in disinformation's service means that course participants have intellectual tools they can use not just to understand how dissemination works, but also apply strategies to protect the public trust.

The CCD also organized a series of trainings for representatives of central executive bodies and, separately, for representatives of regional military and state administrations (OVA and ODA) (The Center for Countering Disinformation conducted a series of trainings for the representatives of the central executive bodies|Center for Countering Disinformation, 2023a; The Center for Countering Disinformation conducted a series of trainings for representatives of the Regional Military Administration and the Regional State Administration|Center for Countering Disinformation, 2023). These sessions reflected the understanding that both central and regional levels of government are key targets for disinformation campaigns, as they serve as direct communicators with the population. The trainings for central bodies focused on developing strategic communication skills, interagency coordination, and the ability to counter disinformation narratives in the media space. The regional administration's trainings placed greater emphasis on crisis communication at the local level, working with local media, and addressing community-level vulnerabilities to information manipulation. By strengthening both central and regional resilience, the CCD contributed to the creation of a multi-level defense system where all layers of governance are prepared to confront disinformation threats.

Apart from civil servants, the CCD has identified the need to strengthen the capacities of Ukraine's security sector institutions. A dedicated training was conducted for the Security Service of Ukraine (SBU) on countering hostile propaganda in wartime conditions (The CCD conducted a training for the Security Service of Ukraine on countering enemy propaganda in times of war|Center for Countering Disinformation, 2023). This initiative proved highly valuable, combining analytical insights with practical skills required for frontline defense against disinformation. It examined how propaganda strives to undermine morale, disorient the masses, and erode confidence in state security institutions. Additionally, the Center contributed to a further advanced course titled "Strategic communications in the conditions of (hybrid) warfare". This was when SBU personnel were trained to use communication technologies to enhance civil resilience against enemy propaganda and respond effectively (The Center participated in the training of SBU employees on strategic communications|Center for Countering Disinformation, 2024). Lectures, practical case analyses and hands-on workshops allowed participants not only to learn how to react to hostile propaganda but develop the new skills needed. They also mastered how to pre-empt manipulative narratives, how to engrain strategic communication into the routine work of the SBU and how to perceive information defense as a task requiring quick reaction patterns, strategic imagination and flexibility in strategy.

In addition to government institutions, the CCD directs attention to state-run enterprises and agencies that are frequently targeted by disinformation due to their strategic significance. A training-intensive program was conducted for the National Nuclear Energy Generating Company "Energoatom" (On March 1, intensive training course was held for «Energoatom»|Center for Countering Disinformation, 2023). As critical infrastructure is often associated with disinformation campaigns designed to provoke fear, panic, or loss of public confidence, this training equipped participants with the knowledge to proactively counter information attacks and develop communication strategies that maintain public trust in nuclear safety and energy security. Similarly, the Center organized a training for the State Service of Ukraine on Food Safety and Consumer Protection in Kyiv, recognizing that economic and consumer sectors are also vulnerable to disinformation, particularly during wartime, when issues of food security become sensitive targets for manipulations (A workshop for employees of the SSUFSCP in Kyiv was held on April 7|Center for Countering Disinformation, 2023).

While each training target specific audiences and challenges, two flagship initiatives stand out, exemplifying the increasing sophistication and internationalization of Ukraine's approach to media literacy and counter-disinformation education. In October 2023, the CCD, together with the Swedish Psychological Defense Agency (Myndigheten för psykologiskt försvar, MPF), hosted the inaugural "Stratcom Weekend 1.0" in Lviv (From October 6 to 9, under the auspices of the Center for Countering Disinformation and the Psychological Defense Agency, "Stratcom weekend" 1.0 was held|Center for Countering Disinformation, 2023). This event was an educational and practical forum where Ukrainian officials, experts, and international partners engaged in in-depth discussions and exercises on strategic communications and countering hybrid threats. "Stratcom Weekend 1.0" became a platform for knowledge-sharing, brainstorming, and joint planning, helping to create a professional community of practitioners capable of acting in a coordinated way in response to disinformation.

The following year, the CCD, together with the Swedish partners, gathered civil servants for what became one of the most memorable initiatives—the four-day "Countering FIMI Weekend" (CCD held Countering FIMI Weekend in Lviv|Center for Countering Disinformation, 2024). Unlike ordinary training, this felt more like an intellectual workshop where people could not only listen to lectures but also argue, test ideas, and learn from one another. The theme of Foreign Information Manipulation and Interference (FIMI) may sound abstract, yet the sessions made it very concrete: participants were asked to walk through real cases, recognize hidden manipulation techniques, and think through how their own institutions should respond. Experts from the United Kingdom and Sweden brought in perspectives that broadened the discussion. British specialists spoke about global patterns of FIMI, showing how Ukraine's experience fits into a much larger struggle. Swedish researchers focused on the role of artificial intelligence, showing how it can be used both to strengthen strategic communications and to detect manipulative campaigns, while also warning about the risks of its exploitation by hostile actors.

Perhaps the most heated conversations came during a presentation on artificial intelligence. On the one hand, AI tools can help analyze vast flows of information and strengthen communication; on the other, they can be turned into powerful weapons of manipulation. For many in the room, this tension felt deeply relevant to their daily work. The weekend closed with an open discussion where participants could question the speakers directly and connect insights to their own practice. What stayed with many was the feeling that they were part of a community facing the same threats and working together to build a stronger shield against them.

Looking back, the cumulative impact of these trainings feels hard to overstate. They did more than simply transfer knowledge from experts to officials. Step by step, they embedded awareness of disinformation into the everyday routines of Ukrainian state institutions, so that this knowledge would not remain locked within one agency but spread across ministries, regions, and sectors. Just as important, the trainings created bonds between people—civil servants who might never have met otherwise found themselves working side by side, building trust and networks that could prove invaluable in moments of crisis.

It also became evident that education, in this context, cannot be a one-time effort. As adversaries continuously adapt their tactics, the state's response must remain equally dynamic, embracing a growth mindset in countering disinformation, constantly learning and evolving. The international dimension amplified this impact, as by engaging European experts to work alongside Ukrainian counterparts, the CCD ensured that Ukrainian officials were not merely passive participants in the global dialogue on defending democracies, but active contributors shaping that conversation.

Ultimately, these trainings demonstrated that countering disinformation is not merely about exposing lies, but about building resilience, fostering critical thinking, and strengthening institutional credibility. In war-torn Ukraine, education itself has become a weapon, quieter than artillery, but no less vital. By investing in the people who staff state institutions, from national ministries to regional administrations, the CCD has helped cultivate a society that is more resistant to manipulation, more confident in its institutions, and better prepared to defend democratic values in the digital age.

> The trainings for central bodies focused on developing strategic communication skills, interagency coordination, and the ability to counter disinformation narratives in the media space. The regional administration's trainings placed greater emphasis on crisis communication

at the local level, working with local media, and addressing community-level vulnerabilities to information manipulation. By strengthening both central and regional resilience, the CCD contributed to the creation of a multilevel defense system where all layers of governance are prepared to confront disinformation threats. Apart from civil servants, the CCD has identified the need to strengthen the capacities of Ukraine's security sector institutions.

6.2 The CCD as a Knowledge Hub

Two manuals that have since become milestones: "Manual on Countering Dis-information" (May 2023) and "Weapons of Information Warfare" (July 2025) ('Handbook on countering disinformation developed by the Center for Countering Disinformation. They were not simply brochures or collections of recommendations. They represented a shift in thinking: the recognition that to resist disinformation, society must not only react to each falsehood but also learn, practise, and teach resilience as a skill.

When war spills not only onto the battlefield but also into the screens of our phones, knowledge becomes a weapon. Ukraine learned this truth early and painfully. Rumours, conspiracy theories, and doctored photos all swirl through newsfeeds alongside reports of real shelling, displacement, and loss. At first, media literacy projects helped ordinary citizens become more cautious, sceptical, and attentive. But it soon became clear: awareness alone was not enough.

In classrooms and lecture halls, and within community groups led by local activists, teachers and their counterparts became the subjects of endless questioning. "Is this video real?" "Can we trust this source?" "What should I do when my students bring this to class?" Scepticism alone was no longer enough—their daily work required guidance and structure. But the available resources were scattered, project-based, and rarely tailored to those standing on the frontlines of community resilience.

This was the moment when the CCD began to assume perhaps its most unconventional role as a security institution. It would not only monitor hostile campaigns or sound alarms. Instead, it would become a knowledge hub, translating analytical expertise into tools that were both practical and pedagogical, yet accessible to all. Few institutions anywhere in the world had attempted such a model, but for Ukraine, this experiment was not a luxury, it was a necessity.

From this decision came two manuals that have since become milestones: "Manual on Countering Disinformation" (May 2023) and "Weapons of Information Warfare" (July 2025) (Handbook on countering disinformation developed by the Center for Countering Disinformation, a working body of the National Security and Defense Council of Ukraine with the support of the European Union Advisory Mission Ukraine|Center for Countering Disinformation, 2023; Handbook "Weapons of Information Warfare"|Center for Countering Disinformation, 2025). They were not simply brochures or collections of recommendations. They represented a shift in thinking: the recognition that to resist disinformation, society must not only react to each falsehood but also learn, practise, and teach resilience as a skill.

6.2.1 Manual on Countering Disinformation

Real case studies from the CCD's own monitoring practice grounded the manual in live reality. Readers can see how hostile campaigns unfolded and how similar patterns appeared across different contexts. What had previously seemed abstract became tangible. Yet the manual is greater than the sum of its chapters: a Ukrainian national security institution has developed an open, instructional capacity-building resource that transforms counter-disinformation work from disconnected donor projects into a state-driven, ongoing process.

The first manual, released in 2023, carried the modest title "Manual on Countering Disinformation". Behind the plain name lay an ambitious idea. This was not to be a campaign slogan, nor a one-time training programme. It was to be a systematic framework for teachers, lecturers, youth workers, and municipal officials, people who often had little technical training but carried the responsibility of guiding others.

Its structure reflected this ambition. The opening chapter examined the nature of information influence more broadly, providing a detailed analysis of how influence campaigns are structured and how they operate. It explored vulnerabilities within the information environment that adversaries exploit, and outlined the techniques commonly used by Russia to manipulate perceptions, spread disinformation, and distort public understanding. This section framed disinformation as a deliberate, strategic tool rather than random error, helping readers understand both the anatomy of hostile campaigns and the mechanisms through which they target society.

The manual then moves to a practical section on hostile information resources and methods for tracking them. It provides step by step guidance on how to monitor and investigate adversary channels across platforms, including traditional media, X, Telegram, YouTube and Facebook, with platform specific techniques and checklists for analysts and practitioners. The chapter also contains a dedicated, detailed module on detecting deepfakes, covering both technical indicators and visual and audio red flags, suggested verification workflows, and recommended tools and best practices for corroboration. This module brings the world of verification into the hands of non-experts. Reverse image searches, metadata analysis, video keyframe checks—tools once reserved for investigative journalists were now presented as step-by-step guides.

Finally, real case studies from the CCD's own monitoring practice grounded the manual in live reality. Readers can see how hostile campaigns unfolded and how similar patterns appeared across different contexts. What had previously seemed abstract became tangible. Yet the manual is greater than the sum of its chapters: a Ukrainian national security institution has developed an open, instructional capacity-building resource that transforms counter-disinformation work from disconnected donor projects into a state-driven, ongoing process. It also lowers the barrier to entry while providing a shared language for discussing manipulation. At the end of the manual, a specially prepared glossary presents CCD's own definitions of key terms, highlighting concepts and practices that the CCD has identified and refined through its operational experience.

6.2.2 Weapons of Information Warfare

> The second manual is based on the premise that disinformation is not merely a collection of isolated falsehoods, but a method of operation – a co-ordinated campaign designed to shape perceptions, sow confusion, and erode resilience from within. To make this clear, the manual is structured around three large thematic blocks. The first unpacks the mechanisms of destructive influence, showing how fake accounts, anonymous authority, and information-alibi, among others, are used to simulate consensus or create illusions of credibility. The second turns to the tactics of manipulation, where the focus shifts from technology to psychology: clickbait, rating, stereotyping, contextomy, and the so-called "information sandwich," where lies are wrapped be-tween truths to make them more believable. The third addresses something that had rarely been systematised before: Russia's use of soft power tools – culture, history, religion, sport, education – as long-term vehicles of influence. By doing so, the manual pointed to a dimension of information warfare that is harder to detect but often more enduring in its effect.

By the time the first handbook was released in 2023, it had already become clear that Ukrainian society needed more than simple tools to identify false information; it also required a deeper understanding of how hostile information campaigns operated in practice. People could be taught what disinformation is, but they often lacked a framework to explain why manipulations spread so effectively and how they fit into broader influence strategies. By 2025, the demand for a more advanced resource was evident. This is how the second handbook, "Weapons of Information Warfare", came into being.

Unlike its predecessor, which targeted beginners, this edition is not intended for entry-level literacy. Its audience consists of educators experienced in conducting workshops, journalists, lecturers, civil society leaders, and communications officers who already possess foundational media literacy skills. They no longer sought a simple "how to spot a fake" guide. Instead, they needed a lens to understand the entire battlefield of information warfare, not just isolated elements.

The second manual is based on the premise that disinformation is not merely a collection of isolated falsehoods, but a method of operation—a coordinated campaign designed to shape perceptions, sow confusion, and erode resilience from within. To make this clear, the manual is structured around three large thematic blocks. The first unpacks the mechanisms of destructive influence, showing how fake accounts, anonymous authority, and information-alibi, among others, are used to simulate consensus or create illusions of credibility. The second turns to the tactics of manipulation, where the focus shifts from technology to psychology: clickbait, rating, stereotyping, contextomy, and the so-called "information sandwich," where lies are wrapped between truths to make them more believable. The third addresses something that had rarely been systematised before: Russia's use of soft power tools—culture, history, religion, sport, education – as long-term vehicles of influence. By doing so, the manual pointed to a dimension of information warfare that is harder to detect but often more enduring in its effect.

What makes the "Weapon of the Information War" striking is its attempt to turn analytical complexity into usable practice. Each chapter combines theoretical explanation with concrete examples. Educators can use it in lecture halls, journalists in workshops, civil servants in local trainings. Participants are invited not just to read but to act: to dissect real disinformation campaigns, map the networks of actors involved, and design counter-strategies that are adapted to their own environment. In this sense, the manual is not just a book—it is a toolkit, a workbook, and a call to action at the same time.

The broader significance of the manual lies in how it reframes the conversation. Where the first manual encouraged individuals to become critical media consumers, the second invites communities to think like strategists. It suggests that defending against manipulation requires not only vigilance but also creativity, cooperation, and the courage to confront influence where it hides behind art, faith, or everyday entertainment. This was a bold step, because it challenged Ukrainians to see disinformation not only in news reports or social media posts, but in the very narratives that shape identity and belonging.

In short, "Weapons of Information Warfare" expanded the horizon of media literacy. It did not discard the foundations laid by the first manual but rather built on them, offering a more ambitious vision: a society capable of recognising the systemic nature of information warfare and prepared to defend itself not just reactively, but proactively, with strategies of its own.

Taken together, these two manuals form a system. The first equips communities with the ability to recognise, question, and verify. The second cultivates the capacity to analyse, anticipate, and lead. One lays the groundwork for civic competence; the other builds the scaffolding for strategic resilience. This system is significant not only for Ukraine but also for other democracies. It shows that national security knowledge can be translated into civic pedagogy without losing precision. It demonstrates that resilience is not simply the sum of individual scepticism but the result of structured, state-supported education. Most importantly, it offers a model of how a society under hybrid attack can defend itself as much with knowledge in classrooms, university auditoriums, and community halls as with weapons on the battlefield.

In the end, these manuals are not merely documents. They are signals of innovation: proof that in times of existential threat, a democracy can respond with creativity, pedagogy, and trust in its citizens. They turn expertise into practice, fear into competence, and fragmented awareness into shared resilience. And by doing so, they remind us that the strongest defence against disinformation is not silence, not censorship, but a society that knows how to read, question, and resist.

Another reason they are significant is that they establish continuity. What was once a scattered series of donor projects or short-term awareness campaigns has now become part of a state-led framework with a long-term vision. This means counter-disinformation is no longer merely reactive; it is also proactive, building citizens' capacity to anticipate manipulation rather than simply respond to it. In this way, the handbooks' function both as educational tools and as a strategic statement: Ukraine is not just combating disinformation day by day, but investing in a culture of resilience that will endure beyond the war.

6.3 What Sets Ukraine's Media Literacy Apart

Ukraine's path is unique. The first difference lies in speed. Where Finland and Estonia had decades of stability to patiently grow their systems, Ukraine was forced to compress this work into a few turbulent years under the pressure of full-scale war. The constant presence of Russian disinformation campaigns turned media literacy from an abstract civic skill into a survival tool. As a result, initiatives such as the CCD's own manuals reached national scale with breath-taking urgency. That rapid pace brought visibility and political weight, but it also entailed costs: uneven quality, dependence on donor financing and a lack of time for careful evaluation. Ukraine's experience shows how a crisis can drive innovation, while also underscoring that lasting resilience cannot be built through emergency measures alone.

Ukraine's engagement with media literacy has never been conducted in isolation. From the outset, it has drawn on international frameworks and best practices—most notably UNESCO's Media and Information Literacy concept, which frames media literacy not merely as a skill but as a fundamental human right and a prerequisite for democracy. The emphasis on lifelong learning, careful observation, and civic empowerment resonated deeply in Ukraine, where the stakes of failing to resist manipulation are measured not in abstract statistics but in human lives. These principles have been integrated into Ukrainian programs, fostering critical thinking, ethical responsibility and healthy scepticism toward narratives that come all wrapped up as truths.

Observers often compare Ukraine with Finland and Estonia, two countries widely seen as two of the champions of national media literacy policy (MLI-report-in-English-22.06.pdf, n.d.). There are, indeed, similarities. Like them, Ukraine has chosen to integrate critical thinking and source evaluation across subjects, rather than confining them to one optional course. Ukrainian educators have been encouraged to adapt methods to local contexts and weave media literacy into lessons in history, languages, or civic studies. This horizontal, integrated model demonstrates that Ukraine's response to disinformation is not a knee-jerk reaction confined to wartime but a deliberate strategy aimed at building long-term educational resilience.

And yet Ukraine's path is unique. The first difference lies in speed. Where Finland and Estonia had decades of stability to patiently grow their systems, Ukraine was forced to compress this work into a few turbulent years under the pressure of full-scale war. The constant presence of Russian disinformation campaigns turned media literacy from an abstract civic skill into a survival tool. As a result, initiatives such as the CCD's own manuals reached national scale with breath-taking urgency. That rapid pace brought visibility and political weight, but it also entailed costs: uneven quality, dependence on donor financing and a lack of time for careful evaluation. Ukraine's experience shows how a crisis can drive innovation, while also underscoring that lasting resilience cannot be built through emergency measures alone.

The second difference is the blurred boundary between education and security. In most democracies, these two domains remain carefully separated: ministries of education design curricula, while security agencies keep their distance to avoid the perception of politicisation. Ukraine has had no such luxury. Here, the CCD, a national security body, stepped directly into the educational sphere—designing manuals, and training sessions that translated the language of security analysis into tools for classrooms and communities. This integration was not a theoretical choice but a necessity: when disinformation is used as a weapon of war, treating education as something detached from security would be artificial, even dangerous. It also raised new questions—how to preserve public trust, ensure transparency, and avoid overreach—questions that will become sharper in the years of post-war reconstruction.

The third distinctive trait is Ukraine's focus on pre-bunking. Instead of simply chasing falsehoods after they spread, Ukrainian projects increasingly aim to prepare citizens in advance, teaching them to recognise manipulative techniques before they encounter them. The CCD-led campaigns have begun anticipating narratives before major political or military events, giving citizens a kind of cognitive vaccine against manipulations. This preventive approach marks a significant shift from reactive fact-checking toward proactive resilience, a strategy that even many established democracies have yet to fully adopt.

All of these features combine to create a dual character for Ukraine's media literacy policy. It can be recognised because it builds on common international principles and draws on models developed in Nordic and Baltic countries. Yet it is also unprecedented, born from the fires of war. The CCD should therefore be seen not simply as an educational initiative, but as a strategy of survival—one that transforms analysis into pedagogy, crisis into innovation, and fear into competence. The lesson from Ukraine is that even under existential threat, a democracy need not respond with censorship or despair. It can instead place trust in its citizens and empower them to think critically. This hybrid nature, both civic and defensive, educational and strategic, is what makes Ukraine's approach a compelling model for other states confronting the realities of hybrid warfare.

6.4 CSC School of Strategic Communications and Information Security

One of the School's cornerstone efforts has been the three-year "Countering Disinformation and Strategic Communications" training project, implemented in partnership with UNDP Ukraine and funded by the Government of Japan. Launched amid Russia's full-scale invasion, this nationwide program targeted regions under acute information pressure or crisis risk. Over 2023–2025 the project delivered intensive trainings across 24 cities – from Mykolaiv in the south to Uzhhorod in the west – focusing on practical skills for crisis response communications and disinformation rebuttal. In total, more than 300 communication specialists participated, including press officers of regional military administrations, local government communicators, and civil society and media representatives.

The School of Strategic Communications and Information Security is a specialized training initiative. The School's mandate is to professionalize and strengthen government communications by training civil servants in strategic communication and countering disinformation. Built on Ukraine's own wartime experience and best practices, the School integrates British Government Communication Service standards (e.g. the UK's *RESIST 2.0* disinformation toolkit) into its curriculum. Its primary goal is to ensure the integrity of the information environment by equipping officials with skills to recognize and rebut information threats, thereby bolstering national resilience. In effect, the School acts as a capacity-building bridge between government, civil society, and international expertise in the fight against malign information influence. By combining national experience with international standards, scaling training across regions, and institutionalising strategic communications within the civil service, the School has built capacities vital for wartime governance and long-term democratic resilience.

One of the School's cornerstone efforts has been the three-year "Countering Disinformation and Strategic Communications" training project, implemented in partnership with UNDP Ukraine and funded by the Government of Japan. Launched amid Russia's full-scale invasion, this nationwide program targeted regions under acute information pressure or crisis risk. Over 2023–2025 the project delivered intensive trainings across 24 cities—from Mykolaiv in the south to Uzhhorod in the west—focusing on practical skills for crisis response communications and disinformation rebuttal. In total, more than 300 communication specialists participated, including press officers of regional military administrations, local government communicators, and civil society and media representatives (Completion of the Center for Strategic Communications' Two-Year Training Program: Over 300 Professionals, 24 Cities, One Shared Goal, 2025). Training modules emphasized developing counter-narratives and rapid-response strategies, crafting effective communication campaigns using the U.K.'s OASIS model (Objectives, Audience, Strategy, Implementation, Scoring), and methods for identifying target audiences and evaluating communication impact. By design, the regional outreach of this project helped build *local crisis communication capacity*—ensuring that frontline communities and authorities can respond swiftly and coherently to emergencies or propaganda surges. This capacity-building effort, supported by UNDP and Japan, has been hailed as vital in strengthening the information security of Ukrainian society during wartime.

Over its first three years 2022–2025, the School of Strategic Communications and Information Security has attained significant results in both training reach and knowledge production. Key achievements from 2022 to 2025 include:

- Over 200 Trainings Conducted: The School organized more than 200 training sessions (both offline and online), ranging from one-day workshops to multi-day intensive courses. Training formats prioritize interactivity, hands-on exercises, and technology-enabled learning, ensuring practical skills uptake by participants.
- Civil Servant Training at Scale: More than 2000 civil servants have been trained through the School's programs as of 2025 (School of Stratcom and Information Security, n.d.). The primary audience is government communication teams—ministries' press officers, central executive agencies, and regional

administrators—who serve as the "first line of defense" against information threats.

- Importantly, officials beyond the communication sphere have also benefited, reflecting the understanding that every public servant today needs basic competency in identifying and countering disinformation.
- Accredited Curricula: Two of the School's key training curricula have been formally certified by the National Agency for Civil Service, integrating them into Ukraine's official professional development.
- These accredited programs are titled "*Russian Disinformation and Ways to Counter It*" and "*Strategic Communications in Public Administration: Crisis Response Strategies*" (Training to counter disinformation—Higher School of Public Administration, 2025). The former provides a comprehensive overview of Kremlin propaganda techniques and countermeasures, while the latter focuses on building communication strategies for government, including how to maintain messaging coherence during crises.
- Strategic Manuals and Toolkits: The School has developed a series of authoritative handbooks to institutionalize knowledge. One major publication is the analytical manual. Another output is the "10 Postulates of Strategic Communications" brochure (produced in collaboration with an EU project)—a concise guide outlining core principles of effective government communication and how to implement them. Similarly, an in-depth "Methodology for Measuring and Evaluating Strategic Communications" was published to provide government communicators with tools to assess the effectiveness of their campaigns (Methodological manual 'Methodology of measurement and evaluation of strategic communications' for civil servants, 2023). This methodological guide explains key performance indicators and evaluation techniques, and when to apply them, thereby introducing a culture of evidence-based assessment into Ukrainian public communication.
- OASIS Model Campaign Guide: In 2025, the School produced a dedicated manual on developing communication campaigns using the OASIS model (a step-by-step framework originally devised by the UK Government Communication Service) (Online training "Communication strategy and plan. OASIS model", 2024). This guide adapts British best practices to Ukrainian realities, walking civil servants through setting Objectives, identifying target Audiences, devising Strategy, implementing plans, and Scoring (evaluating) results. It serves as a practical toolkit for any government agency looking to craft a strategic communication plan aligned with Western standards.
- OSINT Online Course: To broaden its reach beyond live trainings, the School partnered with the NGO Victory Drones to develop a free online course on Open-Source Intelligence (OSINT) and information security. Launched on the Prometheus e-learning platform in October 2024, this course aims to raise the OSINT competencies of a wide audience—from civil society activists and volunteers to journalists and military personnel (OSINT—open source intelligence and information security, 2024). By educating citizens in methods of digital investigation and fact-checking, the course contributes to "national information

security" and empowers the public to detect and debunk disinformation. Within its first weeks, thousands enrolled, underscoring the demand for such skills in Ukrainian society.

- Innovative WhatsApp Training Module: Embracing novel pedagogical methods, the School designed and implemented a two-week mobile learning module via WhatsApp in late 2024. Titled "Proactive and Reactive Methods of Combating Disinformation: Information Attacks," this pilot course (18 Nov–3 Dec 2024) delivered daily micro-lessons and assignments through messaging app chats (School of Stratcom and Information Security, n.d.).
- Participants could study materials at their own pace, complete quizzes and homework to reinforce concepts, and join weekly live Q&A sessions with a mentor and guest experts. This flexible format proved highly valuable under wartime conditions, as it allowed civil servants across the country (including in frontline areas) to continue learning despite travel or schedule constraints. The WhatsApp-based course specifically taught proactive approaches (anticipating and pre-bunking false narratives) and reactive responses (rapid debunking and crisis communication) to information attacks. Its success demonstrated the potential of mobile micro-learning to build capacity even amid ongoing conflict.

6.5 International Information Academy's Contribution to Enhance the Counter Disinformation and Media Literacy

On 1 February 2022, International Information Academy (IIA) conducted in-person training on the general short-term program "Fundamentals of Cyber Security and Countering Disinformation" for civil servants-representatives of the National Council of Television and Radio Broadcasting, the Ministry of Culture and Information Policy of Ukraine, the Ministry of Economy of Ukraine, the State Tax Service, the National Agency of Ukraine for Civil Service, the State Property Fund of Ukraine, the Asset Recovery and Management Agency and other public authorities.

The IIA, a non-governmental organization, was founded in Kyiv, Ukraine, in 2018 with the goal of offering stateless people, foreign nationals, and Ukrainian residents comprehensive assistance in fulfilling their information needs. In order to accomplish this goal, the IIA organizes educational events on information law, information security, disinformation prevention, and cybersecurity; conducts analytical and research activities; offers legal and technological support; and provides information, educational, and training services.

The IIA has actively contributed to bolstering Ukraine's ability to combat misinformation and improve cybersecurity. In general, the contribution of IIA specialists to enhancing media literacy and disinformation resilience among Ukrainian citizens, especially civil officials, as well as among international audiences, may be examined in a number of important areas:

1. Media literacy and counter-disinformation training programs.

2. Dissemination of IIA experts' research findings to domestic and international audiences.
3. Establishment of partnerships with organizations in Ukraine and abroad for the implementation of joint counter-disinformation initiatives.

6.5.1 Media Literacy and Counter-Disinformation Training Programs

At several Ukrainian universities, IIA experts have been offering training programs for the professional development of professionals in governmental and corporate structures in the areas of cyber security and counter disinformation.

Additionally, IIA started a public program called "Truth and Security" in 2022 to improve Ukrainian society's ability to combat disinformation. The project aims to start an expert discussion on the collaboration of Ukraine's civil society and security and defense sector agencies, utilizing emerging technologies like artificial intelligence to identify and respond to disinformation campaigns, awareness-raising campaigns on disinformation, and Russian Federation manipulative operations techniques (The Academy launches a public initiative "Truth and Security" to counter disinformation|International Information Academy, 2022).

On 1 February 2022, IIA conducted in-person training on the general short-term program "Fundamentals of Cyber Security and Countering Disinformation" for civil servants-representatives of the National Council of Television and Radio Broadcasting, the Ministry of Culture and Information Policy of Ukraine, the Ministry of Economy of Ukraine, the State Tax Service, the National Agency of Ukraine for Civil Service, the State Property Fund of Ukraine, the Asset Recovery and Management Agency and other public authorities.

During the classes, the issues of the national cyber security system of Ukraine, development scenarios and methods of counteracting cyberattacks, as well as countering disinformation as an element of cyberattacks were considered (The Academy conducted the first full-time course for civil servants on the fundamentals of cybersecurity and countering disinformation|International Information Academy, 2022).

Following Russia's full-scale invasion of Ukraine on February 24, 2022, IIA experts turned their focus to promoting Ukraine's viewpoint both domestically and internationally, presenting the findings of their research at conferences and workshops on counter disinformation.

6.5.2 Dissemination of IIA Experts' Research Findings to Domestic and International Audiences

Members of the International Information Academy (IIA) have organized and participated in numerous national conferences and European-level summits. Notably, the IIA organized and conducted workshops dedicated to the Ukrainian experience in countering Russian information warfare and cyberattacks, held in Prague on 13 December 2018 and in Brussels on 10 April 2019.

At that time, the Russian disinformation psychological impact on large segments of the Ukrainian population—particularly in Crimea and the Donbas—was significant, as hostile coordinated information operations disseminated false narratives regarding the political situation in the country. These efforts relied on systematic information manipulation and propaganda, supported by controlled Russian-language media outlets and online "internet trolls." Within the broader context of Russia's hybrid warfare campaign against Ukraine, such activities complemented actions on diplomatic and security fronts, sharing the common objective of destabilizing the state and undermining its sovereignty.

The implementation of domestic Ukrainian laws intended to prevent such destabilizing attempts had been accelerated by Russian disinformation campaigns. Additionally, they had prompted the creation of fact-checking organizations and NGOs like IIA, whose mission was to assist Ukrainians in differentiating between authentic and fraudulent news.

IIA suggested to a wide variety of foreign specialists and the media that they leverage Ukraine's expertise and strengthen collaboration in the fight against Russian disinformation and fake news, both against Ukraine and other nations.

Speaking in Brussels in 2019, IIA specialists cautioned that "lessons" from Ukraine's experience may be used to the next European elections, pointing out that combating Russian disinformation is not just a Ukrainian concern but also a global one.

In 2018–2025, IIA experts offered professional advice to propose a procedure for the protection of Ukraine's national interests in the information realm in accordance with democratic principles of freedom of speech while discussing legal and technological issues of countering disinformation at other scientific events. In particular, the National Coordination Center for Cybersecurity at the National Security and Defense Council of Ukraine and the Representation of the U.S. Civilian Research & Development Foundation in Ukraine, CRDF Global, jointly organized the event "Action against disinformation and cyber threats: algorithm of communications on the international arena," where legal principles of content modification as a means to counter disinformation were presented by IIA expert (Academy's Strategic Adviser presented at a meeting of the National Cyber Security Cluster at the National Security and Defense Council of Ukraine|International Information Academy, 2022).

The Support Group for Ukraine, the European Commission, the European Center of Excellence for Countering Hybrid Threats, the European Union Institute for Security Studies, and other experts attended the international forum "Emerging High-Tech Cyber & Hybrid Threats: Building Europe at Peace & Harmony" in Brussels, where IIA expert gave a speech (Emerging High-Tech Cyber & Hybrid Threats: Building Europe at Peace & Harmony|Beyond the Horizon ISSG, 2021).

At the XII International Scientific and Practical Conference "Human Rights in the Age of Digital Transformations," which was attended by representatives of scientific institutions from Mexico, Germany, Poland, Slovenia, Croatia, Georgia, and Ukraine, the IIA's voice was heard. Scientists, notably those in the information sector, backed the Ukrainian people's fight against the Russian invaders (The international conference 'Human Rights in War and the Era of Digital Transformations' was held at NAU, 2022).

At an interdepartmental round table on "Spreading disinformation as a threat to National Security: the search for effective countermeasures," which took place on the premises of the Ukrainian Information Agency Ukrinform on November 29, 2023, the IIA report on disinformation and artificial intelligence: challenges and opportunities was presented. The following issues were discussed during the event:

- review of the latest techniques and tools for combating harmful informational influence;
- study on the vulnerabilities of the Ukrainian information space;
- modern developments in the detection of hostile information influence and effective delivery of information to the target audience in order to prevent its consequences;
- possibilities of linguistic (semantic-textual) and psychological expertise in countering fake news and messages containing signs of manipulation;
- interaction of state and civil institutions in the field of combating the spread of disinformation;
- analysis of international experience in combating hybrid threats (Academy's experts' participation in the round table on countering disinformation in Ukrinform|International Information Academy, 2023).

At the 1st Disinformation Countermeasures and Machine Learning (DisCoML) workshop at ICML 2022 in Baltimore (U.S.A.), IIA expert took part in the panel discussion. DisCoML offered a forum for bringing top researchers together and enabling stakeholders and policymakers to stay up to date on the most recent advancements in the field. Bad actors grow disinformation operations by utilizing ML-enabled bots, deepfakes, cloned websites, and forgeries (Strategic Adviser presented at the 1st Disinformation Countermeasures and Machine Learning (DisCoML) workshop at ICML 2022 in Baltimore|International Information Academy, 2022).

IIA experts took part in the adoption of the Paris Declaration on Multilateral Action for Information Integrity and Independent Media at the 2025 Paris Peace Forum, which had as its topic "New Coalitions for Peace, People, and the Planet." In a world facing more than 60 ongoing conflicts and growing dangers from disinformation and AI manipulation, the Declaration reinforces a worldwide commitment to rebuilding truth, trust, and transparency. In a time of violence and technological disruption, the forum provided an arena for forging new alliances to address global issues (Academy's Expert Joins Global Leaders at the 2025 Paris Peace Forum|International Information Academy, 2025). Additionally, an IIA expert gave a powerful speech in person to members of the Irish Parliament, emphasizing the urgent threats faced by disinformation, cognitive warfare, and artificial intelligence. It was underlined that by eroding public confidence, distorting views of reality, and manipulating vulnerable groups—including children—cognitive warfare poses a direct danger to the fundamentals of democratic societies (AI, Cognitive Warfare, and Disinformation: Academy's Expert Warns Irish Parliament|International Information Academy, 2025).

In a peer-reviewed publication, IIA experts have started publishing research about the challenges of combating artificial intelligence-generated disinformation. One of the studies highlights how crucial it is to match emergency measures against disinformation with international law and the principles of free speech. It also suggests a categorization of Ukrainian authorities' powers with regard to preventive measures and tactics for combating and responding to Russian disinformation, including that generated by artificial intelligence (Marushchak et al., 2025).

In 2018–2025, IIA experts offered professional advice to propose a procedure for the protection of Ukraine's national interests in the information realm in accordance with democratic principles of freedom of speech while discussing legal and technological issues of countering disinformation at other scientific events. In particular, the National Coordination Center for Cybersecurity at the National Security and Defense Council of Ukraine and the Representation of the U.S. Civilian Research & Development Foundation in Ukraine, CRDF Global, jointly organized the event "Action against disinformation and cyber threats: algorithm of communications on the international arena," where legal principles of content modification as a means to counter disinformation were presented by IIA expert.

6.5.3 Establishment of Partnerships with Organizations in Ukraine and Abroad for the Implementation of Joint Counter-Disinformation Initiatives

Like other comparable NGOs, IIA works to expand its operations in other democratic governments in order to fulfil its objective. It does this by sharing lessons learned and providing expert guidance to partner countries. For example, IIA formed partnerships with other European Union think tanks (The International Information Academy has signed the Memorandum of Understanding with Hybrid Core BV, Brussels|International Information Academy, 2021), as well as with he NGO "Ukrainian Center for Research on Security Problems in the name of Dmytro Tymchuk" (The Academy engages partners to the public initiative "Truth and Security"|International Information Academy, 2022).

It was intended to promote initiatives aimed at integration into the European Union, NATO, and UN ecosystems, arrange collaborative research and practical activities, and provide training, particularly in the area of disinformation countering. With a wealth of real-world experience in information warfare, the Tymchuk Center actively combats external threats to Ukraine that arise in the sectors of information security, the economy, and the military (Information resistance, 2026).

The goal of IIA's collaboration and coordination of efforts with the two partners was to enhance the effectiveness of countering Russian disinformation while meeting the demands of Ukrainians, foreigners, and stateless people for accurate, impartial, and high-quality information.

A new stage of international cooperation began on June 27, 2025, when the IIA formally signed a Memorandum of Understanding with INVED, the Institute for Defense of European Democracies (Austia). The collaboration with INVED increases the involvement of Ukrainian experts in the global expert community and gives the IIA new chances to advance democratic velues and information security (The Academy has established a partnership with a new partner|International Information Academy, 2025).

Additionally, in September 2023, IIA has become a member of a leading the pan-European, private–public federation (non-profit) organisation in EU –The European Cyber Security Organisation (ECSO) ('Meet our Members', n.d.). ECSO is a cross-sectoral European organization that supports the growth of the European cybersecurity ecosystem and cybersecurity communities. ECSO unites the public and commercial sectors of European cyber security, including major corporations, startups, universities, research facilities, basic service providers, and national public governments across the continent.

6.6 Challenges and Lessons Learned in Fostering a Media-Literate Ukrainian Society

> One of the most evident challenges has been teacher burnout and a systemic lack of incentives. Ukrainian educators are working under immense strain, facing the daily pressures of teaching during wartime. For many, incorporating media literacy feels like yet another burden on an already overwhelming workload. As a result, the integration of media studies often depends less on formal policy and more on the dedication and passion of individual teachers. It is, therefore, a fragile ecosystem, strong where enthusiasm endures and absent where it does not.

Ukraine's media literacy efforts have, in many ways, been remarkable. In just a few years, they have evolved from isolated initiatives into a nationwide ecosystem, bringing together schools, NGOs, and even security institutions. Yet this rapid progress has also revealed challenges that go far beyond bureaucratic hurdles. These are structural barriers that will determine whether the system can endure and for how long. While such challenges are not unique to Ukraine, the stakes here are especially high: media education is no longer a peripheral "nice-to-have," but a core component of the country's national defense infrastructure.

One of the most evident challenges has been teacher burnout and a systemic lack of incentives. Ukrainian educators are working under immense strain, facing the daily pressures of teaching during wartime. For many, incorporating media literacy feels like yet another burden on an already overwhelming workload. As a result, the integration of media studies often depends less on formal policy and more on the dedication and passion of individual teachers. It is, therefore, a fragile ecosystem, strong where enthusiasm endures and absent where it does not.

The second obstacle lies in the urban to rural divide. Cities such as Kyiv and Lviv have become vibrant hubs for media literacy initiatives, supported by international donors, universities, and NGOs. In contrast, rural schools, which often have limited access to diverse information sources and are more vulnerable to disinformation, remain underserved. The lack of digital infrastructure, shortage of qualified staff, and absence of local partners leave these communities isolated, deepening the social divides that hostile actors are eager to exploit. This gap is further widened by Russia's ongoing occupation of parts of Ukraine's territory, which makes it impossible to develop media literacy and civic resilience among Ukrainians living under occupation. Similarly, in frontline areas, where communities live under bombardment, implementing media literacy programs is extremely difficult. Bridging these divides has therefore become one of the most urgent and complex tasks facing Ukraine's information resilience strategy.

The problem of donor dependence adds another layer of fragility. Many of the most visible programmes run by international organizations exist because of external financing. These funds have been crucial in building momentum quickly, but they come with an expiration date. Project cycles end, priorities shift, and without stable national funding, entire teams of experts risk dissolving just when their experience is most needed. This "stop-start" dynamic has already been felt in several waves, undermining continuity and forcing organisations to reinvent what was already working. For media literacy to become truly institutionalised, Ukraine must move beyond dependency and treat this field as part of its own strategic infrastructure.

Lastly, there is the ceaseless pace of technological change, with AI-generated disinformation representing its latest and potentially most disruptive manifestation. Manuals published in 2023 may already be outdated by 2025; scenarios that once seemed futuristic are now eclipsed by deepfake videos, synthetic voices, and automated propaganda networks. This continual obsolescence undermines trust if not addressed. Teachers cannot be expected to improvise solutions to these threats without timely support, and curricula that fail to keep pace risk being dismissed as irrelevant by students who encounter increasingly sophisticated forms of manipulation online every day.

Despite these difficulties, Ukraine's journey also offers lessons of global importance. The first is that media literacy must be treated as strategic civic infrastructure, not as an optional after-school activity. Just as no state would consider public health or cybersecurity "extracurricular", information resilience requires long-term investment, embedded standards, and stable institutional ownership.

The second lesson concerns balancing coordination with innovation. Ministries must coordinate, and strategies must be integrated. Yet some of Ukraine's most effective breakthroughs have come from NGOs that enjoyed the freedom to experiment, take risks, and innovate outside rigid bureaucratic structures. Any future governance model must preserve this duality: clear central guidance combined with the creativity of grassroots actors.

The third insight is the need to measure impact beyond numbers. It is easy to count how many teachers were trained or how many workshops were held. But the real question is behavioural: are students pausing before sharing a headline? Are families discussing media manipulation at the dinner table? Without measuring these deeper shifts, it is impossible to know whether media literacy is truly working or simply multiplying reports and statistics.

And finally, there is the lesson of agility. In Ukraine, agility has become not just a management buzzword, but a matter of survival. Because disinformation campaigns evolve daily, educational materials must do the same. The CCD has already shown how national security monitoring can feed directly into manuals and community trainings, updating content in near real time. This ability to adapt quickly—to turn analysis into education almost overnight—may be Ukraine's most valuable innovation.

Ultimately, Ukraine's challenge can be described as balancing speed with sustainability. In three years, the country has built what others took decades to achieve. But for these gains to endure, they must be solidified, institutionalized, and financially secured. The Ukrainian experience demonstrates that defending democracy goes beyond tanks and drones: it requires textbooks, classrooms, and citizens equipped to resist manipulations. Media literacy is not an extra-curricular activity; it is an integral part of national defense, and the battlefield runs directly through the minds of the population.

> Yet some of Ukraine's most effective breakthroughs have come from NGOs that enjoyed the freedom to experiment, take risks, and innovate outside rigid bureaucratic structures. Any future governance model must preserve this duality: clear central guidance combined with the creativity of grassroots actors.

6.7 Conclusion

In conclusion, Ukraine's experience demonstrates that media literacy and counter-disinformation education have become central to the country's survival strategy, far beyond a conventional civic skill. The CCD has illustrated that an effective response to information warfare demands both analytical precision and pedagogical creativity, bridging the divide between national security expertise and everyday practice. Through an array of initiatives, from crisis management trainings for senior civil servants to engaging workshops for regional administrators, and from specialized courses for the SBU to animated series for children, the CCD has transformed complex security knowledge into practical, accessible tools that empower citizens at every level. These efforts reveal that resilience is not only about knowing the facts, but also about understanding the mechanisms of manipulation, developing critical thinking, and cultivating a mindset that resists influence before it takes hold.

The manuals "Manual on Countering Disinformation" and "Weapons of Information Warfare" exemplify this layered strategy of resilience. The first equips educators, youth workers, and municipal officials with practical methods for recognizing falsehoods, verifying sources, and fostering critical discussion. The second elevates the conversation, offering a framework to understand the systemic nature of disinformation campaigns, the interplay of psychological and technological tactics, and the strategic objectives behind manipulative narratives. Together, they establish a continuum: from basic recognition of falsehoods to anticipating and countering coordinated influence, cultivating both civic competence and strategic awareness. These educational products, alongside hands-on trainings, have created a shared language and methodology that spans local administrations, state enterprises, and security institutions, knitting together the various layers of society into a cohesive defense against manipulation.

Ukraine's approach highlights that education can itself be a weapon—quieter than artillery yet no less critical. By embedding media literacy across institutions and communities, the CCD has transformed passive awareness into active competence, empowering citizens to act as informed participants in the defense of their democracy. This includes children, whose understanding of digital manipulation and practical strategies for resisting it through initiatives such as the animated series "Dobrochesnist Online". The deliberate targeting of younger audiences ensures that the next generation will not only be media-literate but also capable of contributing to a broader societal culture of critical thinking and informed decision-making.

But the Ukrainian experience is also a reminder of how difficult this mission truly is. The rapid expansion of media literacy initiatives under wartime conditions has revealed deep structural inequalities, donor dependence, and the relentless pace of technological change. Urban centers often attract most of the attention and resources, while rural communities struggle to access the necessary tools, expertise, and infrastructure. The challenge is even greater in frontline and temporarily occupied territories, where constant shelling, instability, and Russian censorship make it nearly impossible to implement educational programs or strengthen civic resilience. At the same time, the rise of AI-generated disinformation and increasingly sophisticated manipulation techniques quickly renders educational materials obsolete. Meeting these constraints requires adaptation, innovation, and long-term strategic planning to remain both relevant and effective. In this regard, the CCD's model of rapid, responsive development—transforming monitoring insights into manuals, training, and public discourse—stands out as a particularly agile and forward-looking strategy that other democracies can learn from.

Finally, Ukraine's experience demonstrates that defending democracy under hybrid attack requires an integrated, whole-of-society effort. It is not enough to reactively debunk falsehoods; true resilience lies in prevention and in embedding critical thinking within the core of national security priorities. By empowering civil servants, educators, children, and community leaders alike, Ukraine has fostered a society where knowledge, vigilance, and analytical thinking are shared civic responsibilities rather than tasks reserved for experts or institutions. It affirms a fundamental principle: the strongest defense against disinformation is not censorship, coercion, or passive awareness, but a society capable of reading, questioning, and responding intelligently.

References

A workshop for employees of the SSUFSCP in Kyiv was held on April 7|Center for Countering Disinformation (2023, 10 April). Available at https://cpd.gov.ua/en/events-en/a-workshop-for-employees-of-the-ssufscp-in-kyiv-was-held-on-april-7/. Accessed 10 November 2025.

Academy's Strategic Adviser presented at a meeting of the National Cyber Security Cluster at the National Security and Defense Council of Ukraine|International Information Academy (2022, 29 May). Available at https://interacademy.info/en/academys-strategic-adviser-presented-at-a-meeting-of-the-national-cyber-security-cluster-at-the-national-security-and-defen%d1%81e-council-of-ukraine/. Accessed 17 January 2026.

Academy's experts' participation in the round table on countering disinformation in Ukrinform|International Information Academy (2023, 6 December). Available at https://interacademy.info/en/academys-experts-participation-in-the-round-table-on-countering-disinformation-in-ukrinform/. Accessed 17 January 2026.

Academy's Expert Joins Global Leaders at the 2025 Paris Peace Forum|International Information Academy (2025, 4 November). Available at https://interacademy.info/en/academys-expert-joins-global-leaders-at-the-2025-paris-peace-forum/. Accessed: 17 January 2026.

AI, Cognitive Warfare, and Disinformation: Academy's Expert Warns Irish Parliament|International Information Academy (2025, 12 October). Available at https://interacademy.info/en/ai-cognitive-warfare-and-disinformation-academys-expert-warns-irish-parliament/. Accessed 17 January 2026.

CCD held Countering FIMI Weekend in Lviv|Center for Countering Disinformation (2024, 30 October). Available at https://cpd.gov.ua/en/events-en/ccd-held-countering-fimi-weekend-in-lviv/. Accessed: 10 November 2025.

Completion of the Center for Strategic Communications' Two-Year Training Program: Over 300 Professionals, 24 Cities, One Shared Goal. (2025). Center for Strategic Communication and Information Security. Available at https://spravdi.org/en/zavershennya-dvorichnogo-czyklu-treningiv-czentru-strategichnyh-komunikaczij-ponad-300-fahivcziv-24-mista-odna-spilna-meta/. Accessed 27 December 2025.

Emerging High-Tech Cyber & Hybrid Threats: Building Europe at Peace & Harmony|Beyond the Horizon ISSG (2021, 14 October). Available at https://behorizon.org/eventsandactivities/emerging-high-tech-cyber-hybrid-threats-building-europe-at-peace-harmony/. Accessed 17 January 2026.

From October 6 to 9, under the auspices of the Center for Countering Disinformation and the Psychological Defense Agency, "Stratcom weekend" 1.0 was held| Center for Countering Disinformation. (2023, 9 October). Available at https://cpd.gov.ua/events/z-6-po-9-zhovtnya-pid-egidoyu-czpd-ta-psychological-defense-agency-vidbuvsya-stratcom-weekend-1-0/. Accessed 10 November 2025.

Handbook "Weapons of Information Warfare"|Center for Countering Disinformation (2025, 28 July). Available at https://cpd.gov.ua/en/manuals/handbook-weapons-of-information-warfare/. Accessed 10 November 2025.

Information Resistance. (2026). Available at https://sprotyv.info/. Accessed 17 January 2026.

Marushchak, A., Petrov, S., & Khoperiya, A. (2025). Countering AI-powered disinformation through national regulation: learning from the case of Ukraine. *Frontiers in Artificial Intelligence*. https://doi.org/10.3389/frai.2024.1474034

Meet our Members. (n.d.). ECSO. Available at https://ecs-org.eu/meet-our-members/. Accessed: 17 January 2026.

Methodological manual "Methodology of measurement and evaluation of strategic communications" for civil servants (2023) Center for Strategic Communication and Information Security. Available at https://spravdi.org/metodychnyj-posibnyk-metodologiya-vymiryuvannya-ta-oczinky-strategichnyh-komunikaczij-dlya-derzhavnyh-sluzhbovcziv/. Accessed 28 December 2025.

Mission of the Center for Countering Disinformation. (2021). Official web portal of the Parliament of Ukraine. Available at https://zakon.rada.gov.ua/go/187/2021. Accessed 10 November 2025.

MLI-report-in-English-22.06.pdf. (n.d.). Available at https://osis.bg/wp-content/uploads/2023/06/MLI-report-in-English-22.06.pdf. Accessed 10 November 2025.

On March 1, intensive training course was held for «Energoatom»|Center for Countering Disinformation (2023, 2 March). Available at: https://cpd.gov.ua/en/events-en/on-march-1-intensive-training-course-was-held-for-energoatom/. Accessed 10 November 2025.

Online training "Communication strategy and plan. OASIS model". (2024). Higher School of Public Administration, 30 October. Available at https://hs.gov.ua/en/online-training-communication-strategy-and-plan-oasis-model/. Accessed: 28 December 2025.

OSINT—open source intelligence and information security. (2024). Prometheus, 1 November. Available at https://prometheus.org.ua/prometheus-free/osint-open-source-intelligence/. Accessed: 28 December 2025.

School of Stratcom and Information Security. (n.d.). Center for Strategic Communication and Information Security. Available at https://spravdi.org/treningy-dlya-derzhsluzhbovcziv/. Accessed 27 December 2025.

Strategic Adviser presented at the 1st Disinformation Countermeasures and Machine Learning (DisCoML) workshop at ICML 2022 in Baltimore|International Information Academy. (2022, 28 July). Available at https://interacademy.info/en/strategic-adviser-presented-at-the-1st-disinformation-countermeasures-and-machine-learning-discoml-workshop-at-icml-2022-in-baltimore/. Accessed 17 January 2026.

The International Information Academy has signed the Memorandum of Understanding with Hybrid Core BV, Brussels|International Information Academy (2021, 15 November). Available at https://interacademy.info/en/the-international-information-academy-has-signed-the-memorandum-of-understanding-with-hybrid-core-bv-brussels/. Accessed 17 January 2026.

The Academy launches a public initiative "Truth and Security" to counter disinformation|International Information Academy (2022, 12 February). Available at https://interacademy.info/en/the-academy-launches-a-public-initiative-truth-and-security-to-counter-disinformation/. Accessed 17 January 2026.

The Academy engages partners to the public initiative "Truth and Security"|International Information Academy (2022, 22 July). Available at https://interacademy.info/en/the-academy-engages-partners-to-the-public-initiative-truth-and-security/. Accessed 17 January 2026.

The Academy conducted the first full-time course for civil servants on the fundamentals of cybersecurity and countering disinformation|International Information Academy (2022, 4 February). Available at https://interacademy.info/en/the-academy-conducted-the-first-full-time-course-for-civil-servants-on-the-fundamentals-of-cybersecurity-and-countering-disinformation/. Accessed 17 January 2026.

The Integrity Online Project. (2022). Available at https://www.youtube.com/watch?v=9mmV2888_KA. Accessed 1 November 2025.

The international conference "Human Rights in War and the Era of Digital Transformations" was held at NAU (2022). Available at https://nau.edu.ua/ua/news/2022/3/v-nau-vidbulasya-mizhnarodna-konferentsiya-prava-lyudini-v-umovah-viyni-ta-epohu-tsifrovih-transformatsiy.html. Accessed 17 January 2026.

The CCD conducted a training for the Security Service of Ukraine on countering enemy propaganda in times of war|Center for Countering Disinformation. (2023, 21 November). Available at https://cpd.gov.ua/en/events-en/the-ccd-conducted-a-training-for-the-security-service-of-ukraine-on-countering-enemy-propaganda-in-times-of-war/. Accessed 10 November 2025.

The Center for Countering Disinformation conducted a series of trainings for representatives of the Regional Military Administration and the Regional State Administration|Center for Countering Disinformation (2023, 22 April). Available at https://cpd.gov.ua/en/events-en/the-center-for-countering-disinformation-conducted-a-series-of-trainings-for-representatives-of-the-regional-military-administration-and-the-regional-state-administration/. Accessed 10 November 2025.

The Center for Countering Disinformation conducted a series of trainings for the representatives of the central executive bodies|Center for Countering Disinformation (2023, 8 May). Available at https://cpd.gov.ua/en/events-en/the-center-for-countering-disinformation-conducted-a-series-of-trainings-for-the-representatives-of-the-central-executive-bodies/. Accessed 10 November 2025.

The Center participated in the training of SBU employees on strategic communications|Center for Countering Disinformation (2024, 29 November). Available at https://cpd.gov.ua/en/events-en/the-center-participated-in-the-training-of-sbu-employees-on-strategic-communications/. Accessed 10 November 2025.

The Center conducted a training on crisis management for the Senior Civil Service Commission|Center for Countering Disinformation (2024, 31 May). Available at https://cpd.gov.ua/en/events-en/the-center-conducted-a-training-on-crisis-management-for-the-senior-civil-service-commission/. Accessed 10 November 2025.

The Academy has established a partnership with a new partner|International Information Academy. (2025, 5 July). Available at https://interacademy.info/en/the-academy-has-established-a-partnership-with-a-new-partner/. Accessed 17 January 2026.

Training to Counter Disinformation—Higher School of Public Administration. (2025). Available at https://hs.gov.ua/navchannya-protydiyi-dezinformacziyi/. Accessed 28 December 2025.

7 Fact-Checking System in Ukraine

Ukraine's fact-checking system did not appear overnight from a single law. It grew gradually, shaped by overlapping needs: to keep public conversation steady, to hold those in power and the media to account, and to resist hostile narratives that spread faster than ordinary reporting could follow. After 2014, and even more intensely after 2022, fact-checking became a part of everyday life. What began as scattered volunteer efforts turned into a living ecosystem with its own balance and rhythm. Independent teams such as StopFake, VoxCheck, Detector Media, and TEXTY.org.ua built transparent practices that anyone could follow: tracing a story to its source, verifying time and place, linking back to original records, and correcting openly when the facts changed. At the same time, the Center for Countering Disinformation (CCD) and other state institutions learned to publish quick, practical guidance that newsrooms could reuse without delay. Together they formed not a single voice, but a shared pulse—an evolving culture that values evidence more than volume, and truth more than speed.

The CCD's purpose is to make verification something people can rely on and repeat. When the CCD's access to official information meets open, transparent methods of showing sources, explaining each step, clarifying what is known and what remains uncertain, truth begins to move farther and faster than any single correction. This is the CCD's essential contribution to Ukraine's fact-checking system: transforming isolated checks into a steady public service that helps society keep its balance under pressure.

A. Marushchak et al., *Counter Disinformation System Development in Ukraine*, Terrorism, Security, and Computation, https://doi.org/10.1007/978-3-032-24731-5_7

7.1 How Fact-Checking Took Root in Ukraine and Became a Source of Resilience

In Ukraine, fact-checking did not grow as a narrow craft taught in journalism schools or confined to newsroom ethics. It developed as an urgent response to hostile influence, becoming a necessary part of national defense in a landscape where information itself is a weapon. Ukrainian fact-checking teams became part of a broader civic shield, working with researchers, and community organizations to expose manipulation and strengthen public trust. Their work reaches far beyond correcting a minister's misquote or a misplaced statistic. It also challenges historical distortions and pushes back against foreign enemy narratives built around the "Russkii mir" (Russian world) concept, which aims to blur or replace Ukrainian identity.

The story of fact-checking in Ukraine did not follow the familiar Western pattern. It emerged from the hard work of rebuilding a nation after the Soviet collapse and from years of information warfare that made verification feel less like newsroom routine and more like a matter of public safety. The early 1990s opened a wide and uncertain space filled with possibility. Many believed that adopting a European model of democracy would quickly bring a normal life. Formal censorship vanished, and with its disappearance came the hope that open conversation could finally take root. Reality arrived fast. The same years brought a vacuum of power, economic shocks, and unstable politics. Old controls were gone, and new safeguards had yet to appear. Newsrooms faced pressure and manipulation from all sides, and there was little time to build common standards for verifying information. Instead of a steady rise in professional practice, Ukraine entered a period when its information space could be seized by the loudest voices and the most determined campaigns.

Out of this experience, a different model took shape. In Ukraine, fact-checking did not grow as a narrow craft taught in journalism schools or confined to newsroom ethics. It developed as an urgent response to hostile influence, becoming a necessary part of national defense in a landscape where information itself is a weapon. Ukrainian fact-checking teams became part of a broader civic shield, working with researchers, and community organizations to expose manipulation and strengthen public trust. Their work reaches far beyond correcting a minister's misquote or a misplaced statistic. It also challenges historical distortions and pushes back against foreign enemy narratives built around the "Russkii mir" (Russian world) concept, which aims to blur or replace Ukrainian identity (Information manipulation and historical revisionism: Russian disinformation and foreign interference through manipulated history-based narratives—PMC, 2023). This is what defines the Ukrainian approach: fact-checking as a form of cognitive defense against systematic disinformation, while still rooted in the principles of honest journalism.

The 1990s in Ukraine are remembered as a time of whiplash change and real danger. The economy collapsed, politics swung from one crisis to another, and organized crime rushed to fill the space left by a fading system. Yet the decade also opened a door. With Soviet censorship gone, newsrooms began to find their own voice—fast, direct, and surprisingly fair for such turbulent conditions. Investigative reporting appeared almost overnight. Journalists followed the money, named names, and treated corruption and violent crime as public matters rather than gossip. It was rough, sometimes improvised, but it was also bold. In the process, it taught audiences to expect something new: evidence, documents, and words spoken on the record instead of in whispers.

From 1991 to 2014, journalism in Ukraine grew in circumstances that made fact-checking a matter of personal discipline rather than institutional routine. Verification depended on a reporter's notes, a bundle of papers, and a phone call to a source who might never respond. The methods were fragile, built on individual honesty instead of lasting systems. As the first stormy years of independence began to quiet, politics found ways to take advantage of those gaps. Without shared rules or strong protections, many media outlets could be influenced, pressured, or simply bought. By the time Ukraine entered a new chapter, it had reporters who knew how to verify facts but still no stable framework to protect that work.

The Orange Revolution began with the presidential election of 2004, and it changed the way the country spoke to itself. Millions of people stood in the cold for the belief that elections should be fair and that those in power should answer to the public. What followed felt like a national awakening. Ukraine chose a democratic path that diverged from Russia's tightening course and, in doing so, set new expectations for what public life could be.

> The modern period of Ukrainian fact-checking began in 2014, as Russia's assault brought the occupation of Crimea and the war in Donbas. The military campaign was accompanied by a wave of disinformation that spread even faster than troops could move. After Viktor Yanukovych fled the country, propaganda intensified, filling television, print, and online media with pre-packaged stories and recycled footage. Thus, journalists and volunteers quickly understood that every event on the battlefield would be followed by a version meant to twist timelines, obscure responsibility, and turn confusion into doubt.

The effect on the media was immediate. The old reflex of suppressing government criticism no longer seemed possible (How Ukraine's Orange Revolution shaped twenty-first century geopolitics—Atlantic Council, 2020). Newsrooms were chaotic and imperfect, yet full of life and ready to argue in public. Editors began to see that audiences now expected evidence, explanation, and open discussion. The Revolution did not create fact-checking organizations overnight, but it did plant something lasting: a public appetite for transparency and accountability. Civil society grew more confident, journalists understood that sources and documents had to be visible, and readers learned to look for proof they could trust. A decade later, when foreign information pressure intensified, that civic habit became a source of strength. It allowed Ukraine to respond from the ground up and gave future fact-checking efforts an audience ready to listen.

The modern period of Ukrainian fact-checking began in 2014, as Russia's assault brought the occupation of Crimea and the war in Donbas. The military campaign was accompanied by a wave of disinformation that spread even faster than troops could move. After Viktor Yanukovych fled the country, propaganda intensified, filling television, print, and online media with prepackaged stories and recycled footage. Thus, journalists and volunteers quickly understood that every event on the battlefield would be followed by a version meant to twist timelines, obscure responsibility, and turn confusion into doubt.

The goal of the campaign went far beyond any single false claim. Its target was the very idea that Ukraine had the right to choose its own path. The same stories surfaced again and again: the post-Euromaidan government labeled "neo-Nazi," Russian speakers portrayed as victims of "genocide," and Ukraine depicted as a "puppet of NATO." Each message followed a familiar pattern, blending fragments of plausibility with emotion and constant repetition. The response that began in 2014 was more than a quick attempt to chase down rumors. It joined rapid verification with context, original records, and open methods that allowed readers to see how evidence was gathered. Fact-checking became both a daily routine and a way of defending memory, showing what was untrue and why each distortion fit a pattern that had been used before and would likely appear again in new form.

> Civil society organizations joined forces with international partners such as UNESCO to expand media and information literacy. The goal was to build a habit of awareness that could live in everyday life: how people read the news, share posts, or question what they see.

In March 2014, as disinformation flooded the public space, a team of faculty, students, and graduates from the National University of Kyiv-Mohyla Academy launched StopFake (About us|StopFake, n.d.). What started as a volunteer project followed a simple rule that anyone could understand: trace each claim to its source, compare it with primary evidence, and explain the result in plain language. The project's beginnings inside a university mattered. The academic environment offered structure, careful documentation, and a sense of responsibility that stood out in a media landscape where speed often overtook verification. Civil society's involvement gave the effort a public face and a kind of trust that no official campaign could imitate.

Growth came quickly because the need was impossible to ignore. The work stayed practical and direct. The team monitored new claims, disproved what could be checked, kept records so patterns could be seen, and identified the narratives that kept returning. Step by step, by combining academic discipline with open publication, they built an international point of reference that readers, journalists, and researchers could examine for themselves. In an information space crowded with noise, that blend of method and civic energy earned a kind of credibility that many established media outlets could no longer sustain. The rise of fact-checking became part of something larger. Across the country, volunteers were delivering supplies, helping evacuees, and supporting soldiers. Verifying information turned out to be part of the same collective effort, another form of defense.

After the emergency work of 2014, Ukrainian fact-checking began to move from instinct to structure. The field matured and expanded, recognizing that its purpose was not only to counter external attacks but also to strengthen standards at home. A major step in this evolution was the creation of VoxCheck by VoxUkraine in 2015 (Colomina et al., 2021, p. 43). The team defined a clear role for itself: to hold domestic politicians and opinion leaders accountable for their words, with particular attention to numbers and the real-world consequences of policy. Professionalization also meant connection with the international community and shared ethical norms. In 2018, VoxCheck joined the International Fact-Checking Network's Code of Ethics (VoxCheck, n.d.), pledging nonpartisanship, transparency, and open correction of mistakes. That commitment opened doors to cooperation with global platforms and showed readers and partners abroad that Ukrainian fact-checkers could meet established international standards. The result is a professional community able to deliver reliable verification quickly, to speak the language of global practice, and to keep searching for stable ways to fund work that serves the public above all else.

As the first wave of debunks began to settle into daily routine, attention shifted from chasing isolated rumors to building resilience. Detector Media stood at the center of this change. Its researchers follow how Russian influence flows through television, news sites, and social networks, tracing the pathways of manipulation and then explaining them in clear, accessible language (NED_Forum-Shielding-Democracy.pdf, n.d.). Around the same time, civil society organizations joined forces with international partners such as UNESCO to expand media and information literacy. The goal was to build a habit of awareness that could live in everyday life: how people read the news, share posts, or question what they see (UNESCO's campaigns on media and information literacy empower millions, 2025).

Policy moved in the same direction. After the Revolution of Dignity, lawmakers introduced rules on transparent media ownership and merged state broadcasters into a single national public service outlet, Suspilne (EBU welcomes new public broadcaster in Ukraine, 2017). The change mattered in daily life. Clearer ownership records made it harder to hide control behind shell companies, while a public service mandate lifted expectations for fairness even in a heated news cycle. Step by step, these reforms helped sketch a broader map for defending the information space. The task was not only to expose falsehoods as they appeared but also to strengthen the domestic media system so it could endure pressure: honest ownership, independent management, and audiences confident enough to ask for evidence.

The full-scale Russian invasion in February 2022 turned the information war into a relentless test of endurance. Within days, fact-checkers faced not only a surge in falsehoods but ones that were sharper and more dangerous: forged mobilization orders, miscaptioned battlefield videos, fake government statements, and recycled footage presented as breaking news. The disinformation did not stop at Ukraine's borders. New narratives were crafted for audiences abroad and funneled through international media spaces to slip past platform rules and sanctions. Old themes resurfaced in fresh forms, from claims that Ukraine "lacked its own agency" to stories meant to divide allies and weaken support.

The relentless pace pushed both verification and media literacy into emergency mode. Teams that once spent days preparing detailed investigations began producing clear, well-sourced checks within minutes. The CCD, originally conceived as a closed analytical hub, has become by the sheer scale of Russian propaganda the important element of the fact-checking system. Its role expanded far beyond internal analysis. The CCD became a visible point of coordination, translating verified information into public guidance and helping sustain a sense of clarity when confusion was a weapon. The goal across all fronts was to stop a harmful rumor before it sparked panic, reinforce public trust with visible proof, and keep the information space functional in the middle of a war.

7.2 Fact-Checking at the Center for Countering Disinformation

CCD analysts follow open sources in several languages, from local Telegram channels to international wire services. Each piece of information is assessed for risk for its accuracy, for its potential impact on public order and essential services. Low-risk items are set aside for routine verification and weekly summaries. High-risk ones move immediately into a fast track, where an analyst, a subject specialist, and a communications lead work together on a single case file.

Fact-checking at the CCD works like an emergency service for the information space. The CCD keeps open lines with ministries, the security and law enforcement community, the diplomatic service, regulators, and regional administrations, so that any claim can reach the right expert within minutes. False rumours about mobilization are checked with the authority that issues the orders. An energy story is compared with grid data. A public health scare goes to the ministry. Because these channels are already mapped, the path from rumour to verified fact is short and predictable. That is why, in fast-moving news cycles, many journalists treat the CCD's updates as the most reliable version of record.

The day at the CCD begins with listening. Analysts follow open sources in several languages, from local Telegram channels to international wire services. Each piece of information is assessed for risk for its accuracy, for its potential impact on public order and essential services. Low-risk items are set aside for routine verification and weekly summaries. High-risk ones move immediately into a fast track, where an analyst, a subject specialist, and a communications lead work together on a single case file. The principle is straightforward: bring the right people into the same thread at the same time, so the response is both precise and quick.

Verification at the CCD relies on open sources, standard journalistic checks, and OSINT methods. Text claims are traced to where they first appeared and then compared with later reposts to catch edits that might change meaning. Images and videos are examined frame by frame, focusing on details that are difficult to fake: street signs, road markings, skyline lines, vegetation. These clues are cross-checked with maps, land registries, business databases, and photographs from ordinary users. Time is verified through shadows, weather archives, and public calendars, which makes it possible to place a misdated clip within a precise window. Documents and supposed leaks are examined for metadata, reused templates, and number formats, then compared with public records such as procurement lists, court files, customs data, or budget portals. When a coordinated push is suspected, analysts look at how the message spreads: clusters of new accounts and matching posting times often reveal an organized campaign.

Institutional cooperation runs in parallel with these checks. When a claim falls within the responsibility of a particular agency, the liaison sends a short request for confirmation or correction. The agency verifies the facts within its area of authority. The CCD then distils what matters for the public and, when necessary, places the claim within a broader narrative pattern. The roles remain distinct. Experts speak for their own fields, while the CCD keeps the message brief, well-sourced, and easy to understand.

Publication at the CCD is designed for reuse. Most often, the CCD releases a short alert that identifies the false claim, states the verified facts, shows one or two decisive checks, and offers practical guidance for readers. When a story spreads widely, the response goes further: an explanation follows that traces how the narrative developed, points out its common variations, and answers the questions people are likely to ask next.

Each note explains what was checked, by whom, and with which sources. Degrees of certainty are stated openly, and updates appear as soon as stronger evidence comes in. At the same time, analysis stays separate from advocacy, so facts do not turn into commentary. Inside the CCD, every significant case ends with a short after-action review that traces how the claim was detected, which checks proved decisive, where delays occurred, and what needs to be added to watchlists. These reviews are not filed away and forgotten. Instead, their lessons feed a living catalogue of recurring narratives and a growing library of worked examples. As a result, every round of verification becomes slightly faster, more confident, and more precise than the one before.

> Partnerships expand reach without weakening independence. NGOs and newsrooms receive early warnings and source materials, then publish in their own voice and format from quick claim-by-claim checks to broader narrative trackers and data visuals. This shared rhythm keeps verification transparent and traceable while opening the conversation to audiences who might not follow official channels. It also strengthens credibility. When several outlets draw on the same verified facts and supporting screenshots, the message holds steady, and repetition begins to work for truth instead of distortion.

Real cases show how the method works in practice. One day, a low-quality video appears online, supposedly showing Ukrainian soldiers claiming that their commanders abandoned them. It is flagged as high risk for morale and quickly sent for verification. On a closer look, the illusion falls apart: the scene is staged, the faces have been swapped, a voice track has been pasted over the footage, and one "soldier" somehow speaks without moving his lips (Telegram: View @CenterCounteringDisinformation, n.d. b). Another case arrives through a mass mailing of a so-called government letter instructing ministries to pack for the west and reduce staff, with lists supposedly meant for mobilization offices. Once examined, it unravels. The number and date break registration rules, there is no record of it in the workflow system, and the language itself feels wrong, its spelling and tone stumble in ways no genuine directive would (Telegram: View @CenterCounteringDisinformation, n.d. c). Both stories point to a single lesson. Start with the simple checks, let the evidence speak, and use language clear enough for anyone to understand.

Partnerships expand reach without weakening independence. NGOs and newsrooms receive early warnings and source materials, then publish in their own voice and format from quick claim-by-claim checks to broader narrative trackers and data visuals. This shared rhythm keeps verification transparent and traceable while opening the conversation to audiences who might not follow official channels. It also strengthens credibility. When several outlets draw on the same verified facts and supporting screenshots, the message holds steady, and repetition begins to work for truth instead of distortion.

What emerges is a state-level fact-checking service that feels practical and close to daily life. The methods remain careful, yet the work moves at the speed of events. Every step leaves a visible trail, from open sources to simple checks that any editor could repeat. The notes are written in plain, human language, the kind a producer can lift for a headline and a reporter can quote without rewriting. In this way, one solid post grows into several reliable stories, the noise begins to fade, and people feel they finally have enough truth to act with confidence.

7.3 Inside the CCD's Partnerships with Fact-Checkers

Credibility grows from a method that is open to scrutiny. At the same time, connection depends on a human voice that explains rather than instructs. When these two qualities meet, fact-checking stops being a narrow journalistic niche and becomes a form of strategic communication that serves defense, diplomacy, and education together. In real situations, a single clear episode can steady a city during a surge of rumors or brief a foreign newsroom following Ukraine in another language.

Cooperation between the CCD and Ukraine's fact-checking community is a living exchange. The CCD scans the information landscape, verifies rapidly through institutional sources, and identifies where a rumour might cause real harm. Independent teams add what institutions cannot: editorial instinct, familiar voices, and audiences that trust them. Working side by side, they move a story from "we're seeing this" to "here's what it is, why it matters, and what to watch next."

Projects span everything from regular briefings and shared watchlists to evidence packets and multimedia explainers designed for people who will never open a policy report. One vivid example is the video collaboration with VoxCheck, where the CCD's verified data meets VoxCheck's storytelling skill and broad reach, creating materials that work equally well on television, and on mobile screens. In this way, fact-checking has evolved into a form of strategic communication that serves defense, diplomacy, and education at once.

Thus, the CCD, together with VoxCheck, created Поговоримо (Let's Talk), a video podcast launched in 2023, when information pressure was relentless (Andriy

Kovalenko About Telegram, Maidan-3 And The Project 'The Second Ukraine' | Podcast 'Let's Talk', 2024). «Let's Talk» treats public education as a genuine conversation that people want to join. The goal was to combine rigorous verification with the approachable tone of influencer-style dialogue, allowing facts to reach audiences in a familiar and trusted voice. The project emerged from a simple realization: straightforward fact checks rarely reach viewers overwhelmed by emotional content and constant scrolling. By bringing the same discipline to a format designed for those feeds, inviting credible guests to carry the message, and letting clear on-screen evidence speak for itself, the team built a form of communication where trust grows naturally.

The concept rests on two complementary strengths. The CCD provides early warnings and verified data, while VoxCheck contributes editorial skill and a network of guests who already speak to different communities. Each episode brings together a fact-checker and a public figure or practitioner from fields such as education, law, media, or the arts. They begin with a claim that has already surfaced in people's timelines and then unpack what the evidence shows, how the story spread, and what habits help viewers recognize the next version when it appears. The tone remains conversational throughout. The questions sound like the ones a person might ask at the kitchen table: Is this real? Who said it first? What would prove or disprove it?

At its core, several lessons are worth keeping. To begin with, credibility grows from a method that is open to scrutiny. At the same time, connection depends on a human voice that explains rather than instructs. When these two qualities meet, fact-checking stops being a narrow journalistic niche and becomes a form of strategic communication that serves defense, diplomacy, and education together. In real situations, a single clear episode can steady a city during a surge of rumors or brief a foreign newsroom following Ukraine in another language. In the end, «Let's Talk» shows that institutional expertise and the creativity of civil society can work within the same format and that education, empathy, and a touch of storytelling can come together to strengthen public resilience.

That same year, in 2023, after months of tracking how talking points about Ukraine resurfaced in foreign coverage, the CCD and VoxCheck launched a series of short video investigations (Tucker Carlson: Love For Putin, Peace Without Zelenskiy, And The Outdated West, n.d.). The brief was simple and ambitious at once: to show how Kremlin-aligned narratives slip into Western media not through official channels, but through familiar journalists, academics, and commentators who present them as "alternative viewpoints". The messages in the videos did not arrive with warning labels, they came wrapped in the language of expertise and credibility.

The partnership worked because the roles were clear, and because each side trusted the other's strengths. The CCD provided structured monitoring across languages and media markets, along with the background needed to place a single quote inside a wider, recurring storyline. VoxCheck, for its part, kept full editorial independence and turned that raw material into concise, engaging investigations that viewers could actually follow. In many ways, this balance became the project's signature. The CCD anchored the facts, VoxCheck shaped the story. Together they created a format that blends rigor with openness.

Each five-to-eight-minute episode focuses on a specific public figure and highlights the exact line under discussion, placing it within a clear, visual timeline. Viewers can see where the statement first appeared, how it was repeated or altered elsewhere, and what changed as it moved across outlets and languages. The themes are familiar to Western audiences—claims that "NATO provoked the war," that "Ukraine is controlled by the West," or that "sanctions hurt Europe more than Russia." Throughout, the tone remains steady and factual. There are no accusations and no labels, only context. The series set out to show the broader landscape in which such claims circulated, helping viewers notice how recognizable narratives reappear, shift shape, and return.

This initiative became a clear example of how security and media can work in sync. When state analysts and independent fact-checkers cooperate openly yet keep their roles distinct, the result becomes a form of resilience that people can sense in daily life. Newsrooms find it easier to explain complex claims when the sources are visible on screen. Audiences, in turn, begin to develop a simple habit: look for the first version of a statement, notice what was added or removed, and decide whether the conclusion still holds.

Ukraine's path looks strikingly different from the gradual buildouts typical of Western democracies. Here, verification routines matured under existential pressure, which forced cross-sector partnerships to take shape in months rather than years. Yet that same urgency became an advantage. Teams now respond within minutes to fast-moving narratives and feel at ease experimenting with formats that meet people where they are. The ethical balance, meanwhile, is hybrid by necessity. Security concerns stand alongside freedom-of-expression norms, so the system leans heavily on transparency and pluralism to keep "truth" from becoming a state monopoly. Independent outlets retain their editorial voice; the state upholds its duty to warn. Both sides benefit and the public can see the difference.

7.4 Conclusion

The fact-checking in Ukraine has firmly moved from the margins to the core of the country's strategic communication. In practice, situational assessments from the CCD began to shape how government institutions briefed one another and addressed the public. At the same time, independent organizations provided verification that could be checked openly and honest feedback from audiences about what confused them and what helped. During moments of crisis, coordinated rapid-response groups treated dangerous rumours as genuine emergencies, bringing the right experts into a single thread and issuing clear guidance within hours rather than days.

In practice, the architecture rests on three interlocking layers that have learned to move in step. At the strategic level sits the CCD, linking intelligence, communication, and public outreach. The CCD coordinates institutional responses whenever a hostile narrative threatens to spill across regions or sectors and provides verified guidance that others can adapt and reuse. At the same time, parts of its work touch the operational field, producing alerts, explanatory notes, and data that flow directly into media and civic channels. Meanwhile, the operational layer (NGOs, research centers) translates verified findings into forms people can actually use: short explainers, visual guides, and course materials that stay in memory. Beneath that, a civic layer of regional fact-checkers, local newsrooms, and educators brings the work home, adapting language and examples to fit their communities. Decentralized yet closely connected, this model has endured wartime pressure precisely because each layer understands its role, shares information quickly, and knows when a case needs to move up or down the chain.

Seen from abroad, Ukraine's path looks strikingly different from the gradual buildouts typical of Western democracies. Here, verification routines matured under existential pressure, which forced cross-sector partnerships to take shape in months rather than years. Yet that same urgency became an advantage. Teams now respond within minutes to fast-moving narratives and feel at ease experimenting with formats that meet people where they are. The ethical balance, meanwhile, is hybrid by necessity. Security concerns stand alongside freedom-of-expression norms, so the system leans heavily on transparency and pluralism to keep "truth" from becoming a state monopoly. Independent outlets retain their editorial voice; the state upholds its duty to warn. Both sides benefit and the public can see the difference.

In the end, the larger lesson is both simple and demanding. Under threat, democracies can adapt and innovate without losing their character. In Ukraine, cooperation between the CCD and independent groups such as VoxCheck has turned verification into a cornerstone of cognitive security. The work itself is deeply social: a public that knows how to ask for sources, institutions that explain their methods, and a media sphere where speed and care can coexist.

References

About us | StopFake. (n.d.). Available at https://www.stopfake.org/en/about-us/. Accessed 11 November 2025.

Andriy Kovalenko About Telegram, Maidan-3 and the Project "The Second Ukraine" | PODCAST "LET'S TALK"? (2024). Available at https://www.youtube.com/watch?v=ftc0ULul19U. Accessed 11 November 2025.

Colomina, C., Margalef, H. S. & Youngs, R. (2021). The impact of disinformation on democratic processes and human rights in the world.

EBU welcomes new public broadcaster in Ukraine (2017). Available at https://www.ebu.ch/news/2017/01/ebu-welcomes-new-public-broadcaster-in-ukraine. Accessed 11 November 2025.

How Ukraine's Orange Revolution shaped twenty-first century geopolitics—Atlantic Council (2020). Available at https://www.atlanticcouncil.org/blogs/ukrainealert/how-ukraines-orange revolution-shaped-twenty-first-century-geopolitics/. Accessed 11 November 2025.

Information manipulation and historical revisionism: Russian disinformation and foreign interference through manipulated history-based narratives—PMC (2023). Available at https://pmc.ncbi.nlm.nih.gov/articles/PMC10509605/. Accessed 11 November 2025.

NED_Forum-Shielding-Democracy.pdf. (n.d.). Available at https://www.ned.org/wp-content/uploads/2023/02/NED_Forum-Shielding-Democracy.pdf. Accessed 11 November 2025.

Telegram: View @CenterCounteringDisinformation (n.d. a). Available at https://t.me/CenterCounteringDisinformation/15788. Accessed 11 November 2025.
Telegram: View @CenterCounteringDisinformation (n.d. b). Available at https://t.me/CenterCounteringDisinformation/14837. Accessed 11 November 2025.
Tucker Carlson: Love For Putin, peace without Zelenskiy, and the outdated West (n.d.). Available at https://www.youtube.com/watch?v=eOfXk8eRR5U. Accessed 11 November 2025.
UNESCO's campaigns on media and information literacy empower millions (2025). Available at https://www.unesco.org/en/articles/unescos-campaigns-media-and-information-literacy-empower-millions-ukraine-think-critically. Accessed 11 November 2025.
VoxCheck. (n.d.). Available at https://voxukraine.org/en/voxcheck. Accessed 11 November 2025.

International Cooperation of the CCD and CSC

8

8.1 CCD's Collaborations with Governmental Bodies

Ukraine now stands not only as a state under siege but also as a frontline partner helping to shape how democracies confront and counter hybrid threats. The CCD's prominent role has become a symbol of resilience and reciprocity, an exchange where Ukraine learns from its allies. Even during war, democratic institutions can adapt without losing their core values – and that openly shared knowledge becomes a powerful instrument of defence.

As Ukraine's central institution for countering disinformation, the CCD consistently represents the country in major international forums dedicated to cognitive security. The experience gained through years of war has given the Center a profound analytical understanding of Russian influence ecosystems, proxy media structures, and complex psychological operations. This frontline expertise is now regularly requested by partner governments and international organizations that seek to enhance their own information resilience, creating a foundation for meaningful governmental and intergovernmental cooperation that strengthens both national and global information security.

Among the CCD's partnerships with governmental institutions, its cooperation with NATO has taken on special significance. What began as a practical exchange of expertise has grown into a relationship built on mutual trust, shared urgency, and a clear understanding that information resilience is central to democratic security. Both the Center and its NATO counterparts regard disinformation as a global test of democratic endurance, a weapon designed to erode confidence, create division, and weaken the moral cohesion that sustains open societies.

The CCD's cooperation with NATO developed along two complementary paths: strategic coordination with NATO Headquarters (HQ) in Brussels and an institutional partnership with the NATO Strategic Communications Centre of Excellence (StratCom COE) in Riga (NATO Headquarters, n.d.; StratCom|NATO Strategic Communications Centre of Excellence Riga, Latvia, n.d.). Together, these directions created a framework that allowed Ukraine to share its frontline experience in

A. Marushchak et al., *Counter Disinformation System Development in Ukraine*,
Terrorism, Security, and Computation, https://doi.org/10.1007/978-3-032-24731-5_8

countering a continuous information offensive while gradually bringing national methodologies closer to Allied cognitive-security standards. Over time, this cooperation moved from consultation to co-creation and from external assistance to genuine strategic alignment.

Within the framework of NATO HQ, the CCD now operates as part of a broader rhythm of analytical exchange and operational coordination. Regular interaction with Ukrainian institutions responsible for countering hybrid threats has made it possible to synchronize situational awareness, enhance analytical compatibility, and strengthen strategic communication during crises. One of the most significant milestones in this cooperation came in 2024, when CCD analysts and NATO experts jointly presented an analytical report to the Ukraine–NATO Council (The CCD deepens cooperation with NATO|Center for Countering Disinformation, 2024). The study examined foreign hostile disinformation campaigns aimed at undermining Allied support for Ukraine and became the first joint assessment with this specific focus prepared by NATO together with a non-member state. This event was meaningful for its analytical depth and for what it represented, marking a change in Ukraine's place within the Alliance's intellectual landscape. The country emerged as a partner capable of producing original expertise and shaping the collective understanding of modern information warfare.

This growing credibility continues to strengthen through the CCD's cooperation with the NATO Strategic Communications Centre of Excellence (NATO StratCom COE) in Riga. Through formalised cooperation mechanisms, participation in exercises and joint research, the CCD and StratCom COE have developed a mutually reinforcing strategic partnership (The team of the Center for Countering Disinformation, a working body of the National Security and Defense Council of Ukraine, represented Ukraine at the Counter Disinformation wargame (CDWG)|Center for Countering Disinformation, 2022). The appointment of a Ukrainian representative within the StratCom COE created a continuous two-way link between Kyiv and Riga, enabling the steady exchange of methodologies, data, and operational insights. This partnership helped Ukraine incorporate NATO's doctrinal approaches into its national system while providing the Alliance with something equally important: practical knowledge gained from real-world information threats, as intentional, harmful, manipulative and coordinated information activities converge in coordinated campaigns, every day.

Gradually, this cooperation began to build on knowledge and shared learning. Ukraine contributes empirically grounded expertise shaped by the realities of war, while NATO offers a networked platform for comparative analysis, joined-up capability development, and coordinated responses. Through this exchange, the Alliance gains direct access to observations that no theoretical model can reproduce, and Ukraine learns to translate its battlefield experience into institutional practices aligned with democratic standards. This process of mutual reinforcement has turned the partnership into a best practice example of how experience and theory, working toward collective defence, can evolve within a single learning continuum.

Through this ongoing collaboration, Ukraine now stands not only as a state under siege but also as a frontline partner helping to shape how democracies confront and counter hybrid threats. The CCD's increasingly prominent role within the NATO StratCom community has become a symbol of resilience and reciprocity, an exchange where Ukraine learns from its allies and enriches the Alliance with lessons drawn directly from the frontlines. This partnership shows that even during war, democratic institutions can adapt without losing their core values—and that openly shared knowledge becomes a powerful instrument of defence.

Building on its cooperation with NATO, the CCD has also strengthened partnerships within the broader European framework of security and governance. This engagement is reflected most clearly in its close work with the European Union Advisory Mission to Ukraine (EUAM), whose support has helped the Center translate strategic guidance into sustainable institutional practice (About Us—EUAM Ukraine, n.d.).

Since 2014, the EUAM has played a central role in reforming and modernising the country's civilian security sector, supporting national institutions in building the capacity to, amongst other things, counter hybrid threats and enhance public communication. Within this framework, the CCD has evolved into both a beneficiary and a committed partner, transforming European strategic guidance into practical tools for everyday work. The cooperation between the CCD and EUAM has become one of the most structured and result-oriented examples of international collaboration in the field of strategic communication and information resilience (In partnership with EUAM, a series of events were held to enhance the Center's public recognition|Center for Countering Disinformation, 2024).

This cooperation is based on a shared belief that disinformation strikes at the very heart of democratic change. The goals of EUAM naturally complement the CCD's mission to identify, analyse, and confront hostile information activity. From the very start, their work develops around three central priorities. The first focuses on strengthening human capacity by improving analytical thinking, communication, and coordination among CCD specialists and partner institutions. The second involves building institutional foundations through the preparation of training materials, methodological guidelines, and joint procedures drawn from European practice. The third centres on public engagement, fostering media literacy and helping citizens understand that disinformation is not a distant irritation but a real threat to national security.

Between 2022 and 2025, the partnership evolved through two complementary streams of capacity building. In the first stream, EUAM experts provided specialised training for CCD personnel on scenario-based crisis communication, open-source intelligence, hybrid-threat analysis, and proactive information management during wartime emergencies (Advanced training in the field of strengthening national security took place|Center for Countering Disinformation, 2023; With the support of EUAM, the CCD underwent a series of trainings to improve their skills|Center for Countering Disinformation, 2023; With the support of EUAM, the specialists of the CCD completed a series of training to enhance professional skills|Center for Countering Disinformation, 2023). These programmes strengthened the CCD's ability to coordinate inter-agency communication, integrate analytical data into strategic messaging, and react quickly to fast-changing information environments. In the second stream, supported by EUAM's methodological and logistical guidance, the CCD organised a nationwide series of trainings for representatives of regional and military administrations as well as central executive authorities (The Center for Countering Disinformation conducted a series of trainings for representatives of the Regional Military Administration and the Regional State Administration|Center for Countering Disinformation, 2023; The Center for Countering Disinformation conducted a series of trainings for the representatives of the central executive bodies|Center for Countering Disinformation, 2023b). These sessions focused on identifying and addressing disinformation at the local level, ensuring consistency between central and regional communication during war. Together, these efforts created more than a professional skill set. They established a sustainable network across Ukraine's public administration, bringing together a generation of communicators capable of acting with confidence under wartime pressure.

At the same time, EUAM organised study visits and online exchanges with European experts (Study visit of the CCDA to the Swedish Psychological Defence Agency and the Swedish Defence University|Center for Countering Disinformation, 2023; The study visit of the Center for Countering Disinformation to Germany took place|Center for Countering Disinformation, 2024; The Center's study visit to Italy|Center for Countering Disinformation, 2025). Through these activities, CCD specialists were able to share their own experience with European counterparts and observe how different institutions across Europe combine monitoring, analysis, and communication into coherent systems. This continuous exchange of knowledge became an important step toward aligning Ukraine's analytical and communication practices with European standards of institutional maturity.

Two significant publications, previously mentioned in earlier chapters, became the most tangible results of this partnership, reflecting how much expertise had been gathered through years of joint work. The Manual on Countering Disinformation (2023), prepared with EUAM's support, introduced the first structured methodology for identifying, verifying, and responding to manipulative content (Handbook on countering disinformation developed by the Center for Countering Disinformation, a working body of the National Security and Defense Council of Ukraine with the support of the European Union Advisory Mission Ukraine|Center for Countering Disinformation, 2023). Two years later, Weapons of the Information Warfare (2025) offered a broader perspective, analysing the systemic nature of information warfare (Handbook "Weapons of Information Warfare"|Center for Countering Disinformation, 2025). Together, these manuals provided practical tools for specialists and confirmed the CCD's position as a national centre of knowledge in the field of information resilience.

Beyond professional trainings and methodological work, EUAM actively supports the CCD's efforts to strengthen its public voice and build trust among diverse audiences. Joint press briefings and expert discussions make it possible to present the Center's mission and values in language that is clear and relatable for journalists, educators, and civil society groups. EUAM's support also has improved the CCD's visual identity, multilingual communication, and openness to international partners. Over time, the Center has begun to be recognised as more than a government institution, becoming a place of expertise that welcomed dialogue with journalists, researchers, and non-governmental organisations.

From a policy perspective, the partnership between the CCD and EUAM illustrates the gradual Europeanisation of Ukraine's information-resilience system. It has created a lasting bridge between EU advisory mechanisms and Ukraine's national security institutions, ensuring that reforms in information policy rest on both democratic values and practical experience. What began as a programme of technical assistance has evolved into the genuine co-production of knowledge. The early stages focused on training and consultation, while later phases led to joint research and shared analytical outputs. As a result, the partnership has moved beyond the traditional donor–recipient model and developed into a strategic relationship in which the CCD increasingly contributes as an equal partner in shaping European approaches to countering disinformation.

From an analytical point of view, this cooperation reflects a dual transformation. On one side, it has strengthened and professionalised Ukraine's counter-disinformation system by embedding European principles of ethics, analysis, and accountability. On the other, it has broadened the European Union's own perspective on disinformation, recognising it as a central element of contemporary crisis management and security governance. Ukraine's frontline experience continues to provide EUAM with tangible evidence and practical insight, while EUAM's methodological discipline reinforces Ukraine's institutional resilience. Together, they represent a model of mutual learning and shared progress.

Bilateral Cooperation and Security Partnerships

Following Russia's full-scale invasion, Ukraine's approach to information-security diplomacy evolved from spontaneous cooperation into a structured network of bilateral partnerships integrated within a broader system of security agreements. Since 2024, Ukraine has signed a series of long-term bilateral security arrangements with partner states such as the United Kingdom, Sweden, Poland, France, and others. Each agreement includes specific commitments to protect the information environment, counter disinformation, and strengthen both national and societal resilience (Kazdobina, 2024). Within this framework, Ukrainian institutions, and the CCD in particular, have assumed a central operational role by working directly with governmental and analytical counterparts in partner countries to implement the information-security components of these agreements. This bilateral approach has helped Ukraine align its cognitive-security efforts with Euro-Atlantic standards while preserving the flexibility needed in wartime conditions.

Among Ukraine's expanding network of bilateral partnerships, cooperation between the CCD and the Swedish Psychological Defence Agency (Myndigheten för psykologiskt försvar, MPF) stands out as one of the clearest examples of how international dialogue can evolve into a practical instrument of cognitive resilience (Psychological Defence Agency, 2025). The partnership emerged from ongoing security consultations between Ukraine and Sweden and soon developed into active collaboration. Both sides recognised that safeguarding democracy and building resilience within the population demands shared discipline, continuous learning, and institutions capable of acting decisively under pressure. The joint work concentrates on three areas central to psychological defence: strengthening institutional capacity, advancing analytical expertise, and improving coordination among agencies involved in countering hostile information activity.

The first stage of this partnership began with a joint training programme on countering malicious information influence, organised by the CCD and MPF (Training conducted by the Swedish Psychological Defence Agency (MPF) under the auspices of the Center for Countering Disinformation|Center for Countering Disinformation, 2023). The course was designed around two interconnected modules that brought together conceptual understanding and practical application. In the opening sessions, participants became acquainted with Sweden's model of psychological defence, which draws on the official Handbook on countering information influence activities (Countering information influence activities: the state of the art: research report. Version 1.4, 2018). Through case studies and guided discussions, they analysed the dynamics of information manipulation, the organisation of influence operations, and the institutional mechanisms that help reduce their impact.

After the introductory stage, the programme moved into a fully practical phase. Ukrainian specialists from different government institutions were divided into inter-agency teams and asked to respond to a simulated disinformation campaign unfolding within a fictional national crisis. The exercise took place in real time, requiring participants to recognise manipulative tactics, assess weak points, and coordinate their response across ministries and agencies. It recreated the tension and uncertainty of an actual hybrid operation and, most importantly, demonstrated that effective cooperation relies on clarity of communication and mutual trust among institutions.

Building on this experience, the CCD and MPF organised an advanced five-day professional training programme titled Countering Information Influence Measures (The Center and MPF held a training on "Countering Information Influence Measures"|Center for Countering Disinformation, 2024). The initiative brought together representatives of government institutions and created a shared learning environment for specialists responsible for shaping Ukraine's information-resilience strategy. The course combined theoretical perspectives from behavioural science and perception management with practical exercises in crisis communication and internal coordination. Participants designed their own teaching modules and short curricula intended for future use in civil-service schools, university media departments, and training centres. By the end of the programme, they had acquired both conceptual understanding and practical skills for developing tailored learning systems that could strengthen their institutions' capacity to withstand targeted information influence.

As the partnership matured, it grew into a steady tradition of annual educational and simulation-based gatherings that blended practical training with international exchange. These events, mentioned in this book in relation to Ukraine's media-literacy movement, were organised under the coordination of the CCD with the valued support of Swedish partners. Over time, they became known as the Strat-Com Weekend and the Countering FIMI Weekend. The first of these, StratCom Weekend 1.0, held in October 2023, brought together Ukrainian officials, communication experts, and international practitioners to rehearse coordinated crisis communication in hybrid-threat environments (From October 6 to 9, under the auspices of the Center for Countering Disinformation and the Psychological Defense Agency, "Stratcom weekend" 1.0 was held|Center for Countering Disinformation, 2023). The following Countering FIMI Weekend, conducted in 2024 and 2025, expanded this approach by integrating open-source intelligence and artificial intelligence tools to enhance analytical capacity and develop proactive strategies for countering foreign information and media influence (CCD held Countering FIMI Weekend in Lviv|Center for Countering Disinformation, 2024; The CCD NSDC together with the MPF held a specialized seminar in Lviv|Center for Countering Disinformation, 2025). Each of these gatherings served both as a training platform and as a meeting point where professionals could test approaches, exchange knowledge, and learn collectively. They encouraged cooperation across institutions, strengthened coordination practices, and helped cultivate a professional culture in which cognitive security became an integral part of everyday communication rather than an emergency response.

Building on these experiences, the CCD and MPF introduced an innovative format called the International Arcade on Countering Disinformation (International Counter Disinformation Arcade, 2023), which took place on 6 December 2023. The event combined elements of competition, simulation, and policy discussion. Representatives of the European Union and partner countries joined the exercise, which featured open debate alongside a game-based challenge. Participants were asked to identify manipulative narratives, design coordinated communication strategies, and evaluate their potential psychological impact on audiences. The atmosphere was both focused and collaborative, turning what might have been a traditional conference into a living experiment in collective problem-solving.

Beyond immediate practical outcomes, the Arcade became a forum for thoughtful reflection on the principles of contemporary information defence. During the event, the CCD set out a proposal for a joint hybrid-threat response mechanism and stressed that durable cognitive security arises from genuine multinational cooperation. Participants exchanged professional insights and endorsed the creation of a transnational network of experts committed to cognitive resilience. The discussions underscored the urgency of bringing democratic societies together around shared principles of transparency and trust, while recognising Ukraine's hard-won experience as a vital contribution to this common effort.

Taken together, these initiatives show how the partnership between the CCD and MPF has matured into true co-development of methodologies for psychological defence. It aligns Swedish conceptual frameworks with Ukraine's wartime operational expertise and creates a learning model rooted in practice that continues to evolve through use. Instead of a lecture-based format, the approach relies on simulation and guided practice, a pedagogy that deepens knowledge while cultivating reflexes, coordination, and sound judgement under pressure. Through the StratCom and Countering FIMI Weekends, as well as the International Arcade, Ukraine has embedded an enduring mechanism of experiential learning in the field of information defence. Seen through an analytical lens, this cooperation shows how a bilateral partnership can turn resilience from an abstract policy aim into operational practice through the joint development of knowledge and skills. The experience of the CCD and MPF therefore serves as a prototype for future multilateral frameworks of cognitive security, where education and strategy come together to protect democratic societies against the evolving pressures of psychological warfare.

Alongside its work with Sweden, the CCD has built a close and forward-looking partnership with the United Kingdom as part of a broader effort to anchor information security within a community of democratic allies, each bringing distinct expertise and institutional practice. In this context, cooperation between the CCD and the United Kingdom has become one of the most structured and enduring pillars of Ukraine's international engagement in the information-security field, in particular through collaboration with the Foreign, Commonwealth and Development Office (FCDO) (Foreign, Commonwealth & Development Office, 2026) and the Zinc Network (Zinc Network, n.d.). Over time, it has evolved into a practical alliance focused on strategic communication, policy design, and professional development.

> The partnership emerged from ongoing security consultations between Ukraine and Sweden and soon developed into active collaboration. Both sides recognised that safeguarding democracy and building resilience within the population demands shared discipline, continuous learning, and institutions capable of acting decisively under pressure. The joint work concentrates on three areas central to psychological defence: strengthening institutional capacity, advancing analytical expertise, and improving coordination among agencies involved in countering hostile information activity.

Cooperation with the Zinc Network began with the development of the CCD's first strategic roadmap in 2021. Building on that foundation, British experts and the Center prepared a second roadmap and expanded the effort into long-term strategic planning that now guides institutional growth. These roadmaps are tailored planning instruments for the Center. They set operational priorities, organise inter-agency coordination, and establish clear measures of progress. They are grounded in the CCD's practical needs and operating environment and they draw on recognised good practice in strategic communication, including insights from behavioural science, risk assessment models, and governance methods that support modern resilience policy. Taken together, the roadmaps give the Center a coherent direction for daily work and a shared language for cooperation with Ukrainian counterparts and international partners.

Cooperation with the FCDO follows a steady rhythm of ongoing collaboration that extends beyond individual projects, with regular working channels connecting CCD analysts and the FCDO team to enable the continual exchange of assessments, narrative trends, and early warning data on Russian information operations worldwide. This continuity has developed into a standing institutional relationship embedded within the broader United Kingdom and Ukraine Security Agreement (Agreement on Security Co-operation between the United Kingdom of Great Britain & Northern Ireland and Ukraine, 2024) and it is reinforced through UK-hosted exchanges and simulation exercises in which CCD specialists take part. Through this iterative learning by doing, Ukrainian experts have adapted proven communication methodologies to the realities of wartime information warfare, which in turn has improved agility and strengthened interoperability with allied systems.

Ultimately, cooperation with the FCDO offers a clear model of strategic co-creation between a national security institution and a democratic partner. It brings innovation together with experience and helps keep Ukraine's counter-disinformation architecture both accountable and forward-looking. By embedding the FCDO's practices in governance and behavioural communication into its own institutional frameworks, the CCD has strengthened its analytical capacity and reinforced the democratic legitimacy of its work. In practical terms, this partnership shows how resilience among allies is built, as one side contributes lessons drawn from real-time hybrid warfare and the other provides the structure and foresight needed to turn those lessons into policy.

The partnerships the CCD has built with institutions in multiple countries show how bilateral cooperation in the information sphere can grow into a wider ecosystem of cognitive resilience, as relationships move beyond formal diplomacy and become a sustained process of mutual learning, professional exchange, and joint development of methods. In practice, this model rests on connected elements that reinforce one another, including joint training and simulation exercises that turn strategic frameworks into applicable skills. It also involves study visits and staff exchanges, which let specialists learn directly from institutional experience, as well as collaborative analytical reports that combine Ukraine's frontline monitoring with European threat assessments to create a shared picture of risk. Finally, it includes coordinated verification and debunking, in which cross-border teams identify and expose disinformation campaigns directed at Ukraine and its allies.

Within the same architecture of applied cooperation, the CCD developed a task-focused partnership with Poland's Government Centre for Security (Rządowe Centrum Bezpieczeństwa, RCB) (Strona główna Rządowego Centrum Bezpieczeństwa—Rządowe Centrum Bezpieczeństwa—Portal Gov.pl, n.d.). First contacts took place in 2022 amid a rapid regional surge in Russian disinformation campaigns (An exchange of experience between the Ukrainian CCD and the Polish RCB|Center for Countering Disinformation, 2022). During the initial exchanges, Polish officials shared practical experience in detecting propaganda and coordinating state communication during crises, and expressed support for Ukraine's effort to formalise verification procedures and to establish a unified national registry of disinformation cases.

Working with RCB, the CCD monitors and exposes Russian narratives in the Polish information space, especially those intended to drive a wedge between Ukraine and Poland. One case involved a forged letter, supposedly from Ukraine's Ministry of Foreign Affairs to Poland's counterpart, asking for data on Ukrainian men under sixty living in Poland for mobilisation purposes. The investigation traced the document to a Russian outlet (Telegram: View @CenterCounteringDisinformation, n.d. a). The episode illustrated how such forgeries are used to harvest personal data and seed distrust, and it demonstrated how coordinated action by the CCD and RCB can contain manipulation before it gains traction.

These coordinated efforts highlight how cooperation between national agencies works in practice. Through shared monitoring and open lines of communication, the CCD and RCB are able to spot hostile narratives early and answer with verified information before they spread. The work also raises public awareness on both sides of the border, reminding people to approach supposed "official documents" on social media with caution and to check claims against verified sources and official websites.

Taken as a whole, these partnerships show how Ukraine's experience has reshaped the meaning of information defence. What began as urgent coordination in wartime has grown into a network of trust that connects institutions, methods and people across borders. Through the CCD's cooperation with European counterparts, resilience has moved from a national priority to a shared democratic practice that treats truthfulness and transparency as strategic assets. In this sense, Ukraine's contribution extends beyond self-protection and helps define what collective security means in the information age.

Through ongoing exchanges, Ukraine has become both a learner and a teacher in the global fight against disinformation. The CCD now works at the center of this network, learning from partners while sharing lessons forged at the front line of hybrid warfare. These ties have shifted information defence from a purely national shield to a common resource that strengthens the cognitive security of the wider Euro-Atlantic community. Over time, what began as survival under pressure has become a cooperative model grounded in openness, and the simple belief that truth, when defended together, travels farther than any lie.

> Partnerships show how Ukraine's experience has reshaped the meaning of information defence. What began as urgent coordination in wartime has grown into a network of trust that connects institutions, methods and people across borders. Through the CCD's cooperation with European counterparts, resilience has moved from a national priority to a shared democratic practice that treats truthfulness and transparency as strategic assets. In this sense, Ukraine's contribution extends beyond self-protection and helps define what collective security means in the information age.

8.2 CCD's Projects with Big Tech and Private Sector Entities and Labeling Social Media Content

The CCD became the state's principal analytical partner, concentrating on the identification of disinformation that violates Ukrainian law or threatens national security. Serving at once as a research hub and an early warning node, the Center connects institutional needs with platform capacities and turns cooperation with global companies into a practical instrument of information defence.

Within this line of work, Ukraine's state institutions together with the CCD maintain close partnerships with major technology platforms, including Meta, Google and YouTube, and TikTok. Each platform now operates a regional contact structure that gives Ukrainian counterparts a direct channel for coordination, which supports rapid responses to incidents, clearer escalation procedures, and greater transparency in moderation. Regular technical calls and situational updates align workflows ahead of sensitive periods such as elections or major security events, while shared analytical notes help teams spot recurring manipulation patterns and prioritise interventions. As a result, the national information space is better protected and platform decisions are easier for the public to understand.

The dialogue with major platforms has developed through the Ministry of Digital Transformation of Ukraine, which established formal channels for communication and put in place crisis response procedures to flag and address harmful content. Building on this foundation, the CCD became the state's principal analytical partner, concentrating on the identification of disinformation that violates Ukrainian law or threatens national security. Serving at once as a research hub and an early warning node, the Center connects institutional needs with platform capacities and turns cooperation with global companies into a practical instrument of information defence.

In 2024, Google and its research unit Jigsaw, in partnership with the CCD and other expert organisations, launched a nationwide media-literacy and prebunking campaign (Don't let yourself and your close ones be manipulated online., n.d.). Based on dedicated research data, there were created 3 educational videos explaining key manipulation techniques in Ukraine such as astroturfing, emotional manipulation and decontextualization, with examples tailored for Ukrainian audiences. CCD specialists influenced the local version by providing insights so that wording and cultural references were accurate and familiar. The campaign reached millions of viewers and became a practical addition to Ukraine's media-education efforts.

Work with TikTok is more operational in character and rests on day-to-day coordination. The CCD became the first institution in Ukraine to establish a direct working channel with the platform, creating a precedent for systematic cooperation between a state body and a global social network (Telegram: View @CenterCounteringDisinformation, n.d. d). Through secure contacts, the CCD sends verified alerts about harmful or manipulative content that may breach Ukrainian law or platform rules. TikTok reviews these submissions within its legal remit and, where appropriate, restricts or removes the material in line with its standards. In parallel, the CCD shares insight on emerging disinformation narratives and influence trends in the Ukrainian information space. This steady exchange improves the effectiveness of moderation and raises user safety, especially for younger and more vulnerable audiences.

One of the most practical lines of cooperation concerns the verification of official Ukrainian accounts and public information projects on social media. In coordination with Meta and TikTok, the CCD helps verify government and educational pages so that users can distinguish authentic sources from impostors. A clear example is the MordorCenter educational project on TikTok, which received verification, enabled the removal of false copies, and strengthened public trust in the genuine channel (TikTok—mordorcenter. Center for Research on the MordoRU, n.d.).

Cooperation with YouTube, in turn, focuses on identifying and reporting videos that contain elements of propaganda or deliberate disinformation, especially those that violate Ukrainian law. The CCD's analysts track emerging trends, flag manipulative content, and share verified findings directly with the platform's team. This collaboration allows for rapid response to harmful narratives, ensuring that videos promoting falsehoods or inciting hostility are reviewed and, when necessary, removed in accordance with platform policies.

Ukraine's experience shows that effective cooperation between the state and global technology companies works when it is grounded in trust, transparency, and the capacity to act quickly. The CCD serves as a bridge between public institutions and private platforms, detecting manipulation, providing verified context, and strengthening the resilience of the information space while protecting free expression.

This approach has created a practical basis for Ukraine's integration into the wider European digital environment. It reflects the principles of the EU Digital Services Act, where responsibility for information integrity is shared and implemented in common frameworks (Regulation (EU) 2022/2065 of the European Parliament and of the Council of 19 October 2022 on a Single Market For Digital Services and amending Directive 2000/31/EC (Digital Services Act) (Text with EEA relevance), 2022). Through open communication and the exchange of data, Ukraine demonstrates that democratic states and technology companies can work together to safeguard the online sphere, and that cooperation remains a more durable form of defence than control.

Ukraine's experience shows that effective cooperation between the state and global technology companies works when it is grounded in trust, transparency, and the capacity to act quickly. The CCD serves as a bridge between public institutions and private platforms, detecting manipulation, providing verified context, and strengthening the resilience of the information space while protecting free expression.

8.3 CSC'S Collaborations with International Institutions

Over 2022–2025 the CSC has actively woven itself into the broader network of international actors confronting Russian information aggression. European and Atlantic officials now regard countering disinformation as a shared priority.

Russia's 2022 invasion dramatically demonstrated the power of information as a weapon. The lines between media, public diplomacy and security blurred: propaganda and disinformation campaigns became extensions of military aggression. Ukraine's leadership responded by elevating strategic communication to a national-security priority. From day one of the war the CSC was on a war footing: it shifted from routine monitoring to round-the-clock analysis of enemy narratives, and it launched large-scale information campaigns to correct misinformation. For example, CSC analysts exposed Russia's "granny with the red flag" narrative as false—finding, interviewing and publicizing the true story of the elderly woman so convincingly that the propaganda symbol was abandoned. Such efforts not only protected Ukrainian resilience at home, but also informed foreign media (BBC, Washington Post, etc.) about the facts of the war, reinforcing Ukraine's credibility abroad. Internally, the CSC helped build "one voice" in government communications: it regularly issued coordinated message-boxes ("Main Positions of Information Response") that guided officials, experts and media on how to discuss battlefield events. These message-boxes have been explicitly adopted by Ukrainian communicators and cited by international observers as authoritative. Thus, the exigencies of war have catapulted strategic communications from a peripheral information function into a core component of Ukraine's defense strategy.

Over 2022–2025 the CSC has actively woven itself into the broader network of international actors confronting Russian information aggression. European and Atlantic officials now regard countering disinformation as a shared priority. During EU High Representative Josep Borrell's October 2023 visit, he explicitly stated that "combating disinformation is a high priority for the EU and Ukraine" and praised the CSC as exactly the kind of "support structure" (Josep Borrell visited the Center for Strategic Communication and Information Security in Kyiv, 2023) needed to resist Moscow's hybrid warfare. In practice, CSC staff regularly engage with EU and NATO bodies. The Centre co-hosts events and exchange programs: for example, its analysts and leaders have spoken at dozens of conferences in NATO countries and elsewhere. In 2023 CSC personnel presented at over 15 international events, including a panel on "Countering Disinformation and Building Strategic Communications" in Brussels and a NATO communicators' conference in Skopje. Similarly, CSC-sponsored forums draw foreign participants: the annual Kyiv StratCom Forum was explicitly organized as a regional platform for sharing Ukraine's experience with NATO partners in Eastern Europe and beyond. The 2023 Forum alone hosted representatives from NATO, the EU, the US, UK and Canada alongside all key Ukrainian agencies.

CSC's collaborations with international institutions extend beyond conferences. Since 2022 it has participated in EU-funded projects and global research networks. For example, CSC analysts joined an EU-backed information campaign on disinformation awareness, co-developing 18 informational products distributed to both Ukrainian and foreign audiences. In parallel, the Centre cooperates with global tech platforms: it maintains formal partnerships with Google, Twitter, Facebook/Meta, and LinkedIn to flag disinformation and to amplify reliable Ukrainian information.

The CSC's evolution from a purely national disinformation office into an international actor reflects deeper institutional learning. Originally chartered to help Ukraine resist propaganda, the Centre has progressively aligned its work … on Ukrainian experience with leading Western strategic communication practices. For instance, its "School for Strategic Communications"—a training program for government communicators—explicitly adopts the UK Government Communications Service's standards and the "Resist 2.0" manual methodology. With British Foreign, Commonwealth & Development Office support, CSC developed courses on proactive and reactive disinformation countermeasures tailored to Ukraine's context. In parallel, the Centre has codified 'one-voice' messaging and other norms by working closely with civil society—explicitly emphasizing dialogue between the state and NGOs when shaping Ukraine's information policy.

The Centre is keenly aware that Ukraine's information struggle is part of a broader security challenge for the Euro-Atlantic community. It frames "FIMI operations" (False Information and Misinformation) as new information-security weapons, mirroring NATO terminology. This conceptual reframing is reinforced by institutional embedding: CSC is funded in part by the EU's "Support to Strategic Communication in Ukraine" program, and its outputs (research, manuals, threat alerts) are actively shared with EU and NATO partners. At the same time, CSC maintains its core role as a national actor. Even as it trains foreign observers (for example, briefing allied diplomats at the Kyiv Stratcom Forum) and recruits international expertise, it continues to prioritize Ukraine-specific priorities and coordinate closely with Ukrainian ministries. Thus, CSC operates as an interlocutor within a developing European strategic communications community.

CSC's international activities can be grouped into several security-relevant dimensions:

- Global Analytics: CSC analysts systematically monitor disinformation abroad. They partner with data startups (like LetsData and Detector Media) to study media landscapes in Europe, Latin America, Africa, the Middle East and Asia. Their studies have identified Kremlin narratives in global south media (e.g. Latin America, Africa, Southeast Asia). By tracking how Russian narratives are adapted to local contexts (religion in Indonesia, anti-West themes in Africa), CSC informs both Ukrainian policymakers and partner governments about transnational propaganda trends.
- Policy Advice and Framing: The Centre uses its analytical findings to advise both Ukrainian officials and foreign stakeholders. CSC publications have

framed strategic issues in security terms—for example, a 2024 analysis urged the West to intensify weapons aid to Ukraine, linking material support to broader strategic outcomes. This piece, aimed at Western audiences, explained "why the efforts currently being made by our partners are no longer sufficient for quality changes on the battlefield". Similarly, CSC briefings helped Ukraine articulate its case in EU security forums: Borrell's visit statements echoed CSC themes (Russian propaganda as hybrid aggression) and explicitly commended Ukraine's need for communication "support structures" like CSC. In these ways, CSC not only counsels Ukraine's own leaders but also contributes to international policy narratives about the war.

- Capacity Building: Training is a cornerstone of CSC's strategy. Domestically it has conducted hundreds of workshops for civil servants, police and military (102 trainings for 837 participants in 2023). Through its School of Strategic Communications it aims to "train communication teams of central executive bodies" to recognize and counter FIMI. Internationally, CSC has transferred its experience by delivering briefings and courses to foreign partners. For example, during the Kyiv StratCom Forum and bilateral meetings, CSC experts have tutored EU and NATO officials on Ukraine's information resilience lessons. It also disseminates curricula based on Western models: the CSC-developed manual "Russia's hybrid war against Ukraine: Winning on the information front" is used as a training text internally and provided to allied communicators through exchange programs.
- Institutional Norm Diffusion: CSC serves as a model and conduit for strategic communications norms. By integrating European practices (e.g. UK's OASIS planning model) into Ukraine's system, CSC effectively exports democratic communications standards. It regularly shares "Main Positions" with international partners, exemplifying the "one voice" principle for crisis response. Its projects (like the Dovidka.info handbook for civilians) have become reference points outside Ukraine. Moreover, CSC's leadership openly engages with allies to spread best practices: it has offered its manuals and research to institutions like NATO's StratCom Centre and to EU media literacy platforms. The European Union's own strategy now cites Ukraine as a case study in building information resilience, often citing CSC data (e.g. on Russia's propaganda failures). Through all these channels, Ukraine's CSC is diffusing strategic communications norms throughout the Euro-Atlantic community.

In 2022–25 the CSC has actively exported its information-security experience to others facing similar threats. Its international conferences and publications effectively package Ukrainian lessons for broader use. For instance, CSC research on "how to counter Russian propaganda" has been cited by Western think-tanks and media as authoritative. Ambassadorial and NATO contacts regularly request CSC analyses of current Kremlin influence campaigns. Importantly, Ukraine's case – as chronicled by CSC – has shaped collective security practices: NATO allies now routinely incorporate counter-propaganda elements into their defense drills (in part inspired by Ukraine's approach), and EU anti-disinformation initiatives often draw on CSC's monitoring reports. The Centre's role in this export is both formal and informal: it hosts foreign observers at its Kyiv StratCom Forum, and provides expert panels at international training exercises. In short, the CSC has become an active conveyor of security communication know-how, helping to seed new norms and capabilities among like-minded governments and organizations.

The evolution of Ukraine's CSC during 2022–2025 offers several lessons for alliance policymakers and strategists. First, the Centre's experience shows that strategic communications should be integrated into national security planning and funded as a core defense capability. The EU High Representative's praise of the CSC underscores that credible, expert-driven centers of strategic communications are now seen as force multipliers. Second, multi-sector cooperation is essential: Ukraine's model of blending government agencies with civil society expertise (and even engaging foreign NGOs and tech firms) enhances legitimacy and effectiveness. CSC's mandate to "strengthen cooperation" with similarly threatened countries highlights the value of formal international networks in information defense. Third, capacity-building (training, forums, manuals) must be prioritized—the CSC's UK-inspired School of StratCom and its digital tools (Dovidka.info, SPRAVDI portal) are concrete templates for other countries facing hybrid warfare. Finally, robust analytics and rapid lesson-learning are vital. CSC's continuous monitoring of global disinformation trends (from EU capitals to African and Latin American media) has provided real-time intelligence that informs both Ukrainian policy and allied understanding. In sum, the CSC's case illustrates how a national strategic communications agency can "go international"—translating domestic wartime learning into contributions to collective security. Future defense frameworks should therefore include institutional links for sharing such experience, ensuring that every societal actor can contribute to building information resilience in today's wars.

The CSC's experience shows that strategic communications should be integrated into national security planning and funded as a core defense capability. Multi-sector cooperation is essential: Ukraine's model of blending government agencies with civil society expertise (and even engaging foreign NGOs and tech firms) enhances legitimacy and effectiveness. Capacity-building (training, forums, manuals) must be prioritized – the CSC's UK-inspired School of StratCom and its digital tools (Dovidka.info, SPRAVDI portal) are concrete templates for other countries facing hybrid warfare. Robust analytics and rapid lesson-learning are vital. CSC's continuous monitoring of global disinformation trends (from EU capitals to African and Latin American media) has provided real-time intelligence that informs both Ukrainian policy and allied understanding.

References

About Us—EUAM Ukraine (n.d.). Available at https://www.euam-ukraine.eu/our-mission/about-us/. Accessed 1 January 2026.

Advanced training in the field of strengthening national security took place|Center for Countering Disinformation. (2023, 14 February). Available at https://cpd.gov.ua/en/events-en/advanced-training-in-the-field-of-strengthening-national-security-took-place/. Accessed: 3 January 2026.

Agreement on Security Co-operation between the United Kingdom of Great Britain & Northern Ireland and Ukraine. (2024). Official website of the President of Ukraine. Available at https://www.president.gov.ua/en/news/ugoda-pro-spivrobitnictvo-u-sferi-bezpeki-mizh-ukrayinoyu-ta-88277. Accessed 18 January 2026.

An exchange of experience between the Ukrainian CCD and the Polish RCB|Center for Countering Disinformation. (2022, 19 December). Available at https://cpd.gov.ua/en/events-en/an-exchange-of-experience-between-the-ukrainian-ccd-and-the-polish-rcb/. Accessed 3 January 2026.

CCD held Countering FIMI Weekend in Lviv|Center for Countering Disinformation (2024, 30 October. Available at: https://cpd.gov.ua/en/events-en/ccd-held-countering-fimi-weekend-in-lviv/ (Accessed: 10 November 2025).

Countering information influence activities: the state of the art: research report. Version 1.4 (2018). Swedish Civil Contingencies Agency, Karlstad; Lund University, Lund.

Don't let yourself and your close ones be manipulated online. (n.d.). Available at https://prebunkingwithgoogle.detector.media/en. Accessed 3 January 2026.

Foreign, Commonwealth & Development Office. (2026). GOV.UK. Available at https://www.gov.uk/government/organisations/foreign-commonwealth-development-office. Accessed 18 January 2026.

From October 6 to 9, under the auspices of the Center for Countering Disinformation and the Psychological Defense Agency, "Stratcom weekend" 1.0 was held|Center for Countering Disinformation (2023, 9 October). Available at https://cpd.gov.ua/events/z-6-po-9-zhovtnya-pid-egidoyu-czpd-ta-psychological-defense-agency-vidbuvsya-stratcom-weekend-1-0/. Accessed 10 November 2025.

Handbook on countering disinformation developed by the Center for Countering Disinformation, a working body of the National Security and Defense Council of Ukraine with the support of the European Union Advisory Mission Ukraine|Center for Countering Disinformation (2023, 23 May). Available at https://cpd.gov.ua/en/manuals/manual-on-countering-disinformation/. Accessed: 10 November 2025.

Handbook "Weapons of Information Warfare"|Center for Countering Disinformation (2025, 28 July). Available at https://cpd.gov.ua/en/manuals/handbook-weapons-of-information-warfare/. Accessed 10 November 2025.

In partnership with EUAM, a series of events were held to enhance the Center's public recognition|Center for Countering Disinformation (2024, 20 May). Available at https://cpd.gov.ua/en/events-en/in-partnership-with-euam-a-series-of-events-were-held-to-enhance-the-centers-public-recognition/. Accessed 1 January 2026.

International Counter Disinformation Arcade. (2023). Available at https://mpf.se/om-oss/nyheter/2023/2023-12-13-international-counter-disinformation-arcade. Accessed 3 January 2026.

Josep Borrell visited the Center for Strategic Communication and Information Security in Kyiv (2023) detector.media. Available at https://detector.media/infospace/article/217531/2023-10-01-zhozep-borrel-vidvidav-tsentr-strategichnykh-komunikatsiy-ta-informatsiynoi-bezpeky-u-kyievi/. Accessed 17 January 2026.

Kazdobina, J. (2024). Making the glass of Ukraine's bilateral security agreements half full.

NATO Headquarters. (n.d.). Organization|NATO. Available at https://www.nato.int/en/about-us/organization/nato-structure/nato-headquarters. Accessed 1 January 2026.

Zinc Network. (n.d.). Zinc Network. Available at https://zincnetwork.com/. Accessed 18 January 2026.

Psychological Defence Agency. (2025). Available at https://mpf.se/psychological-defence-agency. Accessed 3 January 2026.

Regulation (EU) 2022/2065 of the European Parliament and of the Council of 19 October 2022 on a Single Market For Digital Services and amending Directive 2000/31/EC (Digital Services

Act) (Text with EEA relevance) (2022) OJ L. Available at http://data.europa.eu/eli/reg/2022/2065/oj. Accessed 3 January 2026.

StratCom|NATO Strategic Communications Centre of Excellence Riga, Latvia (n.d.). Available at https://stratcomcoe.org/about_us/about-nato-stratcom-coe/5. Accessed 1 January 2026.

Strona główna Rządowego Centrum Bezpieczeństwa—Rządowe Centrum Bezpieczeństwa—Portal Gov.pl (n.d.). Available at https://www.gov.pl/web/rcb. Accessed 3 January 2026.

Study visit of the CCDA to the Swedish Psychological Defence Agency and the Swedish Defence University|Center for Countering Disinformation (2023, 23 June). Available at https://cpd.gov.ua/en/events-en/study-visit-of-the-ccda-to-the-swedish-psychological-defence-agency-and-the-swedish-defence-university/. Accessed 3 January 2026.

Telegram: View @CenterCounteringDisinformation (n.d. a). Available at https://t.me/CenterCounteringDisinformation/11045. Accessed 1 November 2025.

Telegram: View @CenterCounteringDisinformation (n.d. b). Available at https://t.me/CenterCounteringDisinformation/10030. Accessed 3 January 2026.

The team of the Center for Countering Disinformation, a working body of the National Security and Defense Council of Ukraine, represented Ukraine at the Counter Disinformation wargame (CDWG)|Center for Countering Disinformation (2022, 20 September). Available at https://cpd.gov.ua/en/events-en/the-team-of-the-center-for-countering-disinformation-a-working-body-of-the-national-security-and-defense-council-of-ukraine-represented-ukraine-at-the-counter-disinformation-wargame-cdwg/. Accessed 1 January 2026.

The Center for Countering Disinformation conducted a series of trainings for the representatives of the central executive bodies|Center for Countering Disinformation (2023, 8 May). Available at https://cpd.gov.ua/en/events-en/the-center-for-countering-disinformation-conducted-a-series-of-trainings-for-the-representatives-of-the-central-executive-bodies/. Accessed 3 January 2026.

The Center for Countering Disinformation conducted a series of trainings for representatives of the Regional Military Administration and the Regional State Administration|Center for Countering Disinformation (2023, 22 April). Available at https://cpd.gov.ua/en/events-en/the-center-for-countering-disinformation-conducted-a-series-of-trainings-for-representatives-of-the-regional-military-administration-and-the-regional-state-administration/. Accessed 10 November 2025.

The CCD deepens cooperation with NATO|Center for Countering Disinformation (2024). Available at https://cpd.gov.ua/en/events-en/the-ccd-deepens-cooperation-with-nato/. Accessed 1 January 2026.

The Center and MPF held a training on "Countering Information Influence Measures"|Center for Countering Disinformation (2024, 11 April). Available at https://cpd.gov.ua/en/events-en/the-center-and-mpf-held-a-training-on-countering-information-influence-measures/. Accessed 3 January 2026.

The study visit of the Center for Countering Disinformation to Germany took place|Center for Countering Disinformation (2024, 17 April). Available at https://cpd.gov.ua/en/events-en/the-study-visit-of-the-center-for-countering-disinformation-to-germany-took-place/. Accessed 3 January 2026.

The Center's study visit to Italy|Center for Countering Disinformation (2025, 25 March). Available at https://cpd.gov.ua/en/events-en/the-centers-study-visit-to-italy/. Accessed 3 January 2026.

The CCD NSDC together with the MPF held a specialized seminar in Lviv|Center for Countering Disinformation (2025, 28 October). Available at https://cpd.gov.ua/en/events-en/the-ccd-nsdc-together-with-the-mpf-held-a-specialized-seminar-in-lviv/. Accessed 3 January 2026.

TikTok—mordorcenter. Center for Research on the MordoRU (n.d.). Available at https://www.tiktok.com/@mordorcenter. Accessed 3 January 2026.

Training conducted by the Swedish Psychological Defence Agency (MPF) under the auspices of the Center for Countering Disinformation|Center for Countering Disinformation (2023, 18 June). Available at https://cpd.gov.ua/en/events-en/training-conducted-by-the-swedish-psychological-defence-agency-mpf-under-the-auspices-of-the-center-for-countering-disinformation/. Accessed 3 January 2026.

With the support of EUAM, the CCD underwent a series of trainings to improve their skills|Center for Countering Disinformation (2023, 17 May). Available at https://cpd.gov.ua/en/events-en/with-the-support-of-euam-the-ccd-underwent-a-series-of-trainings-to-improve-their-skills/. Accessed 3 January 2026.

With the support of EUAM, the specialists of the CCD completed a series of training to enhance professional skills|Center for Countering Disinformation (2023, 12 June). Available at https://cpd.gov.ua/en/events-en/with-the-support-of-euam-the-specialists-of-the-ccd-completed-a-series-of-training-to-enhance-professional-skills/. Accessed: 3 January 2026.

9 Perspective of the Counter Disinformation System Development in Ukraine

9.1 FIMI Approach in Countering Disinformation

The Center for Countering Disinformation has gradually moved toward a more systemic way of understanding hostile information activity, drawing in particular on the experience and analytical approaches of European partners. A key step in this shift has been the adoption of the Foreign Information Manipulation and Interference (FIMI) framework developed by the European External Action Service.

FIMI is defined by the European External Action Service (EEAS) as a pattern of behavior that jeopardizes or may have a detrimental effect on political structures, procedures, and ideals. These kinds of actions are planned, deliberate, and manipulative. While the main objectives of the EU are to safeguard the information space from harmful external influences, ensure transparency and honesty in information exchange, and strengthen democratic institutions by enhancing resilience to disinformation, the primary goal of this behavior is to influence public opinion, undermine democratic processes, and destabilize society (FIMI-ISAC, n.d.).

Through collaboration with NGOs, academic institutions, and media from Africa and Latin America, the European Union and the United States are strengthening their preparedness for FIMI. To establish a multilateral community with the goal of enhancing collaboration in response to FIMI, they host workshops. To gain a deeper understanding of the disinformation strategies and narratives that are used in these areas, as well as the capacity of local stakeholders to counter them, they also gather data from fact-checking networks. Training in digital competency, media literacy, and development funding channels all improve support for capacity-building. It is also highlighted that maintaining a free and diverse media environment is crucial for countering disinformation and other FIMI (EEAS, n.d. c).

Combating FIMI is essential to preserving national security, upholding democratic processes, and guaranteeing social cohesion within the EU, US, and other countries including Ukraine.

A. Marushchak et al., *Counter Disinformation System Development in Ukraine*, Terrorism, Security, and Computation, https://doi.org/10.1007/978-3-032-24731-5_9

As the information environment becomes more crowded, faster, and more aggressive, it is increasingly clear that simply reacting to individual fakes no longer works. This approach may help to correct a particular falsehood, but it does little to address the broader problem. It resembles treating visible symptoms while leaving the root cause untouched. Over time, this reactive logic exhausts institutions and allows hostile actors to keep the initiative. For this reason, the Center for Countering Disinformation has gradually moved toward a more systemic way of understanding hostile information activity, drawing in particular on the experience and analytical approaches of European partners.

A key step in this shift has been the adoption of the Foreign Information Manipulation and Interference (FIMI) framework developed by the European External Action Service (Information Integrity and Countering Foreign Information Manipulation & Interference (FIMI)|EEAS, 2025). Instead of looking at misleading messages one by one and in isolation, the FIMI logic starts from a different premise: information manipulation is not a series of accidents or mistakes, but a deliberate and sustained activity, usually conducted by foreign state or state-linked actors. In this perspective, hostile campaigns are understood not as a collection of unfortunate distortions, but as instruments of pressure that are systematically used to weaken democratic institutions, undermine social trust, and influence strategic choices.

For Ukraine this way of seeing the problem corresponds closely to lived experience. Practice has shown that the main danger rarely lies in a single false claim that can be disproved with a fact-check. Much more often, the real threat emerges from the way many elements are combined into a single, carefully constructed operation. These campaigns typically rely on narrative engineering, where selective facts, half-truths, and emotional triggers are woven into stories designed to exploit existing societal fractures.

At the same time, these narratives are rarely left to spread on their own. They are artificially amplified and pushed across multiple platforms at once. The same message can appear almost simultaneously in pseudo-media outlets, through anonymous social media accounts, and sometimes even through seemingly respectable or semi-official channels. As a result, an echo chamber is created in which repetition replaces persuasion and volume replaces argument. From this point of view, it becomes clear that the goal is to saturate the information space and make alternative interpretations harder to hear.

Seen through the FIMI lens, such activity reveals its true scale and intent. It is about sustained pressure on the information environment as a whole. This understanding makes it possible to move away from constant "firefighting" and toward a more strategic form of defense. Instead of endlessly chasing individual falsehoods, attention shifts to the structure of hostile campaigns, the logic behind their coordination, and the long-term objectives they serve.

This broader way of looking at information warfare is also supported by recent research on cognitive warfare, in particular by the report of NATO's Chief Scientist (chief-scientist-report-cognitive-warfare-4.pdf, n.d.). It shows that modern conflicts are increasingly fought not only over territory or resources, but over how people think, interpret events, and make sense of reality. In this cognitive domain, influence operations aim at much more than spreading a few false claims. Their real purpose is to gradually reshape patterns of perception, weaken critical judgement, and, over time, undermine the basic trust that holds societies together.

Seen in this light, the value of the FIMI approach becomes even clearer. It allows analysts to step back from individual messages and instead see hostile activity as a coherent, long-term process. This shift in perspective makes it possible to anticipate the strategic effects such campaigns are meant to produce and to design responses that address causes rather than symptoms.

This does not mean that fact-checking loses its importance. On the contrary, it remains a necessary element of information hygiene. Yet assessments by the European External Action Service show that many contemporary influence operations are specifically designed to make simple factual corrections ineffective. Instead of relying on obvious lies, they increasingly play on ambiguity, and selective framing. By mixing facts with interpretation or presenting opinions as neutral descriptions, such campaigns easily slip through mechanisms that depend on a clear distinction between "true" and "false."

One of the main strengths of the FIMI framework is that it helps to uncover the hidden architecture behind such operations. Hostile actors do not act randomly. They build and use coordinated networks that are meant to flood the information space while blending in with legitimate content. The "Doppelganger" operation is a telling example. By copying the visual style, tone, and even the language of well-known media outlets, its organizers created a convincing illusion of credibility without having to rely on crude fabrications ('EEAS-3nd-ThreatReport-March-2025-05-Digital-HD.pdf', n.d.). This made it possible for manipulated narratives to enter mainstream discussions without triggering the usual warning signals.

For Ukraine, this focus on structures and behavior is particularly important. In wartime conditions, hostile actors often operate in grey zones, carefully avoiding clear signatures that would allow for easy attribution. Looking at how networks behave, how content is synchronized, and how amplification works in practice makes it much easier to detect coordinated interference and, crucially, to do so before a campaign reaches its full scale.

Another important step is the mapping of the technical infrastructure behind these operations. This makes it possible to move from discussing what is being said to understanding who is acting and for what purpose. The FIMI logic shifts attention away from endless disputes over the accuracy of individual statements and toward behavioral indicators. These include coordinated timing, attempts to hide real authorship, repeated use of the same hostile infrastructure, and the consistent alignment of narratives with broader geopolitical goals. When these patterns are tracked over time, hostile campaigns can be exposed even if their content looks plausible or carefully worded.

This focus on behavior is particularly vital for Ukraine, where information operations are almost never conducted in isolation. They usually accompany military escalations, cyberattacks, or sensitive diplomatic moments. Available technical evidence shows that such campaigns often intensify during major offensives or around key political decisions, effectively acting as a force multiplier within a broader hybrid strategy.

Focusing on the actors and their methods makes it possible to move toward the systematic exposure of entire networks. The task is no longer just to argue with a particular narrative, but to document recurring patterns of hostile behavior. When this kind of knowledge is shared with international partners facing the same adversaries, it creates a much stronger collective defense. Over time, such transparency raises the political and operational costs for the aggressor. Once the mechanics of manipulation are laid bare, its main advantages, anonymity and surprise, begin to disappear, making information warfare far more difficult and far more expensive to sustain.

Revealing the intent behind a hostile campaign only has real value if it leads to timely and concrete action. In practice, this means being able to notice emerging narratives early, follow their development, and coordinate a response before they gain critical mass. Instead of waiting for the next information crisis to fully unfold, the FIMI logic is built around constant observation and structured information exchange as the basis for early warning. When analytical findings are shared across borders, patterns that might look insignificant in one country can be recognized as part of a much larger operation, and interference can be disrupted before it reaches a wide audience.

> More and more strategic documents now describe foreign information interference not as a problem of "bad content," but as a direct challenge to sovereignty and fundamental rights. This change in perspective creates political space for much closer international coordination. It also makes collective attribution and joint responses more feasible, raising the diplomatic and reputational costs for any state that relies on malign influence as a tool of policy.

Ukraine's counter-disinformation system is gradually moving in this direction. By combining inter-agency monitoring with close international cooperation, analysis is no longer an academic exercise but is increasingly turned into practical input for national security decisions. This reflects a broader shift in thinking.

At the same time, situational awareness cannot be limited to observing the adversary alone. It also requires an honest look inward, at the vulnerabilities within society itself. Experience shows that it is rarely enough to simply point out that a claim is false. What matters just as much is understanding why certain stories resonate, which fears or frustrations they tap into, and where trust is already fragile. By identifying these points of tension in advance, it becomes possible to move from crisis response to prevention.

An equally important part of the FIMI philosophy is its clear normative boundary. Countering manipulation must not slide into censorship or political repression. For Ukraine, embedding this logic into its security thinking helps connect urgent wartime needs with a longer-term commitment to democratic governance. This creates a productive two-way process. On the one hand, Ukraine draws on European frameworks and experience to strengthen its own defenses. On the other, its frontline reality generates unique empirical knowledge. Increasingly, international reports describe Ukraine not only as one of the main targets of foreign interference, but also as a source of practical insight that shapes how these threats are understood across Europe.

Looking ahead, the FIMI approach is likely to develop in several important directions. One of them is deeper institutional integration and closer interoperability. The European External Action Service is steadily building a common language and shared threat assessments among EU member states. For Ukraine, connecting to these systems is a strategic advantage that strengthens cross-border awareness and enables coordinated responses to campaigns that do not respect national borders.

Another direction is the growing role of artificial intelligence in analytical work. While FIMI remains firmly centered on human intent and strategic behavior, future toolkits will increasingly combine expert judgment with automated network analysis and large-scale narrative mapping. In this sense, AI-driven disinformation and the FIMI framework should not be seen as separate challenges. They are parts of the same evolving environment and must be addressed together if defenses are to keep pace with the threats.

A third and equally important trend is the gradual consolidation of these ideas at the normative level. More and more strategic documents now describe foreign information interference not as a problem of "bad content," but as a direct challenge to sovereignty and fundamental rights. This change in perspective creates political space for much closer international coordination. It also makes collective attribution and joint responses more feasible, raising the diplomatic and reputational costs for any state that relies on malign influence as a tool of policy.

In the end, however, the long-term success of this entire approach depends on democratic credibility. Effective countermeasures can only work if they remain transparent and accountable. The real strength of the FIMI framework does not lie in controlling information or restricting debate. It lies in exposing manipulation and strengthening society's ability to withstand it. By keeping these efforts firmly aligned with fundamental freedoms, democratic states ensure that, in defending themselves, they do not erode the very values they are trying to protect.

Revealing the intent behind a hostile campaign only has real value if it leads to timely and concrete action. In practice, this means being able to notice emerging narratives early, follow their development, and coordinate a response before they gain critical mass. Instead of waiting for the next information crisis to fully unfold, the FIMI logic is built around constant observation and structured information exchange as the basis for early warning. When analytical findings are shared across borders, patterns that might look insignificant in one country can be recognized as part of a much larger operation, and interference can be disrupted before it reaches a wide audience.

9.2 Countering AI-Powered Disinformation

Advances in the use of AI have led to the emergence of a greater variety of forms disinformation can take and channels for its proliferation. In this context, the future of legal mechanisms to address AI-powered disinformation remains to be determined. Additional complexity for legislators working in the field arises from the need to harmonize national legal frameworks of democratic states with the need for regulation of potentially dangerous digital content.

Today Ukraine finds itself at a moment where experience alone is not enough. The information environment is changing more rapidly than ever, and the pressure comes from several directions at once. Technological advances, especially in artificial intelligence, have opened new avenues for manipulation that can imitate reality with striking precision. But while these innovations create unprecedented risks, long-standing vulnerabilities have not disappeared. Domestic problems, and deep social anxieties continue to shape how narratives take root. These elements do not function separately, they intersect, amplify each other and create a space where disinformation can emerge quickly, spread widely and influence public behavior before it is fully understood. As a result, Ukraine's primary challenge is shifting from countering visible threats to anticipating the more subtle processes that enable them.

Advances in the use of AI have led to the emergence of a greater variety of forms disinformation can take and channels for its proliferation. In this context, the future of legal mechanisms to address AI-powered disinformation remains to be determined. Additional complexity for legislators working in the field arises from the need to harmonize national legal frameworks of democratic states with the need for regulation of potentially dangerous digital content.

Over the past decade, digital technology and media have advanced enormously. While these developments benefit individuals and societies, driving economic and social development, they also open the door to information manipulation at scale. Benefitting from the pervasive use of social media (SM) worldwide, perpetrators systematically spread disinformation to destabilize societies, interfere in state governance, and radicalize groups. Addressing these advancements and their impact on states and individuals is a pressing issue for legislators at both national and international levels.

The complexity inherent to countering disinformation campaigns from the legal perspective stems from the juxtaposition between the need to regulate cyber operations and the limits of applying regulations and restrictions on freedom of speech. It is not yet clear what regulations are to be applied to cyber operations (including disinformation), especially under the existing international law frameworks.

On the one hand, such operations could be viewed as a part of espionage activities, which are not directly prohibited by international law (Rosen et al., 2023). On the other hand, they could be assessed as a breach of national sovereignty and be sanctioned under national and international law. There is another element adding to the complexity of the issue—given that democratic states constitutionally guarantee access to information and freedom of speech to their citizens, the extent of law applicability in the outlined scenario is not clear. Unrestricted access to information lies at the core of democratic regimes, as it is believed to enable their citizens to participate freely and fairly in the politics and civic life of the nation. At the same time, some of the existing international law frameworks provide the possibility of developing and applying legislative measures to counteract disinformation. For instance, the General Comment on Article 19 of Civil and Political Rights (ICCPR) provides that "When a State party invokes a legitimate ground for restriction of freedom of expression, it must demonstrate in specific and individualized fashion the precise nature of the threat and the necessity and proportionality of the specific action taken" (General comment no. 34, Article 19, Freedoms of opinion and expression, n.d.).

Given that disinformation campaigns are disseminated predominantly through SM, special attention must be paid to this domain. The threat of disinformation for national security is growing because of perpetrators' use of artificial intelligence (AI) tools to create and disseminate false and manipulative messages. In particular, fake news websites, AI-generated personalities, and fraudulent accounts are all used to spread harmful narratives. AI-powered social bots can sense, think, and act on SM platforms similar to humans (Hajli et al., 2022).

At the moment, SM regulation is in incipient stages and varies from state to state. It mostly relies on the legal measures developed in the countries of origin (US or China) over the activity of the very large online platforms (VLOPs). According to Joseph E. Stiglitz, a Nobel laureate in economics and a professor at Columbia University "Big Tech's trade-pact ploy is to create a global digital architecture where America's digital giants can continue to dominate abroad and are unfettered at home and elsewhere (Stiglitz, n.d.). The complexity of VLOPs' corporate regulation is an additional constraint for national governments to address disinformation on SM. Tackling AI-powered disinformation campaigns requires a multipronged approach involving cyber operations and freedom of speech regulations as well as AI-specific legislation and regulation.

This illustrates further that the constraints to addressing the aftermath of disinformation are that in democratic societies, legislation lags far behind the innovation of emerging technology due to the need for consensus decision-making and the lack of technical expertise possessed by legislators. The mitigation of disinformation and its consequences for national security is dependent on freedom of speech guarantees as well as privacy protection regulations. Still, states must ensure that media and SM are free from malign interference and that civil society participates in public space without disinformation, by enacting mechanisms that distinguish the truth from fiction.

Researchers contributed to defining the most appropriate division of the responsibilities between governments, industry, and civil society while addressing disinformation. Namely, Hamilton (2021) recognizes legal exemptions from fundamental freedom of speech based upon National Security concerns, analyzing the existing practice of content moderation. She defined "the modern free speech triangle" (nation-states, SM companies and users) in the context of responsibility for online content production, amplification, and rule creation and enforcement.

Others (Peukert, 2024) pay attention to the justification and the challenges posed by anti-disinformation measures, including the current regulation of counter-disinformation in the EU and the US. Comprehensive analysis of the emerging EU anti-disinformation framework based on the Code of Practice on Disinformation and the Digital Services Act, aimed at minimizing the distribution of false or misleading information has also been conducted (Cavaliere, 2022).

Additionally, scientists identify two strategies for bolstering global AI governance in light of these collaboration issues, which are particularly insightful for our research. These are (a) creating new, centralized international AI institution(s) and (b) enhancing the capacities and coordination of already-existing organizations (Roberts et al., 2024). It has been argued (Roberts et al., 2024), that it is more politically acceptable and practical to fortify the weak "regime complex" of international organizations as they currently stand. Some concerns related to these technologies can be mitigated by inclusive and mutually reinforcing policy change, which in turn would be supported by improved coordination and capabilities amongst the current international organizations controlling AI.

In practical terms, the urgency of the issues introduced above is exemplified at least since Russia's annexation of Crimea. In the context of Russia's full-scale invasion of Ukraine, the Ukrainian government and international experts (Tregubov, 2021) recognize that Russian agents spread the most destructive disinformation developed with AI tools, also known as "real-time" deepfakes. The Atlantic Council, a think tank based in Washington DC, underscores that "the quest to find the right balance between free speech and security will shape and define the decades ahead… and Ukraine's experience should certainly be part of this global conversation." In this review, our aim is to provide the Ukrainian approach to legal regulations to counter Russian disinformation campaigns, particularly amplified by the use of AI.

This way, we tried is to address two concerns. The first pertains to the discrepancy between the pace at which AI technology is advancing and the pace at which national government apparatuses can respond, often hampered by the legal provisions inherent in national laws. The second is to discuss the nexus of security concerns and other legal principles, especially in democracies like Ukraine to address AI-powered disinformation.

9.2.1 AI and Disinformation: Interconnections

As modern reality shows, AI can be both a tool for objective information reaching the masses and a powerful tool for spreading false or manipulative messages. This opens up wide opportunities for those who intend to manipulate public opinion, control the information space, and influence political processes. People can become victims of disinformation without the ability to distinguish truth from manipulation. This is especially dangerous for political and public discourse, where the accuracy of the information can determine the future of a country and its citizens. For the Ukrainian government tackling Russian disinformation sometimes even means saving the lives of the country's citizens.

AI tools are actively used to exert destructive information influence. In particular, fake news websites or voiced AI-generated virtual personalities are used to spread manipulative information. Fake accounts of non-existent people are also being created to promote information needed by the perpetrator. AI can provide more comprehensible and accurate information than people, but it can also generate more persuasive disinformation (Spitale et al., 2023).

In recent years, deepfakes have often been used to exert destructive influence. Ukrainian government notes that Russian propaganda spreads the most dangerous type of deepfakes, called "real-time" deepfakes. "Real-time" deepfake technology poses a serious threat to the information sphere due to its ability to create fake videos instantaneously, potentially deceiving both the public and political elites of various countries, thereby influencing decision-making processes. This technology allows for quick and almost undetectable changes to content, including the faces of politicians or other influential figures, manipulating words and images. In light of such deep-fake capabilities, the threat of trust in information becomes critical for society.

One example of effective use of "real-time" deepfake technology is the propaganda show "Show ViL" by Russian pranksters "Vovan" (Vladimir Kuznetsov) and "Lexus" (Aleksei Stolyarov), known for their conversations with high-ranking officials from various countries. One of their notable uses of "real-time" deepfake was in a conversation with Krišjānis Kariņš, the former Prime Minister of Latvia (Prank c glavoy MID Latvii Krishyanisom Karinsh, n.d.) or former President of Poland Aleksander Kwaśniewski (Prank s Aleksandrom Kvasnevskim, n.d.), where they discussed controversial and sensitive political and geopolitical issues. They used "real-time" deepfake technology to make video calls, pretending to be political figures from certain African countries.

The pranksters conduct video calls with the targeted persons on behalf of other public figures whose images are generated online by AI. Moreover, the generated images and sound are of such high quality that they do not raise any doubts among the victims of the prank. The content obtained in this way is published by the Russian side in the public domain to discredit the persons who became the target of such a propaganda "prank."

Ukrainian Center for Countering Disinformation (CCD), the working body of the National Security and Defense Council of Ukraine (NSDC) uncovered a damaging information campaign against President Volodymyr Zelenskyy constructed with the help of AI. The report "Information Influence Campaign in the African Information Space" (Center for Countering Disinformation, 2024) provides details of the campaign and is a striking illustration of foreign information manipulation and interference (FIMI). Using resources from African media, the campaign's primary objective was to denigrate Zelenskyy and Ukraine in the eyes of international allies. The quasi-state actors disseminated several bogus films and articles under false names through certain African media sources with anti-Ukrainian rhetoric.

A prominent case of this campaign is about the alleged ownership of a villa in Egypt by President Zelenskyy's family. On August 22, 2023, the Nigerian media outlet Punch published an article titled "A Luxury Villa Owned by President Zelenskyy's Family Found on the Coast of Egypt". The material, citing an investigation by "Egyptian journalist" Mohammed Al-Alawi from August 20, 2023, mentioned a villa in the Egyptian resort town of El Gouna, allegedly belonging to Zelenskyy's mother-in-law, Olga Kiyashko. However, the CCD found that the Zelenskyy family does not own any property in Egypt. Moreover, no evidence was found to confirm the existence of Mohammed Al-Alawi, indicating a high probability of AI tools being used to create this persona. Additionally, Mohammed Al-Alawi's YouTube channel (Center for Countering Disinformation, 2024) creation and the video about the villa were dated the same day. This also indicates manipulative tactics.

The dangers of AI technologies in spreading disinformation should be considered broadly, factoring in not only the creation and manipulation of content but also the use of AI to disseminate it, amplify the likelihood of preexisting threats, and profile users with greater precision. AI systems are currently being abused in several fields, and if they are employed more widely, there will be greater opportunities for abuse. On such misuses, decision-makers will feel obliged to step in, but it can be challenging to select the best set of responses (Anderljung & Hazell, 2023). Developers would have a strong incentive to set up organizational procedures for guaranteeing honest and efficient reporting if regulations imposed legal penalties for careless or intentional misreporting. Regulators-approved independent auditors may also be able to help find instances of misreporting (Kolt et al., 2024).

However, it might still be challenging to match the fundamental rights criteria with the decision models of more sophisticated algorithms (Buiten, 2019). Policymakers ought to concentrate on the dangers that they wish to lower. It is demonstrated that defining the primary sources of relevant risks—specific technological strategies (like reinforcement learning), applications (like facial recognition), and capabilities (like the capacity to engage physically with the environment)—better satisfies the requirements for legal definitions (Schuett, 2023).

The legal system faces both conceptual and practical issues as a result of the distinctive qualities of AI and how it can be developed (Scherer, 2015). According to Viljanen and Parviainen (2022), the five layers of AI law are the following: data rules that govern data use, application-specific rules that target AI applications or application domains, general AI rules that apply to a broad range of AI applications, application-specific non-AI rules that apply to specific activities but not to AI specifically, and general non-AI rules that apply generally and across domains. The last two layers are counter-disinformation legislation in our case.

Worries about AI safety have arisen because of AI systems' unpredictability, explainability, and uncontrollability. Because of the complexity of AI systems, limitations in human understanding, and elusiveness of emergent behaviors, it is impossible to predict certain capabilities with any degree of accuracy (Yampolskiy, 2024). Moreover, gaining an awareness of various rule complexes, their dynamics, and regulatory modalities is necessary to comprehend the regulatory environment around AI (Viljanen & Parviainen, 2022). Governments must recognize the significance of adopting a regulatory framework that optimizes AI's advantages while accounting for its hazards. This might entail classifying and categorizing risks according to relevant legal frameworks and country situations, when applicable (The Bletchley Declaration by Countries Attending the AI Safety Summit, 1–2 November 2023, n.d.).

Some scientists find compute governance to be a significant approach to AI governance. Tens of thousands of sophisticated AI chips are needed to train sophisticated AI systems; these chips cannot be purchased or used covertly. AI chips can be supplied to or taken away from specific actors and in certain situations due to their physical nature. Moreover, it is measurable: it is possible to measure chips, their attributes, and their utilization. The extremely concentrated structure of the AI supply chain further enhances the compute's detectability and excludability (Heim et al., 2024). Finally, if mitigations are not implemented for AI-based disinformation including legal regulations, interactive and compositional deepfakes have the potential to bring us closer to a post-epistemic world in which it will be impossible to tell fact from fiction (Horvitz, 2022).

The issue of countering AI-powered disinformation is extremely important, but it is greatly complicated because of the rapid development of the technology for generating deepfakes, including mentioned "real-time" deepfakes. Today, we know for certain about digital visual evidence that may indicate interference with AI content: occlusions, imperfect edges of visual masks, color and light mismatch, etc. However, it is predicted that these image defects will be eliminated in the near future, as AI technologies are developing extremely dynamically. A wide range of significant and urgent threats associated with AI are being discussed more and more by AI specialists, journalists, policymakers, and the public (Statement on AI Risk, n.d.).

There are already technical, legal, regulatory, and educational approaches to counter disinformation in Ukraine—some of which have already been implemented and some of which are just emerging—that can help reduce the level of threat associated with the use of AI. Looking at the case of Ukraine, it is worth paying attention to the activities of some of Ukrainian AI-based platforms (Osavul: AI-Powered Security Against Information Threats, n.d.) which effectively help to detect destructive information influence campaigns in their early stages. Their capabilities are powered by CommSecure and CIB Guard software. CommSecure enables to detect specific narratives in messages on social networks and communities, such as public groups in messengers. This ensures that potentially dangerous information flows are quickly identified and analyzed. CIB Guard, on the other hand, specializes in analyzing public user pages, identifying bots, and determining whether they act in a coordinated manner. This approach allows to quickly recognize coordinated campaigns that may be aimed at manipulating public opinion or spreading disinformation.

9.2.2 Counter Disinformation and AI Regulations

The current international law principle of sovereignty clashes with the cross-border nature of cyberspace and disinformation operations.

Historically, one of the first cases of legally defined misconduct in disinformation is dated January 2019. Then the US a company that created fake SM profiles to make millions of dollars in revenue settled a case with the New York state attorney. The settlement is the first case in which law enforcement has concluded that selling fake SM activity is illegal (Funke & Flamini, n.d.).

As stated above, VLOPs and their platforms are usually to some extent dependent on the laws of the host countries. However, their terms of service are devised based on the legal system of the country of origin, currently predominantly the US and China. VLOPs' intention to develop internal counter-disinformation mechanisms including AI-powered solutions can be affected by commercial and geopolitical apprehensions, e.g. risks of retributory regulation or losing access to market in the host country.

Contrary to the approach to making VLOPs responsible for addressing the disinformation R. Hamilton's opinion (Hamilton, 2021) is that "as a strictly legal matter, there is no reason for the platforms to have developed the elaborate content moderation systems they currently run." VLOPs faced the risks of "wasting" time, finance, and human resources on addressing disinformation by monitoring their networks, detecting fake news and even losing their users if the moderation gives rise to public debate. Thus, VLOPs used to be reluctant to identify perpetrators of disinformation. Nevertheless, VLOPs under pressure or in collaboration with governments, predominantly the US and China, started to develop detection and suspension initiatives, including those relying on AI, aimed at bots and botnets, as well as users exposed to disinformation, reinforcing the visibility of reliable content produced by trustworthy media and fact-checking sources, and vice versa reducing visibility (The Trust Project Helps Readers Identify Reliable News, n.d.) or suspension of sites' disinformation content.

At this point various legal approaches to counter disinformation have been put in place, helping reduce the level of threat associated with the use of AI. According to many reports, legislation governing AI is still in its infancy, with few statutes and other regulatory tools governing the creation and application of AI (Viljanen & Parviainen, 2022). The traditional conundrum of defining AI is exacerbated by the fact that our knowledge of natural intelligence is still incomplete (Mahler, 2021). Overcoming the present shortcomings in global AI governance is complicated by first-order cooperation issues resulting from interstate competition and second-order cooperation issues arising from dysfunctional international institutions (Roberts et al., 2024).

Recently several declarations have been produced at the international level. For instance, UK Bletchley Park hosted the first global summit on frontier AI safety (AI Safety Summit: Introduction, 2023). NATO Washington Summit Declaration adopted on 10 July 2024 also mentioned the intention of the NATO member-states to develop individual and collective capacity to analyze and counter hostile disinformation operations (NATO, n.d.). Additionally, in May 2024 at the AI Safety Summit in Seoul the following AI businesses pledged to uphold a set of international guidelines for AI safety known as the Frontier AI Safety Commitments: Amazon, Anthropic, Cohere, Google, IBM, Inflection AI, Meta, Microsoft, Mistral AI, Open AI, Samsung,—Technology Innovation Institute, xAi, Zhipu.ai (Zhipu.ai is a Chinese company backed by Alibaba, Ant and Tencent) (Frontier AI Safety Commitments, AI Seoul Summit 2024, n.d.).

Finally, authorities like Ukrainian CCD to counteract disinformation have also been developed along regional lines. They've also established the basis of coalitions with such entities as the EU Intelligence and Situation Centre (INTCEN), EU East StratCom Task Force with the flagship project EUvsDisinfo, the Helsinki European Centre of Excellence for Countering Hybrid Threats (counter disinformation capacity), and the NATO Strategic Communication Excellence Centre, among other.

Holding EU candidate status Ukraine is actively harmonizing its legislation with EU legislation and regulations, particularly in measures to counter AI-powered disinformation. The need to legally address the threat is based upon recent EU legal decisions. For instance, advanced disinformation/influence operations campaigns coupled with abuse of AI are listed as a revised line-up of the emerging cybersecurity threats to have an impact by 2030 in the EU (Skills shortage and unpatched systems soar to high-ranking 2030 cyber threats, n.d.). Additionally, the European Union Council on May 21, 2024, approved two documents pertaining to disinformation management—the Future of EU Digital Policy (Council of the European Union, 2024b) and Council conclusions on democratic resilience: safeguarding electoral processes from foreign interference (Council of the European Union, 2024a). The first document seeks to establish the framework for the next five years of digital policymaking and disinformation is listed as one of the detrimental or illegal occurrences that must be combated while promoting entrepreneurship, innovation, and the growth of the capital market. The durability of democracy and preventing outside intervention in electoral processes are the main topics of the second document (Council of the European Union, 2024a). It also provides a comprehensive overview of the legislative, non-legislative, and institutional tools that the EU has established. Both these documents stress the importance of further legal developments in counter disinformation realm. Consequently, they will be reflected to some extent in Ukrainian regulation.

Some norms of the European Media Freedom Act (EMFA) (European Media Freedom Act, 2024) will be harmonized with the Ukrainian legislation as well. As Gamito stated (2023) before enacting EMFA the "online media freedom" was regulated domestically due to the threats of disinformation, without having in mind the European internal market. From the Ukrainian perspective, particularly interesting will be powering the European Board for Media Services (the Board) to engage in dialogue with VLOP to monitor adherence to self-regulatory initiatives aiming to protect users from harmful content, including FIMI. The EMFA emphasizes "insufficient tools for regulatory cooperation between national regulatory authorities or bodies."

With reference to the EU Code of Practice on Disinformation (The Code of Practice on Disinformation, 2024) the EMFA obliges the Board to organize a structured dialogue between providers of VLOPs, representatives of media service providers, and representatives of civil society. This is to foster access to diverse offerings of independent media including as regards the moderation processes by VLOPs and monitor adherence to self-regulatory initiatives to protect users from harmful content, including disinformation and FIMI (Gamito, 2023). The implementation of these norms into Ukrainian legislation is of vital importance to counter Russian AI-powered disinformation at VLOPs platforms.

Another major document is European AI Act (European Parliament, 2024) that contains several provisions on disinformation that need to be reflected in Ukrainian legislation. The European AI Act[1] directly addresses systemic risks posed by general-purpose AI models. These risks include the risks from the facilitation of disinformation. Legally significant is the AI Act definition of "deepfake"[2] as AI-generated or manipulated image, audio, or video content that resembles existing persons, objects, places or other entities or events and would falsely appear to a person to be authentic or truthful (European Parliament, 2024).

Moreover, the European AI Act[3] stipulates the obligations placed on providers and deployers of certain AI systems to enable the detection and disclosure that the outputs of those systems are artificially generated in particular as regards the obligations of providers of VLOPs or very large online search engines to identify and mitigate the dissemination of content that has been artificially generated or manipulated, including through disinformation (European Parliament, 2024). Additionally, the AI Act[4] stipulates that deployers, who use an AI system to generate "deepfakes," should also clearly and distinguishably disclose that the content has been artificially created or manipulated by labelling the AI output. The compliance with this transparency obligation should not be interpreted as indicating that the use of the system or its output impedes the right to freedom of expression and the right to freedom of the arts and sciences (European Parliament, 2024). The requirement to label content (p. 136 of the AI Act) generated by AI systems is without prejudice to the obligation in Article 16 (6) of Regulation (EU) 2022/2065 (Regulation-2022/2065, n.d.)—providers of hosting services shall process any notices that they receive under the mechanisms to allow any individual or entity to notify them of the presence on their service of specific items of information that the individual or entity considers to be illegal content.

[1] p. 110.
[2] p. 60 of the AI Act.
[3] p. 120.
[4] p. 134.

These norms will not be binding for Ukraine and VLOPs' activities in the country until Ukraine becomes an EU member. Thus, the norms should be reflected in Ukrainian regulations on digital services and AI.

Another example of non-legislative regulation in the EU is the Code of Practice on Disinformation of the EU. The Code of Practice was initially signed by Facebook, Google as well as Twitter, Mozilla, advertisers, and parts of the advertising industry, Microsoft and TikTok (The Code of Practice on Disinformation, 2024). In the Code, the signatories recognized "the fundamental right to freedom of expression and to an open Internet, and the delicate balance which any efforts to limit the spread and impact of otherwise lawful content must strike" (The Code of Practice on Disinformation, 2024). Special attention in the Code is given to the case law of The Court of Justice of the European Union (CJEU) on the proportionality of measures designed to limit access to and circulation of harmful content (The Code of Practice on Disinformation, 2024).

It is worth mentioning that Russia has been expelled from the European Court of Human Rights (ECHR) so is no longer a state party to rulings on HR violations by that court, including on Article 10. However, in the recent ECHR Judgment dated 22 October 2024 in the case of Kobaliya and others v. Russia the Court held that there had been violations of the right to freedom of expression, the legislative framework had become considerably more restrictive since 2012, and had moved even further from Convention (European Convention on Human Right) standards" (European Court of Human Rights, n.d.). As a result, such judgments of ECHR will not be currently legally executed in Russia. These make the ECHR mechanism not feasible for counter-disinformation efforts.

Contrary, the CJEU judgments could be a more efficient tool to counter Russian disinformation campaigns based upon the EU's regime imposing restrictive measures on Russian individuals and entities due to Russia's aggression against Ukraine (Pingen & Wahl, n.d.).

Finally, the Code of Practice principles lay out two parts to consider when developing a legal framework for counteracting AI-powered disinformation: (1) no authority for governments to compel content moderation; (2) the content moderation could not be executed only on the basis that messages are thought to be "false."

Another major document is European AI Act (European Parliament, 2024) that contains several provisions on disinformation that need to be reflected in Ukrainian legislation. The European AI Act[5] directly addresses systemic risks posed by general-purpose AI models. These risks include the risks from the facilitation of disinformation. Legally significant is the AI Act definition of "deepfake"[6] as AI-generated or manipulated image, audio, or video content that resembles existing persons, objects, places or other entities or events and would falsely appear to a person to be authentic or truthful (European Parliament, 2024).

[5] p. 110.

[6] p. 60 of the AI Act.

Moreover, the European AI Act[7] stipulates the obligations placed on providers and deployers of certain AI systems to enable the detection and disclosure that the outputs of those systems are artificially generated in particular as regards the obligations of providers of VLOPs or very large online search engines to identify and mitigate the dissemination of content that has been artificially generated or manipulated, including through disinformation (European Parliament, 2024). Additionally, the AI Act[8] stipulates that deployers, who use an AI system to generate "deepfakes," should also clearly and distinguishably disclose that the content has been artificially created or manipulated by labelling the AI output. The compliance with this transparency obligation should not be interpreted as indicating that the use of the system or its output impedes the right to freedom of expression and the right to freedom of the arts and sciences (European Parliament, 2024). The requirement to label content (p. 136 of the AI Act) generated by AI systems is without prejudice to the obligation in Article 16 (6) of Regulation (EU) 2022/2065 (Regulation-2022/2065, n.d.)—providers of hosting services shall process any notices that they receive under the mechanisms to allow any individual or entity to notify them of the presence on their service of specific items of information that the individual or entity considers to be illegal content.

These norms will not be binding for Ukraine and VLOPs' activities in the country until Ukraine becomes an EU member. Thus, the norms should be reflected in Ukrainian regulations on digital services and AI.

Another example of non-legislative regulation in the EU is the Code of Practice on Disinformation of the EU. The Code of Practice was initially signed by Facebook, Google as well as Twitter, Mozilla, advertisers, and parts of the advertising industry, Microsoft and TikTok (The Code of Practice on Disinformation, 2024). In the Code, the signatories recognized "the fundamental right to freedom of expression and to an open Internet, and the delicate balance which any efforts to limit the spread and impact of otherwise lawful content must strike" (The Code of Practice on Disinformation, 2024). Special attention in the Code is given to the case law of The Court of Justice of the European Union (CJEU) on the proportionality of measures designed to limit access to and circulation of harmful content (The Code of Practice on Disinformation, 2024).

It is worth mentioning that Russia has been expelled from the European Court of Human Rights (ECHR) so is no longer a state party to rulings on HR violations by that court, including on Article 10. However, in the recent ECHR Judgment dated 22 October 2024 in the case of Kobaliya and others v. Russia the Court held that there had been violations of the right to freedom of expression, the legislative framework had become considerably more restrictive since 2012, and had moved even further from Convention (European Convention on Human Right) standards" (European Court of Human Rights, n.d.). As a result, such judgments of ECHR

[7] p. 120.
[8] p. 134.

will not be currently legally executed in Russia. These make the ECHR mechanism not feasible for counter-disinformation efforts.

Contrary, the CJEU judgments could be a more efficient tool to counter Russian disinformation campaigns based upon the EU's regime imposing restrictive measures on Russian individuals and entities due to Russia's aggression against Ukraine (Pingen & Wahl, n.d.).

Finally, the Code of Practice principles lay out two parts to consider when developing a legal framework for counteracting AI-powered disinformation: (1) no authority for governments to compel content moderation; (2) the content moderation could not be executed only on the basis that messages are thought to be "false."

AI development and accessibility have generated a lot of discussion, especially when it comes to how they could be abused for malevolent objectives in disinformation and FIMI. Actors in the FIMI rapidly started experimenting with these new tools to produce simulated media (EEAS, n.d. a). The FIMI concept was developed to intercept various tactics used to manipulate society and protect the information space (EEAS, n.d. b). Substantial disinformation efforts aiming at undermining EU members were uncovered following the start of Russian aggression in Ukraine in 2014, marking the first substantial moves in the FIMI approach. Officially implemented as part of EU policy, the specific FIMI effort was part of the European Action Plan Against Disinformation (EU, 2018), which was enacted in December 2018. This action plan called for the establishment of a quick alert system to facilitate coordination amongst EU member states and the development of an operational task force, known as the East StratCom Task Force, to battle disinformation.

As mentioned above the VLOPs' terms of service are developed based upon the legal system of the country of origin, mostly the US one. It is worth paying attention to the US regulations in order to figure out the principles used by VLOPs while addressing AI-powered disinformation.

The US legislation on AI-powered disinformation, which is important for the Ukrainian government to address Russian disinformation domestically and abroad, was drafted in the form of The Deepfakes Accountability Act introduced in June 2019 to combat the spread of disinformation through restrictions on deep-fake video alteration technology (Rep. Clarke, 2019). Additionally, the United States has introduced legal regulation with the Algorithmic Accountability Act (Sen. Wyden, 2022).

On the other hand, proposals for legislative ways to address disinformation in SM networks that give rise to national security concerns could contribute to the ongoing debate in the US and worldwide on the matter of how and by what authority SM networks could be regulated. Taking into account the evolving moderation of online expression, the gap in legal and regulatory terms regarding VLOPs' responsibility affects the national interests of other democratic states. The complexity of the problem derives also from the evolving opportunities for disinformation spurred by technology—for instance, mentioned above "deep-fakes" produced with the use of AI.

However, the US Constitution and case law have not been particularly consistent in the application and interpretation of freedom of speech restrictions. The US Constitution, First Amendment only applies to laws enacted by Congress and to local, state, or federal government agencies, but not to the actions of private VLOPs. Thus, the responsibility of VLOPs regarding freedom of speech and counter disinformation dissemination activities are defined predominantly by corporate policies. The US and other democracies' legal approaches to VLOPs were thus far based upon self-regulation. However, new regulations are currently evolving in AI and counter disinformation domain in the US and EU.

The US Deepfakes Accountability Act 2023 established the "Deepfakes Task Force" particularly to advance efforts of the US Government to combat the national security implications of deepfakes (Rep. Clarke, 2019).

A historic US Executive Order on Safe, Secure, and Trustworthy AI was also issued in late 2023, requiring systems that are far more sophisticated than those in use today to submit reports (The White House, 2023). Additionally, in the US NIST developed the Artificial Intelligence Risk Management Framework: Generative Artificial Intelligence Profile with the preventative action to identify potential content provenance risks and harms in GAI, such as disinformation, deepfakes (AI, 2024).

However, the US legislation on counter disinformation is developing the freedom of speech and freedom of VLOPs' entrepreneurship principles without proper consideration of the national security concerns. For instance, the Disinformation Governance Board Prohibition Act 2023 terminated the Disinformation Governance Board of the Department of Homeland Security (Rep. Bice, 2023). Additionally, the Free Speech Protection Act 2023 prohibits federal employees and contractors from directing online platforms to censor any speech that is protected by the First Amendment to the Constitution of the US (Sen. Paul, 2023).

As a result of a lack of bilateral US-Ukraine governmental collaboration tools, the Ukrainian government needs to develop legal and operational mechanisms to directly communicate with the VLOPs, based in the US, to counter Russian AI-powered disinformation. In this context, the principles of AI self-regulation, voluntarily committed and introduced in 2023 by several AI developers in the US (House, 2023), need to be particularly considered.

To understand the legal prerequisites for countering AI-powered disinformation in Ukraine there is a need to briefly analyze the country's relevant legislation.

Article 43 of the Ukrainian Constitution recognizes article 19 of ICCPR providing: "the exercise of… rights (to freedom of thought and speech) may be restricted by law in the interests of national security…" (Constitution of Ukraine, n.d.) The Ukrainian Law on Information defines "completeness and accuracy of information" (Bulletin of the Verkhovna Rada, 1992) as one of the basic principles of informational relationships. But there is no answer on the criteria of such information, and consequently no clear legal background for a definition of disinformation. Ukraine needs to establish this definition of disinformation in its national legislation. This is even more important considering the harm to the Ukrainian nationals caused by Russian disinformation campaigns. Executing the right to defense from

Russian armed aggression Ukraine has additional justification on the basis of national security to counteract the adversary's disinformation operations. These included, for example, the May 2017 banning of several Russian websites such as VKontakte, Odnoklassniki, Yandex, and Mail.ru.

The first legal concern for Ukraine was to establish and enhance governmental authorities in charge of addressing disinformation. The necessity for the Ukrainian government to guard against foreign meddling in SM is obvious, but it could still potentially impinge upon freedom of expression and result in direct censorship. Another action the Ukrainian government made to counteract Russian propaganda and disinformation was the creation of the appropriate governmental bodies (e.g. Ministry of Culture). As mentioned earlier, in March 2021, the Center for Strategic Communications and Information Security was established with the main objective of joint development of mechanisms to counter disinformation, together with international partners. Further, in line with the National Security Strategy of Ukraine, the CCD was established. The primary goal of this step was to ensure effective countering of propaganda and destructive disinformation campaigns. In May 2021 the President of Ukraine signed the regulation establishing the CCD (Decree of the President of Ukraine No. 106, 2021). The framework of this document establishes that the CCD is tasked with identifying and countering disinformation, propaganda, and destructive informational influence efforts and campaigns, as well as preventing attempts to manipulate public opinion (Mission of the Center for Countering Disinformation, 2021).

With regard to the existing Ukrainian legislative experience in the field of countering disinformation, Ukraine is gradually moving towards developing its own approach to countering the ever-growing information threats. Thus, in recent years, the Ukrainian legal framework has been supplemented by the Laws of Ukraine "On Cloud Services" and "On Stimulating the Development of the Digital Economy in Ukraine", as well as the Law "On Media."

At the same time, it should be emphasized that Ukraine has legislation in place to counter disinformation that provides guarantees of judicial protection and civil rights, among other things: For instance, Article 32 of the Constitution of Ukraine states: "Everyone is guaranteed judicial protection of the right to refute false information about himself or herself and members of his or her family and the right to demand the withdrawal of any information, as well as the right to compensation for material and moral damage caused by the collection, storage, use and dissemination of such false information" (Constitution of Ukraine, n.d.). Further, the Law on Information, Article 278 of the Civil Code of Ukraine, attempts to balance freedom of speech with the protection of legitimate interests, rights, and freedoms of individuals and legal entities. The Criminal Code of Ukraine (CCU) (The Criminal Code of Ukraine, 2011) provides for criminal liability for certain offenses related to destructive information influence, in particular: Article 259 of the CCU ("Knowingly False Reporting of a Threat to the Safety of Citizens, Destruction or Damage to Property") provides for liability for knowingly false reporting of preparations for an explosion, arson, or other actions threatening the death of people or other severe consequences; Article 436 of the CCU ("Propaganda of War") provides for liability for public calls for aggressive war or for initiating a military conflict, as well as for the production of materials with calls to commit such actions for the purpose of their dissemination or distributing such materials. However, none of these legal acts provide for the liability of VLOPs and search services for the dissemination of disinformation, particularly with the use of AI.

In August 2023, the Parliament of Ukraine Verkhovna Rada adopted the "European Integration" law "On Digital Content and Digital Services", which introduced the terms "digital content" and "digital service." This law is aimed at protecting consumer rights when purchasing and using digital content or services. However, this law does not include a human rights part, as the European Digital Services Act (DSA) does. This opens up opportunities for Ukraine to define the legal relationship between VLOPs and users in the context of countering AI-powered disinformation. It should also be emphasized that as part of the implementation of measures to synchronize and harmonize Ukrainian legislation with that of the EU, the Ministry of Digital Transformation and the Verkhovna Rada Committee on Humanitarian and Information Policy are taking active measures to implement the DSA, in particular by amending the Law of Ukraine "On Media."

Specifically, the DSA envisages new responsibilities for platforms and the empowerment of users, which, among other things, will include the following measures for:

Countering illegal content, goods and services: Online platforms should provide users with the ability to flag illegal content, including goods and services. Moreover, platforms should cooperate with "trusted flaggers", specialized organizations whose alerts should be prioritized by the platforms.

Protecting minors: including a complete ban on targeting minors with ads based on profiling or their personal data.

Providing users with access to a complaint mechanism to appeal decisions on content moderation.

Publishing a report on content moderation procedures at least once a year.

Providing users with clear terms and conditions, including the basic parameters on which their content recommendation systems operate.

Appointing a contact person for government authorities and users.

The implementation of the DSA in Ukraine will bring significant benefits in line with the countermeasures against AI-powered disinformation. First, it will increase the transparency of online platforms in Ukraine by forcing them to be open about their content moderation algorithms and procedures, providing users with information about the reasons for content removal or account blocking, and publishing annual reports. Second, it will strengthen the protection of users' rights by providing them with the opportunity to appeal content moderation decisions through special complaint mechanisms, which will help protect the rights to freedom of speech and personal information. Third, the law will help fight illegal content by allowing users to flag illegal content and cooperate with "trusted flaggers." The Concept on development of AI in Ukraine was approved by order of the Cabinet of Ministers of Ukraine on December 2, 2020 No. 1556 (The Concept of Development of AI in Ukraine, 2020), however, there is no law on AI yet in Ukraine.

Finally, it is worth mentioning that Ukraine is actively working to put the FIMI standard into practice right now. The European External Action Service EEAS trained the CCD of the National Security and Defense Council of Ukraine in October 2023, working with the EU Advisory Mission in Ukraine (EUAM Ukraine) to introduce them to the FIMI approach and evaluate the suitability and effects of implementing FIMI for the CCD. The CCD receives from EEAS a complimentary dedicated instance of Open Cyber Threat Intelligence (OpenCTI), a knowledge management and sharing platform for FIMI and cyberspace.

Summing up, AI-powered disinformation campaigns undermine democratic processes, but is it enough to apply the freedom of speech exemptions based on national security concerns? Additionally, what could and should be the legal mechanism to clearly define national interests on a case-by-case basis? The answers are not obvious because of the nexus of domestic and international issues involved and the differences within legal systems. In the current circumstances, the Ukrainian government had legitimate grounds to proceed with banning AI-powered disinformation on VLOPs' platforms based on national security concerns. It is already recognized worldwide that Russia violated international law, and Ukraine had a right to impose anti-disinformation measures as a proportionate self-defense in line with international and domestic law.

9.2.3 Law Applicability in AI and Counter Disinformation Nexus to Address National Security Concerns

There is a complex legal issue centering on the responsibility of VLOPs, with regard to freedom of speech and the laws applicable to certain disinformation dissemination activities. As described above, Ukraine is dependent on corporate policies defining the responsibility of the US-based VLOPs regarding freedom of speech and counter disinformation, including AI-powered.

Despite professing commitment to free speech, the main objective of these companies is profit. The more customer attention VLOPs attract, the more advertising revenue is gained. Provided that disinformation is not defined as illegal and tends to spread further and faster than verified information, VLOPs can be potentially incentivized to engage in its dissemination. VLOPs faced the risks of "wasting" time, finance, and human resources on addressing AI-powered disinformation by monitoring their networks, detecting fake news and even losing their users if the moderation gave rise to public debate; thus, VLOPs used to be reluctant to identify perpetrators of disinformation.

Interestingly, according to the US Communications and Technology Subcommittee and the Consumer Protection and Commerce Subcommittee (The Pressure is on Big Tech, n.d.), the industry self-regulation has failed. This opinion is seconded by scientists, who believe that self-governance is not able to consistently endure the pressure of financial incentives. Assuming that these incentives will always be in line with the public interest is insufficient given AI's huge potential for both positive and negative effects. Governments need to start creating efficient regulatory frameworks right away if they want the development of AI to benefit everyone (Toner & McCauley, n.d.). Let's have a look at some VLOPs' internal policies and trends to counter AI-powered disinformation. VLOPs under pressure or in collaboration with governments, predominantly the US one, started to develop detection and suspension initiatives, including those relying on artificial intelligence, aimed at bots and botnets, as well users exposed to mis- and disinformation, reinforcing the visibility of reliable content produced by trustworthy media and fact-checking sources, and vice versa reducing visibility (The Trust Project Helps Readers Identify Reliable News, n.d.) or suspension of sites' disinformation content.

The creation of the Facebook (Meta) Oversight Board was, for instance, a positive step towards setting principles and rules for the VLOP content moderation. However, with no binding law regarding counter-disinformation, the Oversight Board can only solve its flagged concerns based on the Code of Conduct, which does not provide a clause on disinformation, particularly on AI-powered content. Facebook's (Meta's) policy criteria of importance to public discourse and the number of individuals impacted is vital from the Ukrainian counter-disinformation perspective, such as in the case of the Kremlin-linked TV channels ban, where the need to prohibit broadcasting on SM platforms presented (Dickinson, 2021). Google legal policies (for instance, YouTube's) (Google, n.d.) stipulate the following legal issues to file a complaint: trademark, counterfeit, defamation, stored music policy, other legal issues and complaints (YouTube, n.d.). There is no exact and clear way to counter AI-powered disinformation using legal mechanisms. Even TikTok announces its initiatives to improve platform transparency and prevent covert influence campaigns. The platform claims to have discovered and destroyed networks involved in coordinated acts of inauthentic behavior (Tiktok, n.d.).

However, we should agree with Rebecca Hamilton's opinion (Hamilton, 2021) that, "as a strictly legal matter, there is no reason for the platforms to have developed the elaborate content-moderation systems they currently run." Another complicated legal issue is that AI developers have motivations that are not in line with the interests of the general population. Developers will probably be pushed by financial incentives to underinvest in safety, which would be especially worrying if frontier AI systems result in significant negative externalities. This motivation mismatch indicates that there is also a need for strict supervision of AI developers. Thus, the only consistent solution at the national and/or international level would be to enact enforcement regulations covering VLOPs' operations in addressing AI-powered disinformation.

The case of Ukraine shows that rapid action at times has to be taken, and we want to show some examples of how this may be possible on the legal level. Of course, such rapid action is possible in the unprecedented circumstances of limited freedom of martial law. The legal concern is the extent to which governmental authority respects freedom of speech, privacy, and rule of law principles while addressing AI-powered disinformation. National governments shouldn't be the only ones in charge of addressing AI-powered disinformation. Corporations shouldn't be in charge of self-regulation either. Marsden et al. (2020) propose co-regulation when businesses create their own user regulations, either separately or together, which must then be authorized by democratically legitimate state legislatures or regulators, who also keep an eye on how well they work. Such an approach could be effective in the Ukrainian realm of law while defending from Russian aggression. Accepting the principle that regulatory policies may be more reversible in AI than in other environments (Carpenter, 2024), we propose a "functional approach" (see Table 9.1), based upon the analysis of actions required for countering AI-powered disinformation: prevention, detection, and response to such campaigns.

9.2.4 Prevent, Detect, and Respond to AI-Powered Disinformation

From Ukraine's perspective, the Law on Countering Disinformation could be justified as an emergency measure against internationally recognized Russian military aggression combined with hybrid warfare. However, this law should nonetheless be in line with international law and recognized principles of freedom of speech. We propose the classification of Ukrainian authorities' powers with a set of preventative, detective, and responsive activities to address AI-enabled disinformation.

The development of a reliable news network is one of the first steps to take to prevent AI-powered disinformation. Our opinion is that democratic states should play a less active role in this activity than civil society organizations/traditional media, citizens, and VLOPs because of freedom of speech constitutional guarantees. Exceptions could be made only on the precondition of martial law limits. Strategies for raising awareness about AI-powered disinformation threats to national security should be among the measures for the state to undertake, in order to strengthen society's compliance. As part of regulating and countering AI-powered disinformation, states should provide mechanisms to raise national interest concerns based upon academic research, while taking into consideration intelligence community analysis.

For Ukraine, such a procedure could involve CCD's proposals to NSDC based on Security and Defense agencies' analyses and civil society organizations/traditional media/academia inputs. The vital point of this mechanism is the implementation of NSDC decisions by VLOPs. Public–private cooperation in counter-disinformation requires knowledge-sharing between governments, VLOPs, and other stakeholders. An experience-based, lessons-learned platform, to share knowledge of adversaries' methods and techniques, etc. can be developed in Ukraine, based on the example of disinfocloud.com, an online platform provided by the US Global Engagement Center to connect with relevant stakeholders (Global Engagement Center, n.d.).

Table 9.1 Responsibility of stakeholders in counter AI-powered disinformation activities

Actions	Stakeholders			
	State	VLOPs	Civil Society Organizations/ Traditional media/Academia	Citizen(s)
Prevention				
Development of reliable news network	Support (S) 3	S2 (*number correlates with the level of involvement from 1 – highest to 3 lowest*)	L (*Leading stakeholder*)	S1
Raising awareness	L	S2	S1	S3
Providing mechanism for raising concern about national interests	L	S3	S1	S2
Facilitation of information-sharing platform	L/S1	S2	L/S1	S3
Detection				
Development of/enhancing algorithmic criteria for early detection of disinformation	S2	L	S1	S3
Fact/source-checking	S2	S3	L	S1
Response				
Strategic silence	L	S1	S2	S3
Strategic communication	L	S3	S1	S2
Sanctions and other economic and diplomatic measures	L	S3	S1	S2
Cyber information operations	L	S1	S3	S2
Flagging and dispelling	S3	L	S1	S2

In the EU there is a different approach: an independent, non-profit organization focused on tackling sophisticated disinformation campaigns targeting the EU, its member states, and core institutions—Disinfo Lab (EU DisinfoLab, n.d.). An important action in preventive measures of AI-powered disinformation is the ongoing education and awareness-raising agenda among the actors involved in combating disinformation. This includes a set of measures aimed at raising the level of media literacy and information hygiene among the population.

In an environment where the information space is filled with a large amount of destructive content, the ability to critically evaluate information becomes vital. For example, teaching citizens to distinguish facts from opinions or propaganda helps protect them from disinformation, including from that generated by AI. An important aspect of media literacy is also understanding the algorithmic mechanisms that govern the presentation of content on SM and news platforms, which allows for a better understanding of why people see certain content. Educational activities to improve media literacy and information hygiene should be systematic and cover all age groups. This can be done through educational programs at schools and universities, training for adults, as well as through the media and social networks. Particular attention should be paid to the younger generation, who are active users of digital technologies and are particularly vulnerable to disinformation. Successful implementation of these measures will contribute to the creation of a more resilient society that can effectively resist destructive information influences.

The Russian war against Ukraine has shown that media literacy is not only an academic topic for discussion but also an important process of developing relevant skills that save health and life. In general, the promotion of media literacy in Ukraine is part of a broader strategy aimed at creating an informed society. Recognizing these threats, Ukrainian authority has been actively engaged in public awareness programs and campaigns and cooperation with civil society organizations to promote media literacy as a tool to strengthen the country's information resilience (Horban & Oliinyk, 2024).

Finally, scientists advocate for a global consensus on the ethical usage of GenAI and implementing cyber-wellness educational programs to enhance public awareness and resilience against disinformation (Shoaib et al., 2023).

The best counter AI-powered disinformation response in SM, arguably, are algorithmic approaches to detecting disinformation before it becomes shareable. These actions require clear legal regulation of VLOPs responsibility to detect AI-powered disinformation. AI-powered disinformation campaigns can rarely be detected at the early stages, for instance, adversaries' research on the audience or narratives and fake news preparation including making the AI-powered disinformation credible. Such activities can only be detected by clandestine operations of the intelligence communities.

However, VLOPs actually have the technical capabilities "*to detect mis- and disinformation in real time*" (Bharat, 2017). The basic criteria to qualify some activity as AI-powered disinformation could be if the activity: developed or disseminated by AI system; contains deceptive elements; has the intention to harm; is disruptive; constitutes interference" (Pamment et al., 2018). Such criteria must be available to the public, if used by detection tools.

In terms of impact, the detection of AI-powered disinformation could be made using AI, before fake news dissemination occurs in SM. VLOPs already use their AI-based products to provide feedback to commenters about potential perceived toxicity of content in real-time (for instance Jigsaw's Perspective and Tune). This is a valuable tool for individuals, which allows readers to choose the level of toxicity they will see in comments across the internet (Machine learning can help reduce toxicity, improving online conversation, n.d.). Scientists like Smith et al. (2021) propose an end-to-end system to perform narrative detection, hostile influence operations account classification, network discovery, and estimation of hostile influence operations causal impact; as well as a method for detection and quantification of causal influence on a social network. Such results could be used by the Ukrainian authority to detect AI-powered disinformation.

The technical approach proposed by Dr. Nitzberg (2022) for enabling AI to slow down the amplification of disinformation messages by the employment of time-limitation features for sharing suspected messages, could be efficient at a post-detection stage. If the message is not confirmed to contain fake elements, it could be disseminated at the usual pace; otherwise, it should be flagged or dispelled.

The next action to counter AI-powered disinformation is fact-checking. The authors propose that a fact-checking mechanism be used as a detection activity—before dissemination of what is suspected by AI to be false news. At present, fact-checking occurs after the incriminated fake news has been disseminated. This approach, however, is not sufficient. False information is diffused and has a "*continued influence effect*" (Lewandowsky et al., 2012). Thus, it is vital to develop a proactive counter-AI-powered disinformation detection mechanism. The fact-checking tools developed by VLOPs (mentioned above) and Ukrainian projects like StopFake (StopFake, 2024) and VoxCheck (Russia's Deflections and Denials About Chemical Weapons Use in Ukraine, n.d.) etc., could all contribute to the Poynter Institute's international network (Commit to transparency—sign up for the International Fact-Checking Network's code of principles, n.d.).

There were and still are certain factors that could influence early detection of fake news: for instance, a debate about using encryption, particularly in VLOPs (Decrypting the Encryption Debate: A Framework for Decision Makers, 2018). These debates seriously challenge counter AI-powered disinformation measures at the detection stage, from both a legal and technical perspective.

It may also be necessary for developers to employ identifiers that permit the identification of content produced by AI. One of the ways to counter the above-mentioned is to create special AI-based software that will mark the content in which the visual or audio part has been interfered. This will alert the user about the possible danger of using the "real-time" deepfake. However, the development of such software requires a long time and significant resources, which makes it impossible to counter this destructive influence. Therefore, the Ukrainian experience proposes to counteract "real-time" deepfake calls by carefully verifying the facts of the planned online meeting, staying in contact only through official means of communication, using different communication channels when organizing a video call, and following basic rules of cyber hygiene.

Even though attribution in AI-powered disinformation efforts might be challenging, it's crucial to coordinate attribution and response when sufficient evidence is available and to publicly denounce those who spread false information (Kertysova, 2018). The response actions against AI-powered disinformation are dependent on the attribution of hostile influence campaigns, which is difficult. Response actions are also contingent on jurisdiction, which defines the mechanisms for decision-making as well as the status of data in transit. VLOPs, for instance, can change the data transactions from one jurisdiction to another using their servers' locations and business process requirements. The same could be done by perpetrators to hide the tracks of disinformation dissemination. In consequence, this would severely complicate the attribution of AI-powered disinformation.

Ukrainian experience shows that one of the most important tools for responding to destructive information influence is the development of positive strategic narratives that help build society's resilience to disinformation, particularly that powered by AI. These narratives strengthen trust in official sources and create a positive image of the state in the international arena. The development of such narratives involves the dissemination of new and reliable materials with the involvement of experts from academia, civil society, foreign language experts, media representatives, and partners from other democratic countries. This ensures a high level of diversity and reliability of information. In general, positive strategic narratives should be based on real achievements and events that build trust in information sources. They should be understandable and relatable to the audience, taking into account the values and interests of the latter. This case shows that positive strategic narratives are a powerful tool for countering AI-powered disinformation and strengthening information security and society's resilience to external influences.

The same applies to the identification of negative (hostile) strategic narratives, which is crucial for countering AI-powered disinformation. Identifying dangerous messages aimed at discrediting state institutions, undermining trust in official sources, and creating panic among the population is a top priority. Analyzing the purpose and context of hostile narratives allows us to understand the goals behind the messages. Identifying the tactics and methods used in hostile narratives, such as intimidation, divergence, and fake news enables to develop of strategic countermeasures to neutralize their impact. It is worth noting that developing positive strategic narratives and identifying negative strategic narratives are the primary countermeasures against the influence of destructive information, as through such actions it becomes possible to identify global directions for countering AI-powered disinformation and the main steps towards it.

Another way to respond to AI-powered disinformation—disregard or strategic silence—should be considered in government decision-making taking into account that public opinion would have a tendency to forget quickly. Strategic silence could be used when the risk of danger for national security narratives to be perceived and believed by the population is low. However, this method carries significant potential risks. The main danger lies in the possible incorrect determination of the threat level. If the AI-powered disinformation that is decided to be ignored has a high level of disruptive impact, ignoring it can have serious consequences. For example, it may increase the spread of harmful narratives that can negatively affect public opinion, increase distrust of state institutions, or even cause panic. Therefore, the decision to use strategic silence should be made based on a thorough analysis of the potential impact of AI-powered disinformation. It is important to take into account not only the current state of public opinion but also the potential long-term consequences that may arise from underestimating the threat.

Strategic communication as a way to respond to AI-powered disinformation aims to provide and disseminate new and truthful content; this approach requires time, resources and a systemic framework. The use of humor as a part of responding to disinformation will also help to increase the dissemination of counter disinformation messages on SM platforms. Sanctions and other economic and diplomatic measures are additional legal tools to respond to AI-powered disinformation. One example of a sanction is the US legislation mandating the sale of TikTok based on concerns over disinformation and foreign propaganda (Fung, 2024).

Informational sanctions (flagging or blocking SM accounts) is an approach proposed by the authors, for further consideration and possible use against entities and individuals involved in AI-powered disinformation. In the context of the implementation of the information sanctions mechanism in Ukraine, it is necessary to emphasize a number of important tasks of the CCD at the NDC, including analysis and monitoring of events and phenomena in the country's information space, assessment of the state of information security and analysis of Ukraine's presence in the global information space. One of the key aspects of the CCD's activities is the identification and study of current and predicted threats to Ukraine's information security.

Rapid identification of the main actors generating AI-powered disinformation is crucial for an effective countering of information threats. The CCD closely cooperates with state authorities, law enforcement, and intelligence agencies, including foreign ones, to provide selected and analyzed data on key actors generating AI-powered disinformation. This data is passed on to the appropriate authorities for imposing sanctions and decision-making.

This innovative model of work of the CCD provides a comprehensive approach to countering AI-powered disinformation. It includes not only the identification and analysis of threats but also active cooperation with various national and international organizations, which allows them to respond quickly to changes in the information environment and effectively counter AI-powered disinformation campaigns. In particular, the CCD uses modern technologies to monitor the information space, analyze large amounts of data, and predict potential threats. This includes the use of AI algorithms to automatically detect anomalies in media content. The results of such analysis allow us to accurately identify sources of AI-powered disinformation and assess their impact on society.

Response in the form of cyber information operations is conducted covertly. The malicious use of general-purpose AI for deception and public opinion manipulation is a further topic of concern. AI-powered disinformation can be produced by adversaries and spread more easily even with the aim of influencing political processes.

Response actions include flagging and dispelling fake messages in SM. However, flagging or labeling fake information as "disputed" is not successful because it causes more sharing of the flagged content, and merely labeling information as fake does not lead to a reduction in its spread (Smith, 2017). One of the proposed ways to address the issue of deepfakes is to create a digital watermarking system that can verify the authenticity of media content (Generative AI and deepfakes.

How AI will create disinformation, 2024). Watermarking, which employs an invisible signature to identify digital content as coming from or being updated by AI, is one recommended technique for spotting disinformation (Christ et al., 2024). Although they are helpful, technical countermeasures like content watermarking are typically vulnerable to reasonably skilled offenders (International Scientific Report on the Safety of Advanced AI, n.d.).

The extent of governmental authority to counteract AI-powered disinformation with respect to freedom of speech, privacy, and rule of law principles is shown in Table 9.1.

Authors assign each action mentioned in the table to stakeholders based upon the following considerations: (1) the state cannot exercise influence on the development of a reliable news network and the fact/source-checking process, apart from the official governmental platform; (2) developing and enhancing algorithmic criteria for early detection of AI-powered disinformation, as well as flagging and dispelling it, are the responsibility of VLOPs due to their technical capacity; (3) the state authority should be able to choose the proper response to AI-powered disinformation in order to counter it (excluding flagging and dispelling).

9.2.5 Ukraine's Approach to Counter AI-Powered Disinformation

In today's world, artificial intelligence is changing the way information flows and shapes public perception. For Ukraine, which has endured decades of relentless information attacks, AI represents both a formidable threat and a powerful tool for defense. Unlike previous technologies that simply accelerated traditional manipulation methods, AI magnifies the speed and reach of false narratives, allowing them to penetrate wider audiences and persuade more effectively than ever before. The distinction between content created by humans and content generated by machines is increasingly blurred, making the battlefield of ideas more complex and harder to navigate.

The Organisation for Economic Co-operation and Development's report highlights the dual nature of generative AI. On one hand, these systems can produce synthetic content at remarkable speed, creating videos, images, or text that may be used to mislead, or sow confusion. On the other hand, when carefully incorporated into government processes and civil society initiatives, the same tools can serve as powerful instruments to detect, verify, and curb the spread of false information (Generative AI for anti-corruption and integrity in government: Taking stock of promise, perils and practice, 2024). For Ukraine, these observations reflect real-world developments: hostile actors now use AI to mimic the rhetorical style of Ukrainian officials, generate fabricated battlefield reports, and create synthetic audio or visual content designed to provoke panic. The rapid emergence of these tools has made clear that the battle over information is no longer just about facts, but also about speed, scale, and credibility.

Modern information threats, however, do not operate the same way across political systems. Their effects are shaped by technology, structures of media, governance, and public oversight in each country. Researchers note that the most damaging impacts occur in systems where the state maintains tight control over information, dominates major media channels, limits independent oversight, and uses digital instruments to steer public narratives. The Carnegie Endowment for International Peace highlights that such environments are particularly vulnerable to manipulation and the rapid spread of disinformation (New Digital Dilemmas: Resisting Autocrats, Navigating Geopolitics, Confronting Platforms|Carnegie Endowment for International Peace, n.d.). Ukraine confronts this reality most directly in the context of Russian information operations, which function as a highly coordinated ecosystem. State broadcasters, intelligence agencies, military psychological units, and networks of proxy platforms amplify misleading content, manufacture doubt, and maintain a persistent climate of uncertainty.

Recognizing this complexity, Kyiv has focused not only on technological solutions but also on strengthening institutions, and developing systems that can identify and respond to coordinated information operations in real time. By combining advanced detection tools with structured procedures and close cooperation between government bodies, civil society, and international partners, Ukraine is gradually creating a proactive approach to information defense. This strategy emphasizes that technology alone is not enough, human judgment, professional expertise, and institutional resilience remain essential to countering the sophisticated disinformation campaigns shaping the public sphere.

Building on these systemic challenges, another layer of complexity has emerged with the rise of technologies capable of producing highly realistic audio and video content. Deepfakes and synthetic voices can convincingly imitate Ukrainian political leaders, issue false military orders, or simulate diplomatic statements aimed at undermining international support. These tools allow hostile actors to create content that looks and sounds authentic, making it increasingly difficult for audiences to distinguish truth from fabrication. The Center for Countering Disinformation has documented numerous instances in which such manipulated materials spread rapidly (Telegram: View @TheCenterforCounteringDisinfo, n.d.).

This trend brings a number of serious and immediate risks. Fabricated videos or audio messages that appear to come from military leaders can quickly create confusion and uncertainty among both troops and civilians, especially during critical moments. False statements attributed to foreign officials are often designed to undermine international support, or sow discord among allies. Even seemingly minor rumours about evacuations, chemical threats, or infrastructure failures can spread rapidly, fueling fear and panic far faster than official communications can respond. In a war environment, these manipulations shape perceptions, and have real consequences on the ground.

Beyond the technical sophistication of these manipulations, the real danger lies in how synthetic content interacts with human perception. A convincing video or a familiar-sounding voice can trigger an almost automatic response, with the mind accepting what it sees or hears before reason has a chance to intervene.

Even people who are usually critical or sceptical can experience a fleeting moment of doubt, wondering whether the content might be real. In wartime this effect grows even stronger, as stress, exhaustion and constant exposure to alarming news heighten emotional vulnerability.

To effectively counter distorted information, Ukraine must move beyond reacting to individual incidents and focus on creating a reliable system capable of preventing and verifying false content before it spreads widely. One of the most promising tools in this effort is the C2PA standard (Coalition for Content Provenance and Authenticity), which embeds information about the origin of photos, videos, and documents, allowing journalists and the public to quickly confirm whether a message is genuine (Overview—C2PA, n.d.). Equally important is the establishment of national laboratories where researchers and technical experts collaborate to analyze suspicious materials, reveal new manipulation techniques, and help the public understand how falsified content works. Consistent application of watermarks on official videos, speeches, and emergency alerts further strengthens this framework, making it easier to identify authentic communications even in moments of heightened uncertainty. Together, these measures create a more resilient information ecosystem where fabricated content has far fewer opportunities to take hold.

Building on the measures to verify and secure information, AI also plays a crucial role in enhancing Ukraine's ability to anticipate and respond to emerging threats. These technologies do more than generate content, they can identify patterns in language, track behavioral signals, and detect sudden surges of coordinated messaging, offering a form of early warning before hostile narratives gain momentum. This capability is particularly vital for Ukraine, where waves of disinformation often appear just ahead of attacks on critical infrastructure or military escalations. Drawing from operational experience, timely detection of spikes in misleading narratives has enabled the CCD to alert the public about mobilization rumors, false claims targeting energy systems, and fabricated statements attributed to Western officials, often before such stories could take root or spread widely.

Extending from the role of AI in detection, it is also important to consider how automated systems themselves can unintentionally contribute to the spread of false narratives. Studies indicate that large language models, or LLMs, may sometimes echo Kremlin-aligned talking points, not because they are being deliberately manipulated, but because they function in information environments where reliable sources are limited (HKS Misinformation ReviewLLMs grooming or data voids? LLM-powered chatbot references to Kremlin disinformation reflect information gaps, not manipulation|HKS Misinformation Review, 2025). This is particularly relevant for Ukraine, where accurate and trustworthy narratives are often underrepresented in international datasets. When clear information is scarce, LLMs tend to rely on the most widely available sources, many of which originate from Russian state or pro-Kremlin outlets. This dynamic accelerates the circulation of disinformation and highlights the urgent need for timely, accessible, and verified reporting from Ukraine that can reach both domestic and global audiences.

Addressing these challenges requires understanding that gaps in information are not minor oversights but critical vulnerabilities that can directly impact national security. Ukraine needs a deliberate and coordinated approach to ensure that accurate, verified content reaches audiences effectively. Government reports, expert analyses, and academic research should be made available in multiple languages to maximize their reach both domestically and internationally.

Close collaboration with platforms like Wikipedia and Wikimedia is essential to make reliable information visible and trustworthy on a global scale (Wikimedia, n.d.; Wikipedia, n.d.). Providing open, machine-readable datasets allows international researchers and developers to work directly with authoritative sources, reinforcing the integrity of the information environment. At the same time, Ukraine must advocate for the inclusion of its materials in international transparency and dataset-diversity initiatives. Without these steps, distorted narratives can spread not because anyone intends to deceive but simply because accurate and accessible information is scarce.

In the current information landscape, understanding who is behind a disinformation campaign has grown increasingly difficult. Previously, analysts could rely on consistent markers such as language patterns, behavioral signals, and traces of digital infrastructure to trace content to its origin. Today, adversaries deliberately obscure these signals, adapting messages, translating them across languages, and reshaping narratives to blend into different contexts. As a result, the process of attribution has become far more intricate, with traditional indicators no longer providing the clarity they once did, and the speed of information spread further complicating timely analysis.

Beyond technical challenges, the process of attributing disinformation requires nuanced judgment and contextual understanding. Analysts must weigh evidence carefully and consider the broader political and diplomatic implications of their findings. Modern AI and generative tools intensify these challenges by producing content that leaves almost no traceable metadata or stylistic markers. According to the Center for Security and Emerging Technology, such technologies allow hostile actors to bypass conventional forensic methods entirely, generating misleading content without reusing any prior infrastructure or assets (CSET - AI and the Future of Disinformation Campaigns-Part 2, n.d.). Addressing these risks demands the development of advanced analytical frameworks, agile methodologies, and the combined use of human expertise and technological solutions to preserve the integrity of information and maintain public trust.

In addition to technological manipulation, adversaries have become increasingly adept at mimicking the communication styles of Ukrainian officials, and international partners. Modern videos and social-media posts can replicate not only tone and phrasing but also subtle gestures, facial expressions, and speech patterns. This sophistication makes it far more difficult for audiences to distinguish authentic content from fabricated material, blurring the lines between reality and imitation. In such a context, uncovering the true source of misleading content requires more than a surface-level analysis of the message itself. Analysts must examine the broader narrative ecosystem, tracing how information spreads across platforms, observing the patterns of amplification, and factoring in the geopolitical motivations that drive these campaigns. While the underlying logic of information warfare remains unchanged, the methods have evolved into layered, and convincing forms of deception. Effectively countering them demands combining technical expertise with deep understanding of social, political, and cultural dynamics.

To address these disinformation challenges, Ukraine, together with its international partners, has been developing a multi-layered and adaptive approach to tracking and understanding the flow of misleading content. This strategy goes beyond examining individual posts and focuses on the broader dynamics of information spread. Analysts carefully study patterns of behavior, including the timing and coordination of posts, how narratives are amplified across multiple platforms, and the techniques used to reach specific audiences. They map digital networks to identify botnets, fake accounts, and command-and-control nodes, uncovering the hidden structures that sustain coordinated campaigns. At the same time, analysts trace the life cycle of narratives, observing how stories evolve, mutate, and spread across languages and regions, revealing the ways in which disinformation adapts to different contexts. Verifying the provenance of official content remains a cornerstone of this work, enabling experts to separate authentic messages from forgeries and ensuring that the public and decision-makers can rely on verified information. Taken together, these methods shift the focus from individual content creators to the institutional actors and operational strategies driving disinformation, reflecting a more systemic understanding of the threat. This comprehensive approach is increasingly recognized internationally as a benchmark for effective information integrity and cybersecurity practice, offering lessons for countries facing similar challenges.

While much of the public discussion focuses on the latest and most sophisticated digital manipulation techniques, an equally crucial aspect of defense lies in equipping people to recognize and understand how misleading messages are constructed from the outset. Strengthening public resilience begins long before false information appears in news outlets. Studies have shown that prebunking, which prepares audiences by explaining the underlying logic of manipulation before they encounter it, can significantly improve people's ability to resist deceptive content. Experiments carried out by the University of Cambridge in collaboration with Google Jigsaw illustrate that even short, straightforward videos can make a meaningful difference (Inoculation Science—Video Resources—Truth Labs for Education, n.d.). They help viewers pause, critically assess what they are seeing, and resist narratives that are intentionally designed to provoke immediate emotional reactions. This proactive approach provides citizens with a framework for navigating a digital environment increasingly crowded with misleading and manipulative content, offering them orientation in a chaotic information space.

These prebunking strategies are especially relevant for Ukraine as the country works to strengthen its overall information resilience. Preparing audiences ahead of time allows messages to be crafted with attention to specific age groups, regional language differences, and the particular vulnerabilities that exist in certain communities. For example, educational campaigns can focus on regions most likely to be targeted with rumors about mobilization, false warnings about energy infrastructure, or other narratives designed to create fear and confusion.

From a national security perspective, prebunking offers significant advantages over reactive debunking. It equips citizens with the ability to recognize manipulation before it takes root, effectively building resilience in advance of exposure to false narratives. At the same time, prebunking reduces the public's demand for disinformation, not just the supply, by fostering critical thinking and encouraging people to question and resist misleading content even when some falsehoods manage to circulate. In the context of wartime conditions, where information moves quickly and emotional stress is heightened, prebunking becomes a vital tool for protecting mental resilience, reinforcing trust in reliable sources, and maintaining societal stability in the face of persistent disinformation.

As the international community moves to regulate digital technologies, with initiatives such as the EU's AI Act and OECD recommendations, Ukraine faces the pressing task of creating legal and regulatory frameworks capable of addressing rapidly evolving information threats (Marushchak et al., 2025; Media Development Foundation, 2024; OECD Legal Instruments, 2024). Developing such frameworks is not simply a technical exercise. Any approach to countering disinformation must be guided by clear ethical standards to ensure that it does not infringe upon human rights, suppress legitimate expression, or operate in ways that are opaque to the public.

A strong approach to countering disinformation starts with keeping humans at the center of all important decisions. Automated tools can be useful, but they must be applied transparently, especially when informing the public or assessing potential threats. Efforts to combat false information should target harmful manipulation rather than political disagreement, and privacy protections must be integrated from the very beginning. International research highlights that effective information defense is not just about operational success, it also relies on fairness, accountability, and public trust. For Ukraine, this means developing a regulatory framework that reflects these principles, aligns with EU standards, and at the same time protects democratic values and strengthens confidence in public institutions.

Building on these regulatory and ethical foundations, the future resilience of Ukraine will rely not only on stronger defence measures but also on the careful, responsible, and transparent use of AI in public communication. This is a sensitive field. Civil society and state institutions must operate strictly within legal boundaries, remain transparent, and avoid any practices that could be interpreted as covert influence. At the same time, it is already evident that modern information ecosystems are increasingly shaped by competition among AI systems rather than by human actors alone. In this new environment, the ability to use AI ethically and intelligently becomes essential. It allows institutions to explain complex issues more clearly, support media literacy efforts, strengthen public understanding, and ensure that constructive messages remain visible despite growing noise and manipulation online.

The question is no longer whether AI will participate in shaping public discourse. It certainly will. The real challenge is whether democratic societies can use these technologies in ways that build trust instead of eroding it. For Ukraine, long-term success depends on developing this capacity: cultivating technological competence, grounding practices in law and ethics, and focusing on reinforcing societal resilience rather than attempting to influence it through hidden means.

The issue of countering AI-powered disinformation is extremely important, but it is greatly complicated because of the rapid development of the technology for generating deepfakes, including mentioned "real-time" deepfakes. Today, we know for certain about digital visual evidence that may indicate interference with AI content: occlusions, imperfect edges of visual masks, color and light mismatch, etc. However, it was predicted that these image defects will be eliminated in the near future, as AI technologies are developing extremely dynamically.

9.3 Addressing Other Threats of Disinformation

As Ukraine confronts identity-based vulnerabilities, another powerful factor shapes how disinformation takes root: the psychological weight carried by a society living through prolonged war. Years of constant tension have created unprecedented cognitive pressure that affects how people react to information. Fatigue, uncertainty, and trauma accumulate, making it increasingly difficult to analyse news calmly or question narratives that appear familiar or emotionally compelling.

As Ukraine turns to the broader landscape of information threats, it becomes clear that disinformation is not limited to digital manipulation alone. Even as technologies accelerate the spread of misleading content, the underlying challenge remains deeply rooted in long-standing psychological, social, cultural, and geopolitical factors. Hostile actors continue to blend these methods to influence public opinion, erode trust, and generate confusion. Many of these tactics existed long before the rise of social media, and they continue to evolve as new communication channels appear. Responding effectively therefore requires more than technical countermeasures. It demands an understanding of people, institutions, and the wider international environment, and it requires acknowledging that durable resilience depends as much on an informed, confident society as on any detection system or regulatory tool.

A particularly difficult dimension of this challenge involves the way hybrid influence operations exploit what makes Ukrainian communities diverse. Factors such as language, regional history, religion, and generational experience are often weaponised to exaggerate divisions or portray them as unbridgeable. Russian narratives routinely draw on these differences, attempting to depict Ukraine as a country split between East and West, between Ukrainian and Russian speakers, or between ordinary citizens and political elites. Research and practical experience consistently show that messages linked to identity, belonging, and lived experience resonate more deeply and persist longer than messages based solely on factual claims.

For Ukraine, this presents a strategic dilemma: how to counter polarising narratives while respecting the country's rich cultural, and regional diversity.

Sustainable solutions cannot rely on imposing uniform interpretations or suppressing legitimate differences. Instead, they require communication approaches that emphasise shared citizenship, and democratic values. Strengthening these unifying ideas helps ensure that hostile narratives find less space to grow and that society remains cohesive, and resistant to attempts to manipulate its diversity for political ends.

As Ukraine confronts these identity-based vulnerabilities, another powerful factor shapes how disinformation takes root: the psychological weight carried by a society living through prolonged war. Years of constant tension have created unprecedented cognitive pressure that affects how people react to information. Fatigue, uncertainty, and trauma accumulate, making it increasingly difficult to analyse news calmly or question narratives that appear familiar or emotionally compelling. Research by the Media Development Foundation shows how this strain manifests in daily behaviour. According to their findings, 46.2% of respondents reported that during the six months of 2025 they deliberately avoided news about the war, often because following events felt emotionally overwhelming (Media Development Foundation, 2024). This widespread news avoidance creates gaps where manipulative messages can spread more easily, particularly when they promise clarity or reassurance amid chaos. Psychological studies confirm that audiences under stress are more likely to be influenced by emotionally charged or overly simplistic messages, especially those that offer simple explanations for complex events.

These psychological pressures are not just background conditions, they create openings that hostile actors actively seek to exploit. Manipulators often tailor their messages to resonate with fear, exhaustion, or frustration, spreading stories that suggest Ukraine is destined for defeat, that certain regions have been abandoned, or that political and military leaders have secretly betrayed the public. Such narratives are crafted to trigger anxiety, shame, or distrust, knowing that people under stress may latch onto simple explanations rather than sift through complex realities. Responding to this challenge requires more than presenting accurate information. It calls for communication strategies that acknowledge emotional fatigue, integrate empathy into media literacy efforts, and foreground narratives of solidarity, and recovery. Strengthening resilience, therefore, means supporting people not only intellectually but also emotionally so they can remain grounded despite the constant flow of information and pressure.

At the same time, the influence of disinformation extends well beyond daily news cycles or political rumours. It often operates at a deeper cultural level, drawing on symbols, collective memory, and long-standing narratives that shape how a society perceives itself. In Ukraine's case, the Kremlin has systematically manipulated history for decades, distorting the legacy of the Second World War, romanticising the Soviet past, and reviving imperial myths to justify aggression and delegitimise Ukrainian statehood. These narratives do not simply disinform. They aim to redefine identity, blur historical responsibility, and weaken a shared sense of national continuity.

Because of this, cultural institutions and creative industries will continue to play a vital role in building societal resilience. The preservation of archival materials and the rapid digital documentation of Ukraine's historical heritage help prevent falsification and protect narratives that hostile actors seek to appropriate. Contemporary Ukrainian film, music, and literature speak to lived experience rather than ideology, offering alternative interpretations that challenge imperial myths and reaffirm personal agency. Satire and humour, increasingly visible in wartime theatre, and digital projects, perform a crucial social function. They allow people to process fear, recognise the absurdities and contradictions in hostile messaging, and cultivate psychological endurance.

In addition to psychological pressures and structural weaknesses, the economic dynamics of the digital media landscape will increasingly shape how disinformation spreads. Today's information ecosystem prioritizes content that captures attention, generates clicks, and encourages sharing, often at the expense of accuracy. Stories designed to provoke strong emotions travel more quickly and widely than carefully verified reporting, a pattern confirmed by large-scale research conducted by MIT scholars. Social media platforms, through recommendation systems and engagement-driven algorithms, magnify this effect, enabling even relatively small or localized campaigns to reach audiences far beyond their intended scope. In practice, this means that the digital economy itself can inadvertently reward manipulative narratives, creating fertile ground for disinformation.

For Ukraine, this means that manipulative narratives can spread quickly and widely without sophisticated resources. The opacity of platform algorithms further complicates mitigation, as Ukrainian institutions cannot fully track how hostile narratives circulate, which demographic groups are targeted, or which networks drive amplification. Addressing these risks requires supporting independent journalism, incentivising high-quality Ukrainian content across digital ecosystems, and promoting platform accountability through measures aligned with the EU Digital Services Act.

Building on the challenges posed by economic and algorithmic drivers of disinformation, long-term resilience in Ukraine requires a population that is prepared not just to consume information, but to navigate it critically and thoughtfully. While traditional approaches to media literacy often focus narrowly on fact-checking or evaluating sources, in the context of hybrid warfare, this is no longer enough.

Extending the focus from general media literacy, it is equally important to equip people with what the OECD calls "resilience-oriented digital competence," which combines critical thinking with socio-emotional skills (Fostering societal resilience to disinformation|OECD, 2024). For Ukraine, this insight opens the door to an educational approach that goes well beyond traditional frameworks. Citizens can be trained in AI literacy to recognise deepfakes, synthetic content, and algorithmic bias, while narrative literacy allows them to see how stories frame politics, identity, and social dynamics. Crisis communication training further strengthens the capacity of civil servants, journalists, and local authorities to act decisively and responsibly in high-pressure situations. Complementing these methods, simulation-based exercises offer practical, hands-on experience, allowing individuals to rehearse responses to real-world information threats and build confidence in navigating a complex information environment. By embedding these skills into long-term educational and civic programs, Ukraine can strengthen its democratic foundations and lay the groundwork for post-war renewal.

Recognizing that disinformation knows no borders, Ukraine has increasingly framed resilience as an international effort. The country works closely with partners from the NATO Strategic Communications Centre of Excellence, European Union Advisory Mission, the Foreign, Commonwealth and Development Office of the United Kingdom, and numerous bilateral collaborators to exchange knowledge, and best practices. Yet, experts agree that relying solely on individual projects is no longer sufficient. The next step involves building integrated systems that enable coordinated, real-time responses, allow for shared situational awareness across borders, and strengthen collective preparedness. By fostering such cooperation, Ukraine and its allies can respond more effectively to cross-border information threats while reinforcing a broader network of resilience.

Three strategic pillars can underpin this collective resilience. The first involves interoperable monitoring platforms that allow allied institutions to share information in real time, giving partners a full and up-to-date picture of emerging threats. The second focuses on joint rapid-response mechanisms, enabling coordinated messaging and fact-checking across countries, especially during high-stakes campaigns, such as narratives targeting refugees in Europe. The third pillar envisions regional cognitive-security hubs in key areas like the Baltics, Nordics, and the Black Sea region. These hubs would function as centres for training, scenario-based exercises, and collaborative research, helping to build shared expertise and ensure that teams across borders are prepared to respond quickly and effectively to evolving disinformation challenges.

As Ukraine and its partners look to strengthen collective resilience, they must also contend with a global information environment that is shifting in fundamental ways. Hostile influence campaigns no longer remain confined to one region. Instead, they intersect with local narratives across Latin America, Africa, and Southeast Asia, blending Russian propaganda with regional contexts to create tailored messages that are harder to detect and counter. This decentralised and adaptive ecosystem makes attribution more difficult and allows disinformation networks to persist and evolve over time. At the same time, the actors involved have become increasingly hybrid, combining state services, non-state proxies, extremist groups, and even commercial content producers. These flexible networks can quickly adjust their focus and tactics based on geopolitical priorities, making the information space highly dynamic and challenging to secure.

Effectively countering these threats requires looking at the full lifecycle of hostile narratives, from their initial creation to amplification, cross-platform dissemination, and even offline mobilisation. Modern disinformation no longer exists in isolation, it operates across entire ecosystems, often supported by cyber activities such as attacks on government websites, leaks of falsified documents, and coordinated harassment campaigns targeting officials. Understanding this interconnected landscape is essential to anticipating and mitigating the impact of malicious messaging.

To meet these challenges, Ukraine will continue to develop a more integrated approach, combining digital investigation with careful mapping of how disinformation spreads. Rather than treating each false story as an isolated problem, analysts consider the broader context, observing how narratives move, who amplifies them, and what patterns emerge over time. This perspective allows authorities to understand the strategies behind campaigns, trace the networks that support them, and identify the points where interventions can be most effective. Approaching the task in this way strengthens Ukraine's information space and enhances national security, ensuring that responses are thoughtful, coordinated, and ready before threats gain traction.

The preservation of archival materials and the rapid digital documentation of Ukraine's historical heritage help prevent falsification and protect narratives that hostile actors seek to appropriate. Contemporary Ukrainian film, music, and literature speak to lived experience rather than ideology, offering alternative interpretations that challenge imperial myths and reaffirm personal agency. Satire and humour, increasingly visible in wartime theatre, and digital projects, perform a crucial social function. They allow people to process fear, recognise the absurdities and contradictions in hostile messaging, and cultivate psychological endurance.

9.4 Conclusion

The evolution of Ukraine's counter-disinformation system is increasingly defined by a transition from tactical crisis management to a comprehensive, long-term strategy of cognitive security. Within this framework, the adoption of the FIMI approach marks an important turning point in how information defence is understood and practiced. It reflects a move away from the endless correction of individual falsehoods toward a more mature and strategic way of thinking, one that focuses on the actors, structures, and intentions behind influence operations.

For Ukraine, this shift is not simply a matter of aligning with European policy frameworks; it is a practical necessity shaped by years of confronting information warfare under real wartime conditions. In the years ahead, the success of this approach will depend on whether democratic states can consistently maintain this strategic perspective and act together. When shared analysis is turned into coordinated action, resilience stops being a purely national effort and becomes a collective one. Ultimately, the strength of democracy lies in its ability to protect its information space without closing it, to expose interference without undermining openness, and to remain transparent, confident, and resilient in the face of an information environment that will only grow more complex.

In this strategic perspective, the growing role of artificial intelligence in the information space presents both unprecedented risks and opportunities for Ukraine. AI has transformed the speed, scale, and sophistication of disinformation, enabling the creation of convincing synthetic media, from deepfakes to fabricated audio, which can rapidly mislead civilians, military personnel, and international audiences. This evolution has made traditional approaches to countering false narratives insufficient on their own. Addressing AI-powered disinformation requires a multi-layered strategy that combines technological tools, institutional capacity, and legal frameworks. Standards such as C2PA, national laboratories for analysis, and consistent verification practices strengthen the resilience of Ukraine's information environment, while early-warning systems and analytic monitoring of coordinated messaging help anticipate hostile campaigns before they cause widespread harm. At the same time, gaps in reliable content, especially in international sources, leave vulnerabilities that can be exploited by adversarial AI systems, highlighting the importance of widely accessible, multilingual, and verified Ukrainian information to counterbalance disinformation.

In this context, Ukraine's long-term resilience depends not only on defending against AI-driven threats but also on using AI constructively and responsibly to support public communication. Civil society, state institutions, and international partners must operate within legal and ethical boundaries, ensuring transparency and avoiding practices that could be misinterpreted as covert influence. At the same time, AI offers opportunities to enhance media literacy, and maintain the visibility of constructive narratives despite the growing volume of false content online. The critical challenge for Ukraine and other democratic societies is to integrate AI in ways that build public trust, strengthen societal awareness, and reinforce resilience rather than simply reacting to manipulations.

Even as artificial intelligence accelerates both the creation and detection of disinformation, the underlying human vulnerabilities remain central. In Ukraine, years of war have left people exhausted, and uncertain, creating fertile ground for hostile narratives that exploit fear, and mistrust. Messages suggesting internal division, inevitable defeat resonate particularly strongly in this context. Addressing these threats requires more than factual correction. Effective communication must acknowledge emotional realities, and reinforce shared identity. Empathy, trust-building, and trauma-informed approaches are just as important as accuracy in this struggle.

At the same time, Ukraine faces structural and international challenges. Its perspectives remain underrepresented in global information spaces. Verified Ukrainian reports, expert analyses, and cultural materials are often missing from major world languages, creating data voids where misleading narratives easily take root. Closing these gaps demands a multilingual approach including translating official documents and cultural content, partnering with universities and research institutions to create open-access repositories, and engaging diaspora networks to contextualize complex developments for local audiences abroad. This type of cognitive diplomacy ensures that Ukrainian narratives are visible, and influential on the world stage.

Looking ahead, Ukraine's counter-disinformation system must continue evolving, shifting from reactive measures toward proactive strategies. Inter-agency coordination within a national cognitive-security framework will be essential, integrating narrative mapping, real-time monitoring, and rapid-response mechanisms. Citizens need support through education that combines critical thinking, media literacy, AI literacy, and emotional resilience. Predictive systems can help identify emerging narratives before they spread widely while alignment with international standards reinforces credibility and strengthens partnerships. Cultural and creative initiatives such as films, literature, music, and satire remain key to reinforcing democratic values, countering manipulative narratives, and helping citizens navigate emotionally charged information.

The ultimate goal is cognitive sovereignty, a society that can interpret events independently, recognise and resist manipulative narratives, and participate actively in shaping the global conversation about the war. As research has shown, disinformation spreads most effectively not simply because falsehoods exist, but because gaps in information leave people uncertain and vulnerable. By working to fill these gaps, strengthening resilience, and ensuring the public remains informed and engaged, Ukraine can develop a counter-disinformation system that serves both as a national asset and as a model for protecting democratic societies.

Addressing AI-powered disinformation requires a multi-layered strategy that combines technological tools, institutional capacity, and legal frameworks. Standards such as C2PA, national laboratories for analysis, and consistent verification practices strengthen the resilience of Ukraine's information environment, while early-warning systems and analytic monitoring of coordinated messaging help anticipate hostile campaigns before they cause widespread harm.

References

AI Safety Summit: Introduction. (2023). gov.uk. Available at https://www.gov.uk/government/publications/ai-safety-summit-introduction. Accessed 2 November 2024.

AI, N. (2024). Artificial Intelligence Risk Management Framework: Generative Artificial Intelligence Profile. NIST Trustworthy and Responsible AI Gaithersburg, MD, USA. Available at https://nvlpubs.nist.gov/nistpubs/ai/NIST.AI.600-1.pdf?trk=public_post_comment-text. Accessed 2 November 2024.

Anderljung, M., & Hazell, J. (2023). Protecting society from AI misuse: When are restrictions on capabilities warranted? arXiv. Available at http://arxiv.org/abs/2303.09377. Accessed 1 November 2024.

Bharat, K. (2017). How to Detect Fake News in Real-Time. NewCo Shift, 28 April. Available at https://medium.com/newco/how-to-detect-fake-news-in-real-time-9fdae0197bfd. Accessed: 2 November 2024.

Buiten, M. C. (2019). Towards intelligent regulation of artificial intelligence. *European Journal of Risk Regulation, 10*(1), 41–59. Available at https://www.cambridge.org/core/journals/european-journal-of-risk-regulation/article/towards-intelligent-regulation-of-artificial-intelligence/AF1AD1940B70DB88D2B24202EE933F1B. Accessed 1 November 2024.

Bulletin of the Verkhovna Rada. (1992). Law of Ukraine on Information. Available at https://wipolex-resources-eu-central-1-358922420655.s3.amazonaws.com/edocs/lexdocs/laws/en/ua/ua055en.pdf.

Carpenter, D. (2024). Approval regulation for frontier artificial intelligence: Pitfalls, plausibility, optionality. Available at https://lwp.law.harvard.edu/sites/projects.iq.harvard.edu/files/pegroup/files/carpenter_approval-regulation-for-frontier-ai-regulation-20240111.pdf. Accessed 2 November 2024.

Cavaliere, P. (2022). The truth in fake news: How disinformation laws are reframing the concepts of truth and accuracy on digital platforms. European Convention on Human Rights Law Review. Brill Nijhoff, pp. 481–523. Available at https://brill.com/view/journals/eclr/3/4/article-p481_005.xml. Accessed: 12 November 2024.

Center for Countering Disinformation. (2024). Analytical report «Information Influence Campaign in The African information Space». Available at https://cpd.gov.ua/en/report/analytical-report-information-influence-campaign-in-the-africaninformation-space/. Accessed 2 November 2024.

chief-scientist-report-cognitive-warfare-4.pdf (n.d.). Available at https://www.sto.nato.int/wp-content/uploads/chief-scientist-report-cognitive-warfare-4.pdf. Accessed 12 January 2026.

Christ, M., Gunn, S., & Zamir, O. (2024). Undetectable watermarks for language models. In *The Thirty Seventh Annual Conference on Learning Theory*. PMLR, pp. 1125–1139. Available at https://proceedings.mlr.press/v247/christ24a.html. Accessed 1 November 2024.

Commit to Transparency—Sign Up for the International Fact-Checking Network's code of principles. (n.d.). IFCN Code of Principles. Available at https://www.ifcncodeofprinciples.poynter.org/. Accessed 2 November 2024.

Constitution of Ukraine. (n.d.). Refworld. Available at https://www.refworld.org/legal/legislation/natlegbod/1996/en/42875. Accessed 2 November 2024.

Council of the European Union. (2024b). The future of EU digital policy. Available at https://data.consilium.europa.eu/doc/document/ST-9957-2024-INIT/en/pdf.

Council of the European Union. (2024a). Council conclusions on democratic resilience: safeguarding electoral processes from foreign interference.

CSET—AI and the Future of Disinformation Campaigns-Part 2. (n.d.). Available at https://cset.georgetown.edu/wp-content/uploads/CSET-AI-and-the-Future-of-Disinformation-Campaigns-Part-2.pdf. Accessed 26 December 2025.

Decree of the President of Ukraine No. 106/2021. (2021). Official Internet representation of the President of Ukraine. Available at https://www.president.gov.ua/documents/1062021-37421. Accessed 1 November 2025.

Decrypting the encryption debate: A framework for decision makers (2018). National Academies Press, Washington, DC. https://doi.org/10.17226/25010.

Dickinson, P. (2021). Analysis: Ukraine bans Kremlin-linked TV channels. Atlantic Council, 6 February. Available at https://www.atlanticcouncil.org/blogs/ukrainealert/analysis-ukraine-bans-kremlin-linked-tv-channels/. Accessed 1 November 2024.

EEAS. (n.d. a). 2nd EEAS Report on Foreign Information Manipulation and Interference Threats, European Union. External Action. Available at https://www.eeas.europa.eu/eeas/2nd-eeas-report-foreign-information-manipulation-and-interference-threats_en. Accessed 2 November 2024.

EEAS. (n.d. b). Beyond Disinformation—What is FIMI?. European Union. External Action. Available at https://www.eeas.europa.eu/eeas/beyond-disinformation-what-fimi_en. Accessed 2 November 2024.

EEAS. (n.d. c). TTC Ministerial—FIMI. Available at: https://www.eeas.europa.eu/sites/default/files/documents/2023/Annex%203%20-%20FIMI_29%20May.docx.pdf.

EEAS-3nd-ThreatReport-March-2025-05-Digital HD.pdf (n.d.). Available at https://www.eeas.europa.eu/sites/default/files/documents/2025/EEAS-3nd-ThreatReport-March-2025-05-Digital-HD.pdf. Accessed 12 January 2026.

EU. (2018). Action Plan Against Disinformation, 52018JC0036. Available at https://eur-lex.europa.eu/legal-content/GA/TXT/?uri=CELEX:52018JC0036. Accessed 2 November 2024.

EU DisinfoLab. (n.d.). EU DisinfoLab. Available at https://www.disinfo.eu/. Accessed 2 November 2024.

European Parliament. (2024). Artificial Intelligence Act. Available at: http://data.europa.eu/eli/reg/2024/1689/oj/eng. Accessed 2 November 2024.

European Court of Human Rights. (n.d.). Judgment concerning the Russian Federation, ECHR. Available at https://www.echr.coe.int/w/judgment-concerning-the-russian-federation-16. Accessed: 13 November 2024.

European Media Freedom Act. (2024). Available at http://data.europa.eu/eli/reg/2024/1083/oj/eng. Accessed 2 November 2024.

FIMI-ISAC (n.d.). Available at https://fimi-isac.org. Accessed 2 November 2024.

Fostering societal resilience to disinformation|OECD (2024). Available at https://www.oecd.org/en/publications/facts-not-fakes-tackling-disinformation-strengthening-information-integrity_d909ff7a-en/full-report/component-6.html#chapter-d1e6724-0f21507fbc. Accessed 26 December 2025.

Frontier AI Safety Commitments, AI Seoul Summit 2024 (n.d.) gov.uk. Available at https://www.gov.uk/government/publications/frontier-ai-safety-commitments-ai-seoul-summit-2024/frontier-ai-safety-commitments-ai-seoul-summit-2024. Accessed 2 November 2024.

Fung, B. (2024). Biden just signed a potential TikTok ban into law. Here's what happens next|CNN Business, CNN. Available at https://www.cnn.com/2024/04/23/tech/congress-tiktok-ban-what-next/index.html. Accessed 2 November 2024.

Funke, D., & Flamini, D. (n.d.). A guide to anti-misinformation actions around the world. Poynter. Available at https://www.poynter.org/ifcn/anti-misinformation-actions/. Accessed 2 November 2024.

Gamito, M. C. (2023). The European Media Freedom Act (EMFA) as meta-regulation. *Computer Law & Security Review, 48*, 105799. Available at https://www.sciencedirect.com/science/article/pii/S0267364923000080. Accessed 13 November 2024.

General comment no. 34, Article 19, Freedoms of opinion and expression. (n.d.). Refworld. Available at https://www.refworld.org/legal/general/hrc/2011/en/83764. Accessed 1 November 2024.

Generative AI and deepfakes. How AI will create disinformation (2024). Thumos. Available at https://thumos.global/generative-ai-and-deepfakes/. Accessed 2 November 2024.

Generative AI for anti-corruption and integrity in government: Taking stock of promise, perils and practice (2024). OECD Artificial Intelligence Papers 12. Available at https://doi.org/10.1787/657a185a-en

Global Engagement Center. (n.d.). United States Department of State. Available at https://www.state.gov/bureaus-offices/under-secretary-for-public-diplomacy-and-public-affairs/global-engagement-center/. Accessed 2 November 2024.

Google. (n.d.). How Google fights disinformation. Available at https://storage.googleapis.com/gweb-uniblog-publish-prod/documents/How_Google_Fights_Disinformation.pdf.

Hajli, N., et al. (2022). Social bots and the spread of disinformation in social media: The challenges of artificial intelligence. *British Journal of Management, 33*(3), 1238–1253. https://doi.org/10.1111/1467-8551.12554

Hamilton, R. J. (2021). Governing the global public square. *Harvard International Law Journal, 62*, 117.

Heim, L., Anderljung, M., & Belfield, H. (2024). To govern AI, we must govern compute. Lawfare. Available at https://www.lawfaremedia.org/article/to-govern-ai-we-must-govern-compute. Accessed 2 November 2024.

HKS Misinformation ReviewLLMs grooming or data voids? LLM-powered chatbot references to Kremlin disinformation reflect information gaps, not manipulation|HKS Misinformation Review (2025). Available at https://misinforeview.hks.harvard.edu/article/llms-grooming-or-data-voids-llm-powered-chatbot-references-to-kremlin-disinformation-reflect-information-gaps-not-manipulation/. Accessed 26 December 2025.

Horban, Y., & Oliinyk, O. (2024). Media literacy as a factor in protecting the information space from enemy disinformation in time of war. *Ukrainian Information Space, 13*, 194–205. https://doi.org/10.31866/2616-7948.1(13).2024.300896

Horvitz, E. (2022). On the horizon: Interactive and compositional Deepfakes. In *Proceedings of the 2022 International Conference on Multimodal Interaction.ICMI '22: International Conference on Multimodal Interaction.* ACM, Bengaluru, pp. 653–661. https://doi.org/10.1145/3536221.3558175

House, T. W. (2023). Fact sheet: Biden-Harris administration secures voluntary commitments from leading artificial intelligence companies to manage the risks posed by AI. The White House. Available at https://www.whitehouse.gov/briefing-room/statements-releases/2023/07/21/fact-sheet-biden-harris-administration-secures-voluntary-commitments-from-leading-artificial-intelligence-companies-to-manage-the-risks-posed-by-ai/. Accessed 2 November 2024.

Information Integrity and Countering Foreign Information Manipulation & Interference (FIMI)|EEAS (2025). Available at https://www.eeas.europa.eu/eeas/information-integrity-and-countering-foreign-information-manipulation-interference-fimi_en. Accessed 12 January 2026.

Inoculation Science—Video Resources—Truth Labs for Education. (n.d.). Inoculation Science. Available at https://inoculation.science/inoculation-videos/. Accessed 26 December 2025.

International Scientific Report on the Safety of Advanced AI. (n.d.). gov.uk. Available at https://www.gov.uk/government/publications/international-scientific-report-on-the-safety-of-advanced-ai (Accessed: 2 November 2024).

Kertysova, K. (2018). Artificial intelligence and disinformation: How AI changes the way disinformation is produced, disseminated, and can be countered. *Security and Human Rights, 29*(1–4), pp. 55–81. Available at https://brill.com/view/journals/shrs/29/1-4/article-p55_55.xml. Accessed 2 November 2024.

Kolt, N., et al. (2024). Responsible reporting for Frontier AI development. arXiv. Available at http://arxiv.org/abs/2404.02675. Accessed 1 November 2024.

Lewandowsky, S., et al. (2012). Misinformation and its correction: Continued influence and successful debiasing. *Psychological Science in the Public Interest, 13*(3), 106–131. https://doi.org/10.1177/1529100612451018

Machine learning can help reduce toxicity, improving online conversation. (n.d.). Jigsaw. Available at https://jigsaw.google.com/the-current/toxicity/. Accessed 1 November 2024.

Mahler, T. (2021). Between risk management and proportionality: The risk-based approach in the EU's Artificial Intelligence Act Proposal. Nordic Yearbook of Law and Informatics. Available at https://papers.ssrn.com/sol3/papers.cfm?abstract_id=4001444. Accessed 1 November 2024.

Marsden, C., Meyer, T., & Brown, I. (2020). Platform values and democratic elections: How can the law regulate digital disinformation?. *Computer Law & Security Review, 36*, 105373. Available at https://www.sciencedirect.com/science/article/pii/S026736491930384X. Accessed 29 July 2024.

Marushchak, A., Petrov, S., & Khoperiya, A. (2025). Countering AI-powered disinformation through national regulation: learning from the case of Ukraine. *Frontiers in Artificial Intelligence.* https://doi.org/10.3389/frai.2024.1474034

Media Development Foundation. (2024). Media Development Foundation. Available at https://www.mediadevelopmentfoundation.org/. Accessed 26 December 2025.

Mission of the Center for Countering Disinformation. (2021). Official web portal of the Parliament of Ukraine. Available at https://zakon.rada.gov.ua/go/187/2021. Accessed 10 November 2025.

NATO. (n.d.). Washington Summit Declaration, NATO. Available at https://www.nato.int/cps/en/natohq/official_texts_227678.htm. Accessed 1 November 2024.

New Digital Dilemmas: Resisting Autocrats, Navigating Geopolitics, Confronting Platforms|Carnegie Endowment for International Peace (n.d.). Available at https://carnegieendowment.org/research/2023/11/new-digital-dilemmas-resisting-autocrats-navigating-geopolitics-confronting-platforms?lang=en. Accessed 26 December 2025.

Nitzberg, M., & Zysman, J. (2022). Algorithms, data, and platforms: The diverse challenges of governing AI. *Journal of European Public Policy, 29*(11), 1753–1778. https://doi.org/10.1080/13501763.2022.2096668

OECD Legal Instruments. (2024). Available at https://legalinstruments.oecd.org/en/instruments/OECD-LEGAL-0449. Accessed 26 December 2025.

Osavul: AI-Powered Security Against Information Threats. (n.d.). Osavul. Available at https://www.osavul.cloud/. Accessed 1 November 2024.

Overview—C2PA. (n.d.). Available at https://spec.c2pa.org/?utm_source=chatgpt.com. Accessed 26 December 2025.

Pamment, J., Nothhaft, H., & Fjällhed, A. (2018). Countering information influence activities: The state of the art. MSB. Available at http://lup.lub.lu.se/record/825192b8-9274-4371-b33d-2b11baa5d5ae. Accessed 2 November 2024.

Peukert, A. (2024). The regulation of disinformation: a critical appraisal. *Journal of Media Law, 16*(1), 1–7. https://doi.org/10.1080/17577632.2024.2362485

Pingen, A., & Wahl, T. (n.d.). General court judgments on anti-war sanctions. Available at https://eucrim.eu/news/general-court-judgments-on-anti-war-sanctions/. Accessed 13 November 2024.

Prank c glavoy MID Latvii Krishyanisom Karinsh (n.d.). Rutube. Available at https://rutube.ru/video/f1b81b39c9e83d0b9afedc3b8d8583ad/. Accessed 2 November 2024.

Prank s Aleksandrom Kvasnevskim (n.d.) Rutube. Available at https://rutube.ru/video/2923db90d59af8f76faa9e3b86b0e975/. Accessed 2 November 2024.

Regulation—2022/2065. (n.d.). EU. Available at https://eur-lex.europa.eu/eli/reg/2022/2065/oj. Accessed 1 November 2024.

Rep. Clarke, Y.D. [D-N.-9]. (2019). Deepfakes Accountability Act. Available at https://www.congress.gov/bill/116th-congress/house-bill/3230/text. Accessed 2 November 2024.

Rep. Bice, S.I. [R-O.-5]. (2023). Disinformation Governance Board Prohibition Act. Available at https://www.congress.gov/bill/118th-congress/house-bill/4514/text. Accessed 13 November 2024.

Roberts, H., et al. (2024). Global AI governance: barriers and pathways forward. *International Affairs, 100*(3), 1275–1286. Available at https://academic.oup.com/ia/article-abstract/100/3/1275/7641064. Accessed 2 November 2024.

Rosen, B., Fang, K., & Shah, P. (2023). A right to spy? The legality and morality of Espionage, just security. Available at https://www.justsecurity.org/85486/a-right-to-spy-the-legality-and-morality-of-espionage/. Accessed 13 November 2024.

Russia's Deflections and Denials About Chemical Weapons Use in Ukraine. (n.d.). VoxUkraine. Available at https://voxukraine.org/en/category/voxcheck. Accessed 1 November 2024.

Scherer, M. U. (2015). Regulating artificial intelligence systems: Risks, challenges, competencies, and strategies. *Harv. JL & Technology, 29*, 353. Available at https://heinonline.org/hol-cgi-bin/get_pdf.cgi?handle=hein.journals/hjlt29&section=15&casa_token=UARIsum5qXcAAAAA:576caHV0xCik40JTtfvCkzRyVYiizzDtuzfgt_jhKNdl8kTRJisQXxcmjBdujdImd5DajBw. Accessed 1 November 2024.

Schuett, J. (2023). Defining the scope of AI regulations. *Law, Innovation and Technology, 15*(1), 60–82. https://doi.org/10.1080/17579961.2023.2184135

Sen. Wyden, R. [D-O.] (2022). Algorithmic Accountability Act of 2022. Available at https://www.congress.gov/bill/117th-congress/senate-bill/3572/text. Accessed 2 November 2024.

Sen. Paul, R. [R-K.] (2023). Free Speech Protection Act. Available at https://www.congress.gov/bill/118th-congress/senate-bill/2425/text. Accessed 13 November 2024.

Shoaib, M.R., et al. (2023). Deepfakes, misinformation, and disinformation in the era of frontier AI, generative AI, and large AI models. In *2023 International Conference on Computer and Applications (ICCA)*. IEEE, pp. 1–7. Available at https://ieeexplore.ieee.org/abstract/document/10401723/. Accessed 13 November 2024.

Skills shortage and unpatched systems soar to high-ranking 2030 cyber threats (n.d.). ENISA. Available at https://www.enisa.europa.eu/news/skills-shortage-and-unpatched-systems-soar-to-high-ranking-2030-cyber-threats. Accessed 2 November 2024.

Smith, J. (2017). Designing against misinformation. Design at Meta, 20 December. Available at https://medium.com/designatmeta/designing-against-misinformation-e5846b3aa1e2. Accessed 2 November 2024.

Smith, S. T., et al. (2021). Automatic detection of influential actors in disinformation networks. *Proceedings of the National Academy of Sciences, 118*(4), e2011216118. https://doi.org/10.1073/pnas.2011216118

Spitale, G., Biller-Andorno, N., & Germani, F. (2023). AI model GPT-3 (dis)informs us better than humans. *Science Advances, 9*(26), eadh1850. https://doi.org/10.1126/sciadv.adh1850.

Statement on AI Risk. (n.d.). Center for AI Safety. Available at https://www.safe.ai/work/statement-on-ai-risk. Accessed: 2 November 2024.

Stiglitz, J. E. (n.d.). Why big tech's digital trade rules are harmful, foreign policy. Available at https://foreignpolicy.com/2024/04/04/big-tech-digital-trade-regulation/. Accessed 13 November 2024.

StopFake. (2024). StopFake. Available at https://www.stopfake.org. Accessed 1 November 2024.

Telegram: View @TheCenterforCounteringDisinfo (n.d.). Available at https://t.me/TheCenterforCounteringDisinfo/9399. Accessed 26 December 2025.

The Criminal Code of Ukraine. (2011). Available at https://zakon.rada.gov.ua/laws/show/2001-05#Text.

The Trust Project Helps Readers Identify Reliable News. (n.d.). Santa Clara University. Available at https://www.scu.edu/news-and-events/press-releases/2017/nov-2017/the-trust-project-helps-readers-identify-reliable-news.html. Accessed 2 November 2024.

The Concept of Development of AI in Ukraine. (2020). The Parliament of Ukraine. Available at https://zakon.rada.gov.ua/go/1556-2020-%D1%80. Accessed 13 November 2024.

The Bletchley Declaration by Countries Attending the AI Safety Summit, 1–2 November 2023 (n.d.) gov.uk. Available at https://www.gov.uk/government/publications/ai-safety-summit-2023-the-bletchley-declaration/the-bletchley-declaration-by-countries-attending-the-ai-safety-summit-1-2-november-2023. Accessed 29 July 2024.

The White House. (2023). Safe, secure, and trustworthy development and use of artificial intelligence, federal register. Available at https://www.federalregister.gov/documents/2023/11/01/2023-24283/safe-secure-and-trustworthy-development-and-use-of-artificial-intelligence. Accessed 1 November 2024.

The Code of Practice on Disinformation. (2024). European Commission. https://digital-strategy.ec.europa.eu/en/policies/code-practice-disinformation. Accessed 2 November 2024.

The Pressure is on Big Tech. (n.d.). House Committee on Energy and Commerce. Available at https://energycommerce.house.gov/posts/energycommerce.house.gov. Accessed 1 November 2024.

Tiktok. (n.d.). Countering influence operations. Tiktok. Available at https://www.tiktok.com/transparency/en/countering-influence-operations/. Accessed 2 November 2024.

Toner, H., & McCauley, T. (n.d.). AI firms mustn't govern themselves, say ex-members of OpenAI's board. The Economist. Available at https://www.economist.com/by-invitation/2024/05/26/ai-firms-mustnt-govern-themselves-say-ex-members-of-openais-board. Accessed 2 November 2024.

Tregubov, V. (2021). Ukraine raised the alarm over weaponized social media long before Trump's twitter ban. Atlantic Council, 14 January. Available at https://www.atlanticcouncil.org/blogs/ukrainealert/ukraine-raised-the-alarm-over-weaponized-social-media-long-before-trumps-twitter-ban/. Accessed 1 November 2024.

Viljanen, M., & Parviainen, H. (2022). AI applications and regulation: Mapping the regulatory strata. *Frontiers in Computer Science, 3*, 779957. https://doi.org/10.3389/fcomp.2021.779957/full

Wikimedia. (n.d.). Available at https://www.wikimedia.org/. Accessed 26 December 2025.

Wikipedia. (n.d.). Available at https://www.wikipedia.org/. Accessed 26 December 2025.

Yampolskiy, R. V. (2024). On monitorability of AI. *AI and Ethics*. https://doi.org/10.1007/s43681-024-00420-x

YouTube. (n.d.). Legal policies. Available at https://support.google.com/youtube/topic/6154211?hl=en. Accessed 2 November 2024.

The manufacturer's authorised representative in the EU is Springer Nature Customer Service Centre GmbH, Europaplatz 3, 69115 Heidelberg, Germany. If you have any concerns regarding our products, please contact ProductSafety@springernature.com

Printed and bound by CPI Group (UK) Ltd, Croydon, CR0 4YY
05/10/2026
02228057-0001